RESEARCH IN MARKETING

Volume 4 • 1981

RESEARCH IN MARKETING

A Research Annual

Editor: JAGDISH N. SHETH
Department of Business
Administration
University of Illinois

VOLUME 4 • 1981

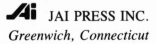 JAI PRESS INC.
Greenwich, Connecticut

CONTENTS

LIST OF CONTRIBUTORS

Paul F. Anderson
*Department of Business
Administration
Virginia Polytechnic Institute
and State University*

Donald J. Bowersox
*Department of Marketing
and Transportation
Michigan State University*

Lawrence A. Brown
*Department of Geography
Ohio State University*

Marilyn A. Brown
*Department of Geography
University of Illinois*

David J. Closs
*Department of Marketing
and Transportation
Michigan State University*

C. Samuel Craig
*Graduate School of Business
Administration
New York University*

S. Watson Dunn, Dean
*College of Business and
Public Administration
University of Missouri*

Thomas P. Hustad
*Graduate School of Business
Indiana University, Indianapolis*

John T. Mentzer, Jr.
*Department of Business
Administration
Virginia Polytechnic Institute
and State University*

Theodore J. Mitchell
*Faculty of Management Studies
University of Toronto*

Otto Ottesen
*Copenhagen School of Economics
and Business Administration
Denmark*

P. S. Raju
*Department of Marketing
University of Illinois,
Chicago Circle*

Vithala R. Rao
*Graduate School of Business
Cornell University*

Darius Jal Sabavala
*Graduate School of Business
Cornell University*

Jeffrey R. Sims
*Sears Roebuck and Company
Chicago, Illinois*

Jagdish N. Sheth
*Department of Business
Administration
University of Illinois*

PREFACE

The fourth volume of *Research in Marketing* consists of nine research papers of considerably varying lengths and highly diversified topic areas. However, they all seem to have one thing in common: Nontraditional thinking with which they pave new avenues of theoretical and empirical research in marketing.

For example, the first paper, by Paul Anderson, suggests how financial investment theories and criteria can be and should be incorporated in marketing investment decisions. He clearly favors the three new approaches of capital asset pricing model (CAPM), its logical successor, namely, the arbitrage pricing theory (APT), and finally the time-state preference approach developed by Banz and Miller over the more traditional criteria of return on investment (ROI), risk-return frontier analysis and the weighted average cost of capital (WACC) methods of investment analysis. In my opinion, this paper is likely to act as a catalyst for greater borrowing from other business disciplines which have been traditionally ignored or looked down by marketing scholars because of their greater behavioral and environmental orientation as well as presumed scientific and methodological superiority of more pure disciplines in behavioral sciences.

In a similar manner, Brown, Brown and Craig provide a new conceptual framework for the traditional area of diffusion of innovations by incorporating the supply function with the demand function as codeterminants of rate and level of adoption of innovations. They propose a three-stage model consisting of diffusion agency's (change agent's) organization structure, its strategy for promotion of the innovation and finally the market infrastructure representing the demand function. They rightfully suggest that the first two stages have been sadly neglected in the diffusion literature and demonstrate their impact on the diffusion process by comparing several innovations such as friendly ice cream, cable television and other case histories. Finally, they describe a statistical model which incorporates all the three factors deemed critical in successful diffusion of innovations. This paper has one additional distinctiveness in that it represents joint research by scholars from geography and marketing, again reflecting the trend toward more macrotheory in marketing and thereby disassociating from the behavioral sciences.

The research paper by Bowersox, Closs, Mentzer and Sims summarizes a model for short-range forecasting and distribution operations. It is a simulation model which combines, as a systems approach, the four stages of assessing market demand uncertainty including desired demand patterns, performance of physical distribution operating capabilities for these demand patterns to generate sales forecasts, replication of the physical distribution system to simulate customer stock and facility replenishment outcomes, and finally management reporting and performance measures for the distribution system. Each stage has several options, especially in the area of generating sales forecasts and measuring market uncertainties.

The uniqueness of this paper is the systems approach to physical distribution. In some ways, it reminds the reader of the classical simulation model for warehouse location decisions proposed by Kuehn and Hamburger. Once again, what is conspicuously missing is the microlevel behavioral orientation and a presence of strong emphasis on macromarketing factors in the simulation model. This paper also reflects the growing interaction between the academics and the practioners of marketing.

The research paper by Watson Dunn discusses the issue of regulation of advertising. After reviewing the substantive aspects of advertising regulation as well as who regulates what, Dunn discusses the role of research in improving the regulation of advertising. He suggests that both the regulators and the regulated need organized educational effort about what to expect from behavioral research, that we should establish standards for comparing advertising and consumer behavior on a continuous basis and that an organized dialogue is needed between researchers and research users. In many ways, this paper reflects similar sentiments expressed earlier by Bauer and Greyser about the dialogue that never takes place between industry and regulation and what to do about it.

The fifth research paper by Mitchell and Hustad describes a new approach to new products screening based on the Analysis of Options technique proposed by Nigel Howard as part of development of metagame theory. The Analysis of Options is a team approach to new product screening in which a task force plays roles of different resource managers each one taking a stakeholder perspective. The partisan view of each resource manager is represented by playing "what if" scenarios and their impact on the rest of the system. In many ways, the Analysis of Options is a more formalized approach to consensus management popular among the Japanese companies. Mitchell and Hustad then compare the Analysis of Options approach with more traditional practices in new product screening such as checklists, ad hoc procedures, weighted checklists and mathematical modeling. They favor the Analysis of Options method due to its flexibility, simplicity, efficiency and variety.

In a very nontraditional and somewhat controversial viewpoint, Otto Ottessen suggests a model of short run advertising effects. The basic proposition is that advertising has a *diminishing returns* relationship with sales and, therefore, advertising budgets should not be too large, media should be dispersed rather than concentrated, and advertising messages should be targeted to several segments. He shows several examples from the Scandinavian markets utilizing what he calls Market Maps. While the theory is based on individual response functions and depends heavily on the behavioral sciences, the theoretical propositions for advertising effectiveness and the managerial implications for advertising decisions are unique and opposite to the traditional norms.

The next research paper, by Raju, is concerned with the increasingly popular area of exploratory behavior manifested by consumers and its implications for marketing practioners. After reviewing several theories and propositions in psychology and consumer behavior, Raju proposes a two-component model for consumer exploratory behavior: novelty component and conflict component associated with a stimulus which generates exploratory behavior. He then derives a curvilinear relationship between stimulus novelty and stimulus preference. Finally, he adds one more component labeled as the extrinsic component to explain those situations in which consumers still prefer a stimulus even though it is boring and/or conflict-provoking. I think once we have the theoretical underpinnings for consumer exploratory behavior, it is likely to generate a stream of empirical research.

The research paper by Rao and Sabavala is the first serious effort to integrate our substantive knowledge about the marketing mix and then begin to raise questions about constructing mathematical models appropriate for the integrated framework. This is refreshing in view of the fact that most researchers have tended to be technique-oriented in building marketing models. Rao and Sabavala then discuss the problem of micro-macro consistency (aggregation problem) as well as issues of functional forms, interdependence, simultaneity and controllability aspects of integrating the marketing mix variables.

In the last paper, Sheth provides one more theory to the discipline, this time focusing on psychology of innovation resistance. Noticing the pro-change bias among scholars and practitioners in the diffusion of innovation area, Sheth suggests that people who resist change may be more normal and their resistance more rational than those who adopt innovations. Citing the negative personal, social and global consequences of technological changes as well as the emerging deviant profile of the innovators, he suggests that researchers must learn and respect why people resist innovations rather than channel marketing efforts to overcome their resistance. He suggests that habit for existing practice as well as perceived risks associated with the innovations are the prime determinants of innovation resistance. Based on habit-risk typology, Sheth suggests a typology of innovation resistance for different types of innovations.

As usual, the papers are listed alphabeticlaly.

Jagdish N. Sheth
Series Editor

MARKETING INVESTMENT ANALYSIS

Paul F. Anderson

I. INTRODUCTION

It has long been recognized that many of the more important marketing decisions which a firm must face may be viewed as investment decisions [20,38,39,55, 86,87]. An investment may be defined as an outlay of cash in the current period which is expected to generate cash returns in future periods. As such, decisions to introduce new products, to commit more resources to sales territories, or to improve the long-term efficiency of distribution channels may all be classed as marketing investments [17]. It is the intention of this paper to assess the current state of the art in marketing investment analysis and to explore the possible future directions in this area. The former task will involve a review of the marketing and traditional finance literatures, while the latter task will require an exploration of the leading edge of financial theory.

The paper begins with a brief review and critique of contemporary procedures for analyzing marketing investments. This is followed by a discussion of the

Research in Marketing, Volume 4, pages 1–37
Copyright © 1981 by JAI Press Inc.
All rights of reproduction in any form reserved.
ISBN: 0–89232–169–5

important relationship between corporate goals and marketing investment analysis. The next section of the paper develops in some detail the traditional capital asset pricing model approach to investments and illustrates some potential applications in marketing. Then the theoretical and practical problems with this approach are explored and recently developed alternative models are introduced. Finally, the implications of these developments for marketing are discussed and directions for future research are suggested.

II. CONTEMPORARY METHODS OF MARKETING INVESTMENT ANALYSIS

We begin by posing the basic marketing investment problem through the use of a hypothetical example. Assume that a firm faces the alternative of investing in either of the new products whose estimated net cash flows are shown in Table 1. Both investments require an initial outlay of $2 million, but the timing and amount of their cash flows differ. Moreover, the two new products differ in terms of their risk characteristics. The essential marketing problem is this: how does the firm decide which new product investment furthers the attainment of corporate goals?

Two basic methods of analyzing investment opportunities are popular in the marketing literature. The first may be referred to as the average rate of return on investment (ROI) approach.

A. Return on Investment

ROI is calculated as the ratio of the average annual net income generated by the project to the average investment in the project:

$$\text{ROI} = \frac{\text{Ave. Annual Net Income}}{\text{Ave. Investment}} \tag{1}$$

Investment opportunities whose returns exceed some predetermined cutoff rate are accepted, and all others are rejected.

Many variations on the form and use of this approach are to be found in the literature [19,37,55,71,78,86,87]. In some cases cash flow or contribution margin is substituted for net income. In other cases, the return is calculated as a single rather than a multiple period measure. In addition, ROI is frequently employed as a control as well as an evaluation tool.

There are at least two serious problems with the ROI approach to investment evaluation. Its first and foremost difficulty is that it ignores the time value of money. Projects are evaluated solely on the basis of their return to investment ratios. The rapidity with which returns are realized is not considered. Its second major problem is that ROI fails to consider the differential risk of investment projects. Investment rankings based on ROI alone can be misleading. Quite often

Table 1. Forecasted Cash Flows for Two New Product Investments

Year	Product A ($000s)	Product B ($000s)
0	-2,000	-2,000
1	+700	+200
2	+750	+300
3	+500	+800
4	+450	+700
5	+300	+600
6	+200	+400
Total	+$900	+$1,000

high return opportunities carry with them high levels of risk. Clearly, a prudent marketing manager would wish to consider both risk and return in selecting among alternative investment strategies.

B. Discounted Cash Flow

The other major approach to the evaluation of marketing investments involves the use of discounted cash flow (DCF) techniques [18,55]. There are two discounted cash flow procedures in the literature: the net present value (NPV) and the internal-rate-of-return (IRR) methods. The NPV technique simply calculates the present value sum of the net cash flows resulting from a project:

$$NPV = \sum_{i=1}^{n} \frac{A_i}{(1 + k)^i} \qquad (2)$$

where
  NPV = the net present value of the project,
  A_i = the net cash flows resulting from the project in year i (this includes both cash inflows and outflows),
  n = the expected life of the project in years, and
  k = the firm's weighted average cost of capital (WACC).
The firm's decision rule is to accept the proposal if NPV is equal to or greater than zero. This implies that the return on the project equals or exceeds the firm's cost of capital.

The IRR method, on the other hand, solves the discounting formula for the rate which equates the present value of the cash inflows with the present value of the cash outflows. This is accomplished by determing k* in equation (3):

$$0 = \sum_{i=1}^{n} \frac{A_i}{(1 + k^*)^i} \tag{3}$$

where k* is the internal rate of return on the investment. The firm should accept the project if k* equals or exceeds the firm's cost of capital.[1]

Unlike the ROI approach, discounted cash flow methods take into account the time value of money. The discounting mechanism automatically adjusts for the differential timing of cash flows. As such, the present values or internal rates of return of projects with different cash flow configurations can be compared directly.

Another advantage of DCF over the return on investment approach is that the former employs cash flow as the return criterion. Cash flow, not net income, is the accepted measure of investment return [1,98]. An investment is essentially a commitment of immediate cash in anticipation of cash returns extending over some period of time. Cash is the important criterion because only cash receipts can be reinvested in other projects or paid to stockholders as dividends. Net income, on the other hand, is an accrual accounting concept which results from an attempt to match expenses to benefiting periods regardless of when the actual cash outflow occurs [94].

Unfortunately, traditional discounted cash flow techniques do not consider the risk element in investment analysis. In order to deal with the problem of risk, various modifications of the DCF procedures have been suggested. Four of the more widely known approaches will be presented here.[2]

1. *Risk-Adjusted Hurdle Rate.*   The risk-adjusted hurdle rate approach is employed with internal rate of return methodologies. The technique involves a subjective adjustment of the firm's cost of capital to account for the riskiness of various investment projects [24,97]. For example, assume that Firm J is considering four new-product investments represented by the letters A, B, C, and D. The expected internal rates of return for the new products are as shown below:

Product	IRR
A	18.7%
B	9.7%
C	14.0%
D	7.9%

In the traditional IRR approach, the firm would use its weighted average cost of capital (WACC) as the hurdle rate for each of the four products. Thus, if the WACC was 11.5 percent, products A and C would be accepted, and products B and D would be rejected.

However, management may believe that the riskiness of products A and C is such that a higher hurdle rate is necessary. Thus, a risk-adjusted rate of 16.0% might be applied as a cutoff criterion. With this approach, only product A would be considered an acceptable investment opportunity.

2. Risk-Adjusted Discount Rates. The risk-adjusted discount rate approach is formally equivalent to the risk-adjusted hurdle rate technique. Here, however, the risk-adjusted cost of capital becomes the discount rate used to determine the net present value of the investment alternatives [97]. All investment opportunities whose NPVs equal or exceed zero are accepted. Once again, this is equivalent to requiring the return on the project to equal or exceed the risk-adjusted cost of capital.

3. Certainty-Equivalent. The certainty-equivalent approach is generally employed with net present value methodologies. It involves the application of a risk-adjustment factor to the cash flows in the NPV formula:

$$\text{NPV} = \sum_{i=1}^{n} \frac{C_i A_i}{(1 + R_f)^i} \qquad (4)$$

where
C_i = the certainty-equivalent coefficient for year i, and
R_f = the risk-free rate of interest (this is usually approximated by the return
The certainty-equivalent coefficient can take on values between 0 and 1.00 and will vary inversely with the level of risk in the cash flows. The coefficient is determined by management's subjective risk preferences and may assume different values for different years. Thus, if management views risk as increasing over time, the certainty equivalent coefficient will decline over the expected life of the project. The risk-free rate is used to discount the cash flows because the adjustment for risk takes place in the numerator. The riskless rate simply accounts for the time value of money.

Robichek and Myers suggest that the certainty-equivalent approach is theoretically superior to the risk-adjusted discount rate method [79]. They have demonstrated that the risk-adjusted discount rate implies increasing risk over time. While it is true that the assumption of increasing risk may be correct, they argue that certainty-equivalents allow management to explicitly consider the exact nature of the time pattern of risk.

4. Kotler's Risk-Return Criterion The risk-return approach suggested by Kotler is conceptually similar to the capital asset pricing model approach to be discussed in a later section of this article [55].[3] Both approaches rest on the assumption that investment analysis is essentially a process of identifying the trade-offs between the risk and return of various investment opportunities.

In order to explicate the risk-return trade-offs, Kotler employs a graphical device similar to that shown as Exhibit 1. Here, rate of return is plotted along the

Exhibit 1.   Kotler's Risk-Return Model

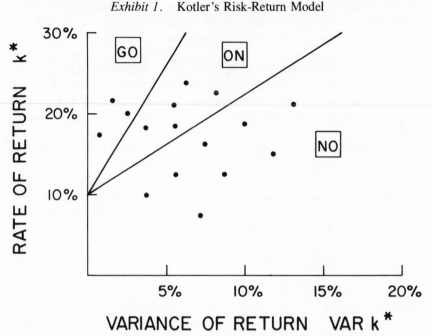

Source: Adapted from Philip Kotler, *Marketing Decision Making* (New York: Holt, Rinehart and Winston, 1971), p. 265.

vertical axis, and risk, as measured by the variance of return, is plotted along the horizontal axis.[4] Each point in this two-dimensional diagram represents the risk-return ordered pair of a potential investment project.

The risk-return space is divided into three decision regions. The area in the upper left is known as the GO region because management looks favorably upon projects with relatively high return and low risk. The cutoff line for the GO region has an intercept of 10 percent because this is the minimum return which management is willing to accept. The slope of the line represents management's subjective trade-off of risk for return. For example, if the slope of this line were 2.5, it would mean that management requires an increase in return of 2.5 percent to compensate for a 1.0 percent increase in risk (variance).

The ON region contains projects with questionable risk-return profiles. Kotler suggests that additional marketing research should be conducted on these proposals to clarify their risk-return potential. With additional information, management should be able to reclassify the projects in either the GO or the NO regions. Investments falling in the NO region are deemed to be unacceptable to management and are rejected.

Of course, projects falling in the GO region must still be ranked in terms of their attractiveness. This is especially important if the firm operates under self-imposed capital rationing.[5] Kotler suggests that this can be accomplished with reference to management's "utility function" for risk and return. If such a function can be identified, it is a simple process to rank order the investments in the GO region.

C. Criticisms of Risk Analysis Methodologies

The four risk analysis methodologies presented above all have a number of potential limitations. One problem is that risk-adjusted rates and certainty equivalents are highly subjective risk measures. Because of individual differences in risk preferences and estimating abilities, their application is likely to be inconsistent across projects and time periods. Indeed, there is always the danger that risk estimates may reflect the vested interests of various decision makers. Given the subjective nature of the task, it is not at all difficult to select and justify discount rates or certainty equivalents which ensure the acceptance of "pet" projects.

A related problem is that these estimates reflect the preferences of management and are not necessarily those of the firm's stockholders. (This criticism also applies to Kotler's approach). Ideally, investment decisions should be made in accordance with the risk-return preferences of the firm's shareholders. As the owners of the firm and the ultimate risk-bearers, it is the stockholders who should determine the levels of return they wish to attain and the risks they are willing to assume.

A second potential problem related to the Kotler model concerns the use of return variance as the risk surrogate. This is known in the financial literature as the total-project-risk approach [33]. Unfortunately, financial theorists are uncertain as to whether return variance is an appropriate risk measure for firm investment decisions.[6] In a subsequent section, this issue will be reviewed and its implications for marketing investment analysis will be developed.

III. CORPORATE GOALS AND MARKETING INVESTMENT ANALYSIS

In the previous section, it was suggested that investment decisions should be made in accordance with the risk-return preferences of the firm's shareholders rather than its management. This view is widely held among financial theorists and is reflective of the fact that modern investment theory is built upon the assumption that shareholder wealth maximization is the firm's ultimate objective [31].[7] It should be noted that this is not necessarily the same as the objective of profit maximization. There are at least three significant problems with the profit maximization objective which make it a less than adequate criterion for investment analysis.[8]

The first problem with profit maximization is its vagueness. The firm has a wide variety of profit measures which it could seek to maximize. For example, should the firm maximize the dollar amount of profits or earnings per share? What about return-on-equity versus return-on-assets? Should the firm focus on long-run or short-run profits? Finally, should accounting profits be measured or is cash flow more appropriate? The particular definition of profit employed has important implications for managerial decision making.

A second problem with the profit maximization criterion is that it cannot provide management with guidance in selecting alternatives which differ in the timing or duration of their cash flows. For example, should the firm invest in a project which returns $200,000 five years from now or one which produces $30,000 in each of the next five years? According to a pure profit maximization criterion, the former investment opportunity is the obvious choice. However, if the firm can reinvest the returns from the second alternative at a certain 15 percent, it will find that by the end of the fifth year it will have a total return of $202,271. Obviously, the firm must take into account the time value of money when evaluating investment opportunities.

A third, and possibly the most important, concern with the profit maximization criterion is that it does not consider the risk or uncertainty of investment returns. As noted previously, risk is frequently defined as the variability in the possible returns from a project [34,98]. Exhibit 2 shows the probability distributions of the returns for two investment projects. Both have average expected annual returns of $5,000. However, the variability in the return of project Y is expected to be much greater than that of project X. Thus, project X is the preferred alternative on the basis of its lower level of risk. Application of a strict profit maximization criterion to this decision would not have differentiated between the two alternatives.

Exhibit 2.   Return Distributions for two investment projects

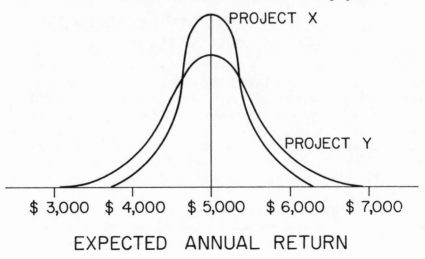

Because of the problems associated with the profit maximization objective, financial theorists have adopted the broader and more comprehensive objective of maximizing shareholder wealth. Maximization of shareholder wealth—i.e., maximizing the price of the firm's stock—provides the firm with the operational criterion it needs to make investment decisions. It is unambiguous, and, as will be demonstrated, it allows for the consideration of timing, duration, and risk differences in the returns of alternative investments. More importantly, it is fully consistent with the optimal allocation of society's economic resources.

The basic and most fundamental rationale for shareholder wealth maximization is that such an objective is in the best interests of society as a whole. It is founded on the premise that society seeks to allocate its scarce resources in such a way as to maximize total economic welfare. Thus, economic resources should flow to those firms which do the best job of satisfying consumers' economic wants and needs. The capital markets accomplish this allocation process on the basis of security prices. That is, those firms which do the best job of satisfying consumer's needs should have the best future investment prospects. As a result, investors will tend to bid up the prices of these securities and capital resources will be allocated to these firms. Thus, a firm which seeks to achieve shareholder wealth maximization through customer satisfaction is not only operating in the best interests of the stockholders, but is also acting in the best interests of society as a whole.[9] As Van Horne notes, the use by the firm of any objective other than shareholder wealth maximization "is likely to result in the suboptimal allocation of funds and therefore lead to less than optimal capital formation and growth in the economy as well as a less than optimal level of economic want satisfaction" [98, p. 9].

Of course, the adoption of wealth maximization as the firm's objective does not preclude the existence of other goals. It simply asserts that all other goals are subordinate to the firm's primary mission of maximizing share price. This is, in effect, a hierarchy-of-objectives approach. In order to achieve its ultimate objective, the firm must set subsidiary goals which, in turn, ensure the attainment of the primary corporate goal. Thus, market share, sales revenue, gross margin, and contribution margin objectives are all appropriate. Indeed, they are essential to the implementation and control of marketing programs. However, the firm must never lose sight of the fact that these objectives must dovetail in such a way as to accomplish the corporate mission of wealth maximization.[10]

It should also be noted that the objective of share price maximization does not mean that management must make all decisions with one eye on the stock market ticker. Indeed, the short-term movements in stock prices are much too volatile to provide a useful guide for corporate action. Rather, what is implied by the wealth maximization criterion is that corporate investment decisions should be made according to a set of principles which are designed to ensure that shareholder wealth will be enhanced. These principles should be derived from the modern theories of investor and capital market behavior. In the following section, the traditional capital asset pricing model approach to these issues will be presented.

IV. INVESTOR AND CAPITAL MARKET BEHAVIOR

In order to enhance shareholder wealth, the firm must understand the nature of
investor behavior. In effect, it must have a theory of stockholder decision making. In 1952, Markowitz provided one such theory in his paper on portfolio
selection [66]. The Markowitz approach eventually created a revolution in financial theory. Until recently his work has been viewed as the "theoretical substruc-
ture of finance" [85, p. 167].

Markowitz set out to develop a normative model of investor behavior in a
security market in which participants are uncertain about future events. He noted
that the tendency of investors to diversify their security portfolios cannot be
explained by the traditional maxim that investors seek to maximize the discounted returns from their holdings. If this were true, investors would never
diversify. Each market participant would hold only one security—the one which
he believed would generate the highest discounted returns.

Markowitz suggested that diversification is essentially an attempt by risk-
averse investors to lower their total risk exposure by purchasing a broad range of
securities. The underlying assumption is that while some securities may fall upon
hard times and their returns may decline, others will do well and will offset those
stocks whose returns have fallen. The recognition that shareholders are concerned with risk as well as return led Markowitz to offer his "mean-variance"
maxim in place of the maximization-of-discounted-returns rule.

This approach suggests that investors view uncertain security returns in terms
of a probability distribution similar to those portrayed in Exhibit 2. Furthermore,
investors are assumed to make their stock selection decisions on the basis of only
two attributes: (1) the mean or expected value of the probability distribution of
returns, and (2) the variance of the return distribution.[11] The variance of returns
is used as the risk surrogate—measuring as it does the variability in returns from
some expected value. Markowitz assumes that investors make decisions on the
basis of a single period time frame, i.e., a week, a month, a year, etc. The
expected return and variance are the investor's subjective estimates of these
parameters during this single time period.

Markowitz noted that when securities are combined into a portfolio, the expected return on that portfolio is a weighted average of the expected returns on
the component securities. However, the variance of the portfolio's return is not a
simple weighted average of the variances of the individual securities. Portfolio
variance is also a function of the correlation or covariances among the returns of
the securities. Markowitz demonstrated that this fact allows investors to reduce
portfolio variance without lowering the portfolio's return by combining securities
which have less than perfect positive intercorrelations (as measured by Pearson's
product-moment correlation coefficient) [34]. This procedure is referred to as
Markowitz efficient diversification. In effect, by combining stocks with less than
perfectly correlated returns, we find that a portion of each security's variation is

canceled by a complementary variation in the returns of other securities [68].

This diversification process can be demonstrated in terms of covariances. Markowitz shows that the variance of a portfolio's return is given by:[12]

$$\sigma_p^2 = \sum_{i=1}^{N} w_i^2 \sigma_i^2 + \sum_{i=1}^{N} \sum_{j=1}^{N} w_i w_j \, COV_{ij} \tag{6}$$

where

$\sigma^2{}_p$ = the variance of the return on the portfolio,
w_i = the proportion of the portfolio's value represented by security i,
σ_i^2 = the variance of the return of security i,
COV_{ij} = the covariance in the returns of securities i and j, and
N   = the number of securities in the portfolio.

Assume that equal dollar values are invested in each of the N securities such that

$$w_i = 1/N, \text{ for } i = 1, \ldots, N.$$

Equation (6) may then be written:

$$\sigma_p^2 = \frac{1}{N^2} \sum_{i=1}^{N} \sigma_i^2 + \frac{1}{N^2} \sum_{i=1}^{N} \sum_{j=1}^{N} COV_{ij} \tag{7}$$

If the largest variance of the securities included in the portfolio equals M, the first term on the right-hand side of (7) must satisfy

$$\frac{1}{N^2} \sum_{i=1}^{N} \sigma_i^2 \leq \frac{NM}{N^2} = \frac{M}{N}.$$

This expression will be smaller the larger the value of N. Thus, for very large portfolios the first term on the right-hand side of (7) will approach zero, leaving:

$$\sigma_p^2 \approx \frac{1}{N^2} \sum_{i=1}^{N} \sum_{j=1}^{N} COV_{ij}. \tag{8}$$

The mean of the covariance in the portfolio is

$$\overline{COV}_{ij} = \frac{\sum_{i=1}^{N} \sum_{j=1}^{N} COV_{ij}}{N(N-1)}. \tag{9}$$

Substituting (9) into (8) yields:

$$\sigma_p^2 \approx \frac{N-1}{N^2(N-1)} \sum_{i=1}^{N} \sum_{j=1}^{N} COV_{ij} = \frac{N-1}{N} \overline{COV}_{ij} \tag{10}$$

Equation (10) demonstrates that the variance of a portfolio approaches the average covariance of its component securities as the number of securities increases (as N increases, $(N-1)/N$ approaches 1). This means that the risk of a portfolio depends largely on the covariances of its individual securities. Thus, the risk contribution of a single security depends on its covariance with securities already in the portfolio rather than on its individual variance.

Once a portfolio is well diversified, its return becomes very highly correlated with the return on the security market as a whole. That is, the return on the portfolio tends to move in lock step with the weighted average return of all securities in the market. This occurs because much of the variation in stock returns due to firm specific events (e.g., product failures, strikes, management errors, etc.) has been eliminated through Markowitz efficient diversification. The variability that remains is due largely to macroeconomic events which impact all securities (e.g., the business cycle). This variability is known as systematic risk. Systematic risk is the portion of a security's return variance which cannot be diversified away because it is more or less common to all securities. The firm-specific variance, on the other hand, is known as unsystematic risk and can be largely eliminated by diversification.

As a result, in a market in which Markowitz efficient diversification is the rule, investors are basically concerned with systematic risk. Since all investors hold fully diversified portfolios, additions to portfolios are evaluated solely on the basis of their systematic risk levels. Of course, securities differ with regard to the amount of systematic risk they bring to a portfolio. For example, a firm which manufactures consumer durables is much more likely to have its fortunes affected by the business cycle than the producer of a staple food item. As such, the systematic variability of the former's stock is likely to be greater than that of the latter.

The most widely used index of systematic risk is the so-called beta coefficient.[13] This is simply the slope coefficient of a linear regression of the security's return (the dependent variable) on the market's return (the independent variable) for some ''representative'' number of periods:[14]

$$R_{ij} = \alpha_j + \beta_j R_{im} \qquad (11)$$

where

R_{ij} = the return on security j during period i,
α_j = the intercept coefficient for security j,
β_j = the beta coefficient for security j, and
R_{im} = the return on all market securities during period i.

Since the returns of almost all securities are positively correlated with the return on the market as a whole, high positive beta coefficients indicate a high level of systematic risk.

For example, using data from the period 1959 to 1969, Weston has estimated that Chrysler Corporation's beta is approximately 2.94 [100]. This means that for every 1 percent change in the market return, the return on Chrysler's stock can be expected to change by 2.94 percent. Because of its high level of volatility vis-à-vis the market, Chrysler's stock is a relatively unattractive candidate for inclusion in a portfolio.[15] As such, investors will bid Chrysler's price down (which is equivalent to bidding its return up) until its return is sufficient to compensate investors for assuming such a high level of systematic risk.

An opposite process occurs with low beta securities. Stocks with betas of less than one are known as defensive securities because they are particularly good candidates for inclusion in portfolios. Defensive securities tend to lower the systematic risk of fully diversified portfolios. As a result, these stocks are in high demand. This high demand for low beta securities pushes their prices up and drives their returns down. The adjustment process continues until the return on each security and portfolio in the market is commensurate with its systematic risk level. High-risk securities and portfolios will have relatively high returns, and low-risk securities and portfolios will have relatively low returns.

Sharpe demonstrated that when beta is used as the index of systematic risk, the risk-return relationship is not only positive, but also linear [88]. This linear relationship, known as the security market line (SML), is shown in Exhibit 3. Sharpe's equation for the security market line is given by:

$$E(R_j) = R_f + [E(R_m) - R_f]\beta_j \tag{12}$$

where

$E(R_j)$ = the expected return on any security j,

R_f = the risk-free rate of interest (often estimated by the return on U.S. Treasury bills),

$E(R_m)$ = the expected return on all securities in the market (often estimated by the return on the Standard & Poor's 500-stock index), and

β_j = the beta coefficient for security j.

According to Sharpe, when the capital market is in a state of equilibrium—that is, when the competitive bidding process has adjusted the securities to their proper risk-return levels—all portfolios and securities in the market should plot on the SML. The security market line is, in essence, a model of capital market behavior. Since investors are assumed to make their decisions on the basis of two factors—expected return and systematic risk—the SML purports to describe the equilibrium prices of all securities in the market. Thus, the SML is frequently referred to as the capital asset pricing model (CAPM).

V. MARKETING INVESTMENT ANALYSIS AND THE CAPM

In theory, the applicability of the CAPM should reach far beyond the major stock exchanges. It has been noted that it should be possible to plot all income-producing assets in the risk-return space of Exhibit 3. As long as investors are free to enter any market they desire, the competitive process will ensure that the risk-return ordered pairs of all assets plot on the security market line. This includes stocks and bonds, Treasury bills, real estate, and even the capital investment projects of business firms.

Consider, for example, Firm J, whose securities plot on the SML as shown in

14   PAUL F. ANDERSON

Exhibit 3.   The Security Market Line

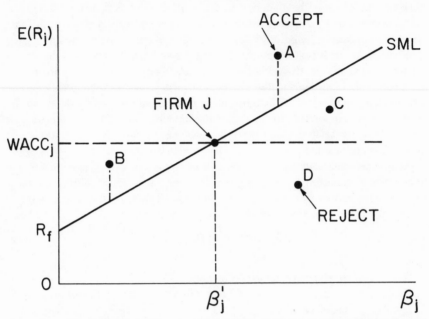

Source: Adapted from J. Fred Weston, "Investment Decisions Using the Capital Asset Pricing Model," *Financial Management,* Vol. 2 (Spring, 1973). pp. 25-33.

Exhibit 3. From the viewpoint of the investors, Firm J is simply a collection of real and intangible assets (e.g., plant and equipment, patents, managerial acumen, brand franchises, etc.) held for the benefit of the shareholder. Firm J's systematic risk level is indicated by its beta coefficient, β_j'. The expected return on the firm's securities is given by $WACC_j$ (this is also the weighted average cost of capital for the firm).[16] Let us once again assume that Firm J is considering four new-product investments represented by the letters A, B, C, and D. Acceptance of a project requires an investment outlay to cover the research and development, production, and marketing of the product. The return on this investment is the estimated after-tax cash flow generated by the new product.

The expected return and risk levels for each project are shown in Exhibit 3. Note that projects A and B both plot above the security market line. This means that the return on these projects is in excess of that which is required to induce an investor to accept their risk levels. Since their returns more than compensate the firm for assuming the risk, acceptance of the projects will result in an upward revision in the firm's share price. Once the projects are combined with the firm's other assets, the firm's own risk-return ordered pair will be in temporary disequilibrium, i.e., it will plot above the SML. Investors will then act to restore equilibrium by bidding up the price of the firm's shares and lowering its expected yield to the security market line. Thus, all investors holding Firm J's shares just prior to the acceptance of projects A and B will realize a subsequent wealth increment due to the increase in share price [85]. On the other hand, projects C and D both plot below the SML. This means that their returns are not sufficient to compensate for their risk levels. As such, Firm J should reject these projects.

It may be instructive at this point to compare the CAPM's decision rules with those of the traditional weighted average cost of capital approach. The weighted average cost of capital (WACC) for Firm J is given by the horizontal dashed line in Exhibit 3. (Since Firm J is financed entirely with equity, its cost of capital is the return which stockholders require to induce them to accept Firm J's risk level). In employing the cost of capital criterion, the firm accepts all investment projects whose returns exceed the WACC. As can be seen in Exhibit 3, this leads to decision which are different from those generated by the market model. The WACC approach would accept project C and reject project B, while the market model would reject C but accept B. The difference, of course, is that the security market line adjusts for the differential risk of the projects and the WACC does not. Indeed, the WACC is only applicable for projects in the same "risk class" as the firm [85].

Proponents of the CAPM approach suggest that it offers important advantages over the traditional cost of capital or the various risk-adjustment approaches discussed earlier. First, it provides the firm with an objectively determined risk measure (the beta coefficient) which reflects the systematic rather than the total variability of project returns. Since only nondiversifiable or systematic risk is relevant to investors who operate in Markowitz efficient security markets, beta becomes the "correct" risk measure for shareholder wealth maximizing firms. In addition, the CAPM's risk-return trade-off function represents the preferences of the firm's shareholders rather than those of management. Thus, the market model allows for the direct incorporation of shareholder preferences in firm investment decisions.

A. Operationalizing the Capital Asset Pricing Model

Even proponents of the CAPM approach to investment analysis realize that it is not without its operational difficulties. In particular, various measurement problems have limited its application in real-world settings.[17] (Chief among these problems is the estimation of beta coefficients for investment projects.) However, some progress has been made in recent years in developing approaches which circumvent some of the problems [13,14,98,100]. One such methodology will be presented here.

Consider the case of Firm J, which is trying to decide if it should enter a new product (Product D) in an established market. Firm J does not now compete in this market but has developed Product D as a technological spinoff from its main line of endeavor. After extensive marketing research covering such factors as market structure, consumer preferences, potential competitive reactions, available production and marketing resources, and a myriad of other factors, the firm has developed a ten-year revenue and profit forecast (it is expected that the product will have a ten-year life cycle). From this information, the firm determines the net after-tax cash flow which should result from the new product venture. These cash flows are then entered into the traditional net present value discounting formula to determine the investment worthiness of the project:

$$NPV_d = \sum_{i=1}^{n} \frac{A_i}{(1 + R_d)^i} \tag{13}$$

where

NPV_d = the net present value of the investment in Product D,

A_i = the net after-tax cash flow in year i,

n = the expected life of the product in years, and

R_d = the required rate of return for Product D calculated from the SML.

Equation (13) is simply an updated form of the risk-adjusted net present value method. The only difference between this approach and previous formulations is that the CAPM is used to generate the risk-adjusted discount rate. The discount rate R_d is calculated by using Sharpe's formula for the security market line [Eq. (12)]. Note that the components of Sharpe's equation are all market-wide constants. This implies that the required return for Product D will be the same for every firm in the economy. While the cash flow expectations will vary from firm to firm (because of differences in marketing and production expertise, synergism, and so forth), the discount rate will be constant across firms.[18]

With the exception of beta, the components of Sharpe's equation are easy to estimate. Both the risk-free rate R_f and the return on the market R_m can be estimated from published sources. Beta, on the other hand, is a more difficult matter. Unlike securities, new product investments are not traded on stock exchanges. Thus, it is difficult to determine their potential levels of systematic risk.

One approach to the problem is to employ the average beta coefficient of a group of companies engaged exclusively, or almost exclusively, in the manufacture and sale of the product under consideration. Since systematic risk is largely a function of the response of a firm's product line to variations in economic activity, it is suggested that this surrogate approach should provide a reasonably good estimate of the product's beta coefficient.

Assume, for example, that the average beta of firms which market Product D is approximately 1.9. If Firm J expects the return on the market to average 10 percent and expects the risk-free rate to be in the neighborhood of 4.4 percent, Sharpe's SML equation will generate a required return of 15 percent:

$$E(R_j) = R_f + [E(R_m) - R_f]\beta_j \tag{12}$$

$$15.0 = 4.4 + (10.0 - 4.4)1.9.$$

This, then, becomes the rate at which the expected cash flows from Product D are discounted in Eq. (13). The decision rule is to invest in the new product if its net present value is equal to or greater than zero. (This is equivalent to requiring Product D's return to plot on or above the SML). Alternatively, the internal rate of return for Product D could be determined by using Eq. (3). If the IRR equals or exceeds R_d, the investment in the new product should be made.

A third approach involves the computation of risk-adjusted hurdle rates for each of the firm's existing product lines. This methodology has been employed at the Quaker Oats Company to determine the required rates of return on present products. Quaker's products range from ready-to-eat cereals and pet foods to industrial chemicals and restaurants. Employing a surrogate approach and a slightly modified version of the SML, Bower and Jenks determined individualized hurdle rates for four of Quaker's major product categories: grocery products, toys, industrial chemicals, and restaurants [13]. The rates ranged from a low of around 8 percent for restaurants to a high of almost 12 percent for chemicals. The significance of these rates is that they may be employed to evaluate any new investments in each of the firm's product lines. For example, if Quaker Oats wishes to expand its industrial chemical line, it knows that it must earn at least 12 percent on any new investments in this category. In addition, these rates may be employed as a control device to evaluate the ongoing performance of each of Quaker's product lines or product divisions.[19] The major advantage here is that the required rates are tailored to the unique systematic risk levels of the various markets in which they compete.

Of course, it is not always a simple matter to estimate betas via the surrogate approach. In some cases, it will be difficult to find firms which deal exclusively with the product of interest. Indeed, in such instances it may be necessary to use a surrogate product which has similar systematic risk characteristics. For example, in calculating the individualized rates for Quaker Oats, Bower and Jenks reported difficulty in identifying wholly adequate surrogates for such products as pet foods, mixes, hot cereals, and industrial chemicals.

Another problem with the CAPM approach concerns the need to estimate the net cash flows resulting from the investment. Cash flow is usually estimated by determining net accounting income and adding back depreciation and other non-cash expenses [1]. However, net accounting income can only be determined by fully allocating all costs to the new venture. The potential distortions which can result from the arbitrary allocation of marketing costs have been well documented in the literature [19,35,53,71,78]. Given the current state of the art in distribution cost accounting, the Sharpe model is probably more applicable to relatively "free-standing" marketing investments in which the costs of the venture are somewhat easier to separate from other marketing activities. Depending upon the firm, this could include such major marketing ventures as the decision to introduce a new product, the decision to enter a new territory (or country), or the decision to acquire a new subsidiary. In addition, the CAPM has potential applications in the areas of new product pricing, product line extension and abandonment, divisional control, and many others. In the following sections, some of these applications will be reviewed.

1. New Product Pricing.   The CAPM may be employed to identify optimal pricing strategies for new products. An example problem will be used to illustrate this application. Consider a firm which is trying to determine if a price of $20, $25, or $30 is appropriate for a new product introduction. Unit sales forecasts and cash flows for each price alternative are shown in Table 2. For simplicity, it is assumed that the product will have a five-year life cycle. (After this time, its position in the product line will be filled by a technically superior model). It is further assumed that the forecasted cash flows reflect programmed adjustments in each price as a result of competitive reactions and the expected rate of inflation.

As can be seen from Table 2, the low, middle-range, and high-price strategies are expected to generate internal rates of return of 6.9 percent, 12.0 percent, and 10.7 percent, respectively. Obviously, the middle-range price of $25 results in the highest return. To determine if this return is commensurate with the risk of the new product, the firm could consult the CAPM. Assuming the following values for the SML's components,

$$R_f = 5.0\%$$
$$E(R_m) = 10.0\%$$
$$\beta = 1.2\%,$$

the required return on the new product is 11.0%:

$$E(R) = R_f + [E(R_m) - R_f]\beta \qquad (12)$$

$$11.0 = 5.0 + [10.0 - 5.0]\ 1.2.$$

Since the expected return on the $25 price is 12.0 percent, this represents the wealth-maximizing alternative.

Of course, most of the estimates involved in this decision process are subject to forecast error. As such, managerial judgment could be significantly enhanced through the use of sensitivity analysis. This would provide decision makers with information on the amount of forecast error in each variable necessary to change the outcome. A similar approach is demonstrated by Allen, Martin, and Anderson [3].

2. Product Line Extension, Proliferation, and Abandonment   One of the more interesting aspects of the CAPM concerns its implications for product line diver-

Table 2. New Product Pricing Example

	Price = $20		Price = $25		Price = $30	
Year	Unit Sales	Cash Flow	Unit Sales	Cash Flow	Unit Sales	Cash Flow
0	0	-$19,800	0	-$19,800	0	-$19,800
1	1,000	4,000	920	4,600	750	4,200
2	1,100	4,400	1,010	5,060	825	4,950
3	1,210	4,840	1,110	5,570	910	5,450
4	1,330	5,325	1,220	6,120	1,000	5,990
5	1,460	5,850	1,350	6,739	1,100	6,590
Total	6,100	$4,615	5,610	$8,280	4,585	$7,689
IRR		6.9%		12.0%		10.7%

sification. It was once believed that the investment projects of corporations could be treated like securities which are traded in the capital markets. This led a number of authors to apply the Markowitz portfolio approach to the firm's capital budgeting problem [76,96,99]. The same approach has been applied to the product mix problem by Kotler [55] and the new product decision by Burger [16]. Of course, application of the Markowitz portfolio model to the product investment decision will necessarily lead to product line diversification. Firms will seek to attain product portfolios which are fully diversified and "efficient" in a Markowitz sense [55].

However, this approach fails to consider what has come to be known as the "homemade diversification" theorem [2,69,72]. This theorem recognizes that shareholders can diversify their own holdings more easily and more efficiently than corporations. Thus, further diversification by the corporation becomes redundant. That is, product line diversification per se is not a thing of value from the standpoint of the stockholders [85]. On the other hand, corporations may be able to attain synergistic effects between products which the stockholder cannot duplicate in the market. In these instances, diversification can actually enhance shareholder wealth.

For example, consider the case of a data processing equipment marketer which wishes to expand its product offering by adding a line of office copiers. After considering all options, the firm decides that the acquisition of a medium-sized copier manufacturer would be its best vehicle for entry into the market. However, given that the firm's stockholders can easily acquire shares of the copier manufacturer in the securities market, is the acquisition a thing of value to the shareholders? This will depend upon the extent to which the merger generates synergistic effects [14]. For example, the fact that the data-processing firm has a recognized brand franchise and an effective marketing organization will probably increase the profitability of the copier line over and above what it would be without the merger. Similarly, the addition of copiers to the product line will likely enhance sales of data processing equipment. Thus, the synergy between the product lines will generate returns to shareholders in excess of those they would realize if they owned the stock of each firm as a separate concern.

Of course, similar reasoning can be generalized to new product investments which do not involve acquisitions or mergers. In this regard, the CAPM greatly simplifies the product line diversification decision. The general rule is to invest in all new products whose expected returns exceed the required return generated by the security market line. Of course, the expected returns must reflect expected synergistic effects between and among product lines. Thus, while the CAPM does not imply product line diversification per se, its decision rules may lead to some diversification if synergy is present.

As a result, a rigorous application of the CAPM would probably minimize much of the product line proliferation which is common in some industries. The discipline of the model would force product managers to quantify the cash flow benefits from the "full-line" strategy which is so often the justification for product proliferation. Unless it could be demonstrated that the *total* return (including incremental returns to other products) generated by the new addition is sufficient to compensate for its risk, the product line should not be expanded.

In theory, the product abandonment problem can be handled in much the same way as the product line extension decision. Periodically, the expected sales and returns of existing products should be reforecasted. If the return over the product's remaining life falls below its required security market line return, the product should be abandoned.

However, great care must be taken in calculating the product's return. If the cash flows reflect fixed costs which would not disappear with abandonment, or if the marginal returns from interrelated products are not considered, the CAPM could signal an incorrect abandonment decision.[20] Given the measurement problems involved, it may be necessary for the firm to fall back on more conventional procedures in dealing with this problem. Thus, contribution margin analysis may be a more appropriate device in some product abandonment cases. In effect, the use of the CAPM can be limited by the inability of distribution costing techniques to identify the cash flows of individual products or product lines.

3. Divisional Screening Rates.   In many companies, the marketing organization constitutes a separate division of the firm. Moreover, in many of the larger corporations individual product lines are organized into separate divisions. Given this type of organizational structure, it is clearly inappropriate to apply the corporation's weighted average cost of capital as a return standard for all divisions. Systematic risk differences across product lines require separate evaluation standards.

Consider, for example, a firm with one division which markets industrial machinery in a mature market and another which markets a household appliance which is in the growth stage of its product life cycle. It is clear that the business cycle will impact these products differentially [91]. As a result, the systematic risk of the two divisions will vary. The firm's cost of capital cannot serve as an evaluation standard since it reflects the "average" risk of the combined divisions. What is required are divisional screening rates which reflect the unique risk-return relationships of the product lines. The use of these rates by the Quaker Oats Company has already been discussed. In this section, one approach to the calculation of divisional screening rates will be presented.

The basic problem in determining the required rate of return for a corporate division is that, unlike the corporation itself, the division does not have securities which are traded in a capital market. Thus, the usual regression procedures for estimating the beta coefficient of a firm are closed to us. Fortunately, an alternative procedure has been suggested by Gordon and Halpern [40].

Given that the standard regression method for estimating beta,

$$R_j = \alpha_j + \beta_j R_m, \tag{11}$$

is not possible for a nontraded division, Gordon and Halpern offer a surrogate approach. They suggest that there may be a statistic $\hat{C}_j$ available from company records which is highly correlated with the firm's beta coefficient. If this is the case, the following regression may be run to determine estimates of the parameters λ_o and λ_1:

$$\hat{\beta}_j = \lambda_o + \lambda_1 \hat{C}_j \tag{14}$$

where

$\hat{\beta}_j$ = firm j's beta coefficient,

λ_o and λ_1 = regression parameters, and

$\hat{C}_j$ = a variable based on company records which is highly correlated with $\hat{\beta}_j$.

Once λ_o and λ_1 are determined, they may be substituted into Eq. (15) to estimate the beta coefficient of division s:

$$\hat{\beta}_{js} = \lambda_o + \lambda_1 \hat{C}_{js}, \tag{15}$$

where

$\hat{\beta}_{js}$ = the beta coefficient of the sth division of firm j,

λ_o and λ_1 = the regression parameters from Eq. (14), and

$\hat{C}_{js}$ = a variable based on divisional records which is comparable to $\hat{C}_j$.

The estimated beta for the division can then be used in the SML model to generate the screening rate for division s:

$$k_{js} = R_f + [R_m - R_f]\hat{\beta}_{js} \tag{16}$$

where k_{js} equals the required return on the division and the other variables are as previously defined.

Gordon and Halpern provide fairly strong theoretical and empirical support for using the rate of growth in net or operating income as the surrogate variables $\hat{C}_j$ and $\hat{C}_{js}$. Thus, the estimation Eqs. (14) and (15) would become

$$\hat{\beta}_j = \lambda_0 + \lambda_1 \hat{g}_j \qquad (14')$$

and

$$\hat{\beta}_{js} = \lambda_0 + \lambda_1 \hat{g}_{js} \qquad (15')$$

where

$\hat{g}_j =$ the growth rate of net or operating income for the corporation, and

$\hat{g}_{js} =$ the growth rate of net or operating income for the division.

Of course, serious estimation problems arise in determining either the net or operating income of a division. However, these estimation problems must be faced regardless of the method used in evaluating the financial performance of the division.

Once screening rates have been developed for each of the firm's product divisions, they can be used as a standard for all new investments made by the divisions. In addition, the screening rates can be used to evaluate the performance of division or product management. The real advantage of using divisional rates in this fashion is that managers are evaluated on the basis of the unique risk-return relationships in their individual markets. The CAPM automatically adjusts the required return to account for the systematic risk of the division. Thus, product managers are not held to a single standard which is not applicable to any particular product line.

Of course, care must be exercised in employing return standards as a performance evaluation tool. The problems involved in using a rate of return requirement for divisional control purposes have been well documented in the literature [21,22,42,48]. In general, a rate of return standard may tend to encourage behavior which is not in the best interests of the firm as a whole. For example, in an attempt to improve their rates of return, managers may lower their investment bases by scrapping productive assets or by leasing equipment when purchase is more advantageous.[21] Similarly, managers may be reluctant to dilute the return on their divisions by investing in products whose returns, while acceptable, are below the current rate being earned by the division.

One approach for dealing with the latter problem involves the use of Solomons' residual income technique [70,93]. With this procedure, the return standard becomes a "cost of capital" charge which is deducted from divisional revenue. Management is then evaluated on the basis of the division's contribution margin as shown in Table 3. Since the focus is on contribution margin and not return-on-investment, there is no incentive to avoid certain investments which might lower divisional ROI. There is, however, the danger that managers

Table 3. Division Contribution Margin: Residual Income Approach

Divisional Revenue		$5,000,000
Variable Costs	$2,500,000	
Fixed Costs	$1,000,000	
Investment Costs (12% divisional cost of capital x $5,000,000 divisional investment)	$ 600,000	
Total Costs		$4,100,000
Division Contribution Margin		$ 900,000

may tend to prefer investments with low payback periods in order to improve short-run contribution margins. As such, the investment evaluation procedure must still be prescribed and monitored by corporate management to ensure that the market model standards are employed.

B. The CAPM: Problems and Limitations

The general concerns with the application of the CAPM fall into two categories. First, questions have been raised concerning the applicability of the CAPM to the complex multiperiod firm investment decision. Second, there is the empirical issue of whether Sharpe's security market equation represents the return generating process in the capital markets.

The former concern relates to the issue of whether a positive theory of equilibrium security prices can be applied directly as a normative tool for corporate investment analysis. For example, the discount rate generated by the SML is a single-period rate calculated as shown in Eq. (5). Some have questioned the accuracy of applying this rate to the multiperiod cash flows of a firm's investment project [14,98]. This issue has been investigated by both Fama [29] and Myers and Turnbull [73]. Fama shows that if the production and marketing activities of the firm are not expected to change much over time, and if the parameters of the CAPM remain constant, it is reasonable to discount a multiperiod cash flow at a single risk-adjusted rate. Similarly, Myers and Turnbull show that any errors introduced by employing the market model in the multiperiod investment context are generally small. However, they go on to demonstrate that estimating beta via the surrogate approach is more difficult than originally believed. They note three problems with the surrogate approach. First, there will always be measurement error in any regression estimate of beta. Second, the surrogate firms must have the same beta coefficient as the project under consideration. That is, they should be matched on "asset life, growth, patterns of expected cash flows over time, the characteristics of each component of the cash flows, the relative contribution of the components to the firm's value, and possibly on other factors" [73, p. 331]. Finally, the estimated beta will generally lead to a biased discount rate if the surrogate firms have significant growth opportunities.

Another category of concern relates to the assumptions underlying the CAPM. It is said that if these assumptions do not hold, it is inappropriate to apply the CAPM in a firm investment context. For example, one of the key assumptions of the market model is that the cost of bankruptcy to the equity holders is zero [98]. That is, if insolvency occurs, the firm's assets can be sold at their full economic values without legal or disposal costs. If this assumption holds, investors will be able to diversify away a firm's unsystematic risk. However, if bankruptcy costs are positive (as they are in most real-world liquidations), the investor will be unable to fully diversify his portfolio. Since bankruptcy depends on both systematic and unsystematic risk, it would be inappropriate in this setting for the firm to make investment decisions according to the market model. On the other hand, the probability of bankruptcy for many large corporations is rather remote. If this is the case, Van Horne suggests that it is perfectly appropriate for the corporation to employ the CAPM to make firm investment decisions [98, p. 183].

In a similar fashion, the theoretical basis for the CAPM requires minimal "imperfections" in the capital markets. For example, it is assumed that investors can lend or borrow funds at the same rate of interest, that there are no transactions costs involved in buying or selling securities, and that market information is equally available to all investors [34]. Of course, these assumptions do not hold in the real world; however, many believe that the actual impact of such "imperfections" on the CAPM is probably small [98, p. 183].

The far more serious concern with the applicability of the CAPM is the empirical issue. Almost from the beginning, tests of the CAPM generated negative findings. One of the best known tests of the SML was conducted by Blume and Friend in 1973 [12]. As with most of the subsequent tests of the CAPM, they used regression analysis to determine if security returns are in fact a positive linear function of their beta coefficients.[22] Using data from the New York Stock Exchange (NYSE), they found no relationship existing for the 1955–1959 period, a negative relationship for the period 1960–1964, and the anticipated relationship only for the 1965–1968 period. Similar inconsistent results were also found by Jacob [51].

In an attempt to determine if returns might be a function of both systematic and total risk, empirical enquiries were conducted by Arditti [7], Douglas [25], and Lintner [61]. In these studies, security returns were regressed on both risk measures simultaneously. Arditti and Douglas found that beta's impact on return was either insignificant or in the wrong direction. On the other hand, Lintner found significant effects for both systematic and total risk. These studies were then subjected to a detailed analysis by Miller and Scholes [67] and by Black, Jensen, and Scholes [10]. Both studies concluded that various statistical problems severely limited the validity of the research findings.

Black, Jensen, and Scholes (BJS) [10] then proposed and tested a revised version of Sharpe's equation. Their so-called two-factor model takes the form:

$$R_j = (1 - \beta_j) R_z + \beta_j R_m, \qquad (17)$$

where R_z equals the return on the zero-beta portfolio (i.e., a portfolio which is uncorrelated with the market return). Based on empirical testing, they conclude that the two-factor model is a better representation of the return generating process than Sharpe's "single-factor" model. Fama and MacBeth extended the BJS work by testing a more complex four-factor model of the SML [30]. They concluded that the overall data are consistent with the two-factor model of BJS.

More recently, however, Roll has demonstrated that these tests of the CAPM are meaningless [80]. The problem arises because it can be shown that the linear relationship between return and beta is a tautology. Given this fact, empirical studies which focus on the linearity of the SML are not true tests of the mean-variance capital asset pricing model. Roll demonstrates that there is only one testable hypothesis generated by the capital asset pricing theory. This hypothesis is that the market portfolio is mean-variance efficient. That is, if all risky assets in the economy are treated as a portfolio, none of the portfolio's components (taken individually or as subportfolios) can attain a superior risk-return relationship, i.e., more return for the given risk or less risk for a given return. The linearity of the relationship between expected return and beta follows from the market portfolio's efficiency and is not independently testable [80, p. 130]. Moreover, in order to test the efficiency hypothesis the exact composition of the market portfolio would have to be specified. Since this includes all risky assets (e.g., stocks, bonds, options, coins, houses, land, human capital, etc.) the identification problem is enormously difficult. Even if researchers could agree on a proxy portfolio, the econometric problems involved may be insoluble. As a result, Roll concludes that "there is practically no possibility that such a test can be accomplished in the future" [80, pp. 129–130]; and, he suggests that the CAPM should be abandoned in favor of Ross's arbitrage theory of capital asset pricing [82,83].

Ross, on the other hand, believes that a test of the CAPM is possible, but he recognizes that the problems involved will be formidable [84, p. 893]. He also notes that if the empirical difficulties with CAPM prove to be insurmountable, the arbitrage pricing theory (APT) is its logical successor (assuming that the APT is not rejected by empirical testing).

C. The Arbitrage Pricing Theory

The APT itself is deceptively simple. Ross assumes that returns on assets are generated by the following mechanism:

$$\tilde{R}_i = E_i + \beta_{i1}\tilde{R}_{p1} + \beta_{i2}\tilde{R}_{p2} + \ldots + \beta_{ik}\tilde{R}_{pk} + \tilde{\epsilon}_i \qquad (18)$$

where

$\tilde{R}_i$ = the return on a given asset,

$E_i, \beta_{i1} \ldots \beta_{ik}$ = constants,

$\tilde{R}_{p1} \ldots \tilde{R}_{pk}$ = economic factors, and

$\tilde{\epsilon}_i$ = a random disturbance term independent of the $\tilde{R}_p$ and $\tilde{\epsilon}_j$.

In essence, Eq. (18) states that returns on assets are a linear function of various economic indicators. For example, returns may be a function of such factors as industrial production, the consumer price index and the prime rate of interest. (The identity of the $\tilde{R}_p$ is an empirical question which is not addressed by Ross.) Through a process similar to Markowitz efficient diversification, investors will be able to eliminate the residual risk term $\tilde{\epsilon}_i$. Furthermore, if all arbitrage opportunities have been exhausted in the capital markets, the expected return on an asset will be given by:

$$E_a = E_0 + (E_{p1} - E_0)\beta_{a1} + (E_{p2} - E_0)\beta_{a2} + \ldots$$

$$+ (E_{pk} - E_0)\beta_{ak} \qquad (19)$$

where

E_a = the expected return on an asset a,

E_0 = the expected return on a riskless asset,

$\beta_{a1} \ldots \beta_{ak}$ = the beta coefficients for each of the k factors, and

$E_{p1} \ldots E_{pk}$ = the expected returns on portfolios of securities which have a beta coefficient of 1 when regressed on the kth factor and a beta of zero on all others.

Equation (19) is nothing more than a multifactor version of the CAPM. Instead of a single beta coefficient related to the return on the market, the APT has multiple beta coefficients—one for each factor which generates asset returns. Indeed, Eq. (19) reduces to Eq. (12) (Sharpe's SML) when the only factor generating returns is the return on the market as a whole (R_m).

The APT has two major advantages over the CAPM. The first is its minimal assumption set. The APT requires only that $\bar{\epsilon}_i$ can be diversified away and that all arbitrage opportunities have been exploited. Its second major advantage is that the APT is clearly testable if the factors generating the returns in (18) are identified.

The APT's application to marketing investment analysis is a straightforward extention of the CAPM procedure. The required return on a marketing investment would be generated by Eq. (19) and compared with the expected return. Investments whose expected returns exceed the required return should be undertaken. Of course, the major unresolved issue is the identification of the factors which generate the returns on marketing investments. This is a crucial empirical issue which will require much additional research before it is clear if the APT has practical potential for marketing. In the meantime, a recently developed approach to the investment problem based on time-state preference theory may offer a practical alternative to parameter preference models.

VI. A TIME-STATE PREFERENCE APPROACH TO MARKETING INVESTMENT ANALYSIS

For many years the time-state preference approach associated with the names of Arrow [8] and Debreu [23] has been the major theoretical competitor of parameter preference models such as the CAPM. Unfortunately, implementational problems have retarded the development of time-state models as practical corporate investment tools. However, recent work by Ross [81] and by Black and Scholes [11] has led the way to the development of such a model by Banz and Miller [9]. This approach should have particular appeal for marketers because of its similarity to expected value and decision tree models extant in the marketing literature [18,55].

Banz and Miller's basic valuation equation is given by:

$$\text{NPV} = \sum_{i=1}^{n} v_i \bar{X}_i \qquad (20)$$

where

NPV = the net present value of the investment,

$\bar{X}_i$ = the expected cash flows in each future state of the economy $i = 1, 2, \ldots, n$, and

v_i = the current market-determined price of a security which pays \$1 in state i and zero otherwise.

The v_i or state prices adjust the future cash flows for risk. The v_i range between 0 and $+1$ and adjust for the risk preferences of investors and the probability of the occurence of state i. To apply the model an anlyst must estimate the state-contingent cash flows generated by an investment.

An illustration may help to clarify the model's application. Assume that a firm is considering the introduction of a new product which is expected to be a fad item with a three year life cycle.[24] Further assume that the firm can forecast cash flows for the product under three alternative economic scenarios as shown in Table 4. Using state prices calculated by Banz and Miller, the net present value of the new product investment is:

$$\text{NPV} = -\$750(.1672) + \$3,000(.1693) + \$1,000(.1686) - \$1,500(.2912)$$
$$+\$2,000(.2915) + \$800(.2903) - \$2,500(.5398) + \$1,000(.5333)$$
$$+\$500(.5313) = \$379[25] \tag{20}$$

Since the net present value exceeds zero, the firm should invest in the new product.

Of course, the model is highly dependent on the accuracy of Banz and Miller's state prices. These are calculated by employing a variant of the Black-Scholes options pricing model [11,15]. The Black-Scholes model was designed to price European-type call options on common stock. Such an option allows the holder to purchase a certain number of shares of the stock at a certain price on a given day. Ross has shown that by combining such options in a hedge portfolio with their underlying securities a unique contingent claim can be formed which will pay off in only one future state of the world [81]. If the prices of such contingent claims could be estimated, they would provide the v_i for Eq. (20).

In an attempt to estimate these state prices, Banz and Miller employ the predictive distributions of stock market returns developed by Ibbotson and Sinquefield [49,50]. The predictive distributions are derived from simulations based on fifty years of actual past returns. Banz and Miller employ the return on the stock market as their index of the state of the "economy." For example, in developing estimates for a three state world, they define a "recession" as a

Table 4. State-Contingent Cash Flow Forecasts

	State of Economy		
Year	Boom	Normal	Recession
1	-$750	-$1,500	-$2,500
2	$3,000	$2,000	$1,000
3	$1,000	$800	$500

return on the market between -86.47 percent and $+0.06$ percent, "normal" as a return between $+0.06$ percent and $+20.42$ percent, and "boom" as a return be tween $+20.42$ percent and $+171.83$ percent. The categories reflect "states" which have occurred with roughly equal probability over the last fifty years. Banz and Miller also develop estimates for 5 and 20 state worlds. The resultant state prices are published in tables in their article [9].

Thus, to employ the state-preference approach, an analyst merely forecasts a project's state-contingent cash flows and employs the Banz and Miller tables and formula to estimate its net present value. However, at this stage of its development, one would be advised to use the model with caution. There are many crucial assumptions implicit in the Banz and Miller computations. Moreover, their work has not yet been subjected to independent evaluation and critique. We can expect further development and refinements in this area in the years to come.

VII. ASSESSMENT AND DIRECTIONS FOR FUTURE RESEARCH

Given the various empirical, practical and theoretical problems with the invest- ment models presented in this paper, where does this leave us with respect to marketing investment analysis? An answer to this question must consider both the theoretical and practical dimensions of the problem. From a theoretical standpoint, it is clear that the financial literature has advanced well beyond the approaches which we find in the marketing literature. In part, this reflects the fact that financial theorists have adopted shareholder wealth maximization as the ultimate goal of the firm. As such, the risk adjustments in contemporary financial models attempt to represent the risk preferences of stockholders rather than those of management. Thus, in the CAPM, the APT and the time-state preference approaches we see the use of market-determined measures of risk. Unfortu- nately, much more empirical and theoretical work will be necessary to determine which, if any, of these models will emerge as the accepted basis for investment analysis. Given the amount of work involved, it appears that it will be many years before a consensus is reached.

In the interim, what guidance can the financial literature provide the marketer who must decide between investments in two mutually exclusive marketing ventures? This brings us to the practical dimension of the issue. What is required, of course, is a "second-best" theory. Given that an investment analysis model which is both theoretically "correct" and operationally practical has not yet emerged, which approach will provide the marketer with "nearly right" an- swers. Unfortunately, the financial literature can provide little insight on this point. Until the optimal model is known, it is impossible to specify the close approximations.

Perhaps the most reasonable approach for marketers to take is to employ a combination of methodologies in assessing the investment worthiness of marketing projects. For example, a firm might be advised to use one of the traditional risk-adjustment approaches (e.g., certainty-equivalent, risk-adjusted discount rate or Kotler's risk-return criterion) with one of the more recently developed models (e.g., Banz and Miller's time-state preference approach). If the signals from both methodologies are consistent, the firm should have greater confidence in following the indicated decision. Of course, a problem arises when the models give inconsistent signals, as is likely to occur with more marginal projects. In this situation it may be important to recall that the largest potential source of error in such computations surrounds the estimates of the cash flows and not the risk-adjustments. As Banz and Miller note, it is hard to understand why practitioners who have been "swallowing whole herds of camels" in the form of cash flow forecasts would "strain at the gnat or two of imprecision" in the discount rate estimates [9, p. 654].

Thus, from a practical standpoint, marginal investments must be viewed with caution because of the forecast error which is not accounted for by any of the financial risk adjustment methodologies. This may suggest to some firms that consistent "accept" decisions must be generated by alternative models before funds are committed to marketing projects.

It is also suggestive of an important avenue for future research. The problem of forecasting the cash flows generated by new projects is one of the major barriers to improved marketing investment analysis. While much progress has been made in improving our forecasting tools, less emphasis has been placed on quantifying the forecast error inherent in these procedures. This is particularly true of the diffusion models which are widely used in forecasting new product sales [55, pp. 524–36]. Moreover, little attention has been paid to the problem of incorporating forecast error in the investment decision calculus.

In addition, only moderate progress has been made in improving our ability to associate cash flows with specific marketing ventures, e.g., products, customers, territories, etc. Improved forecasts must be built upon better historical estimates of segmental cash flows. This will require the development of new methods of distribution cost accounting. Our present methodologies are wholly inadequate for the task at hand. Indeed, contemporary full-allocation procedures differ very little from those developed fifty years ago [6].

It would be unfortunate if the limitations of modern distribution cost analysis were allowed to inhibit the wider application of financial technologies in marketing. While the current trend toward contribution margin and segmental analysis approaches is to be applauded, it must be recognized that such methodologies are primarily useful for short-run decision making and control purposes. For longer term decisions, an investment (i.e., discounted cash flow) approach provides the more appropriate framework [31,98]. Indeed, if inordinate emphasis is placed on contribution margin approaches, research effort may be diverted from full-allocation methods.

Of course, a resolution of the basic theoretical issues in investment analysis remains as the first research priority for financial theorists. Empirical tests of the APT and, if possible, the CAPM are needed to provide a solid theoretical basis for their potential application as normative capital budgeting tools. Moreover, continued investigation of the Banz and Miller state-preference approach is clearly warranted. In particular, the accuracy of their assumption set and the resulting state-prices requires scrutiny.

Marketers and others outside the field of finance may find that they can make contributions to this research effort. For example, both marketers and economists may be particularly useful in identifying the return generating factors in the arbitrage pricing model. Of particular interest to marketing are the factors related to the return on new products. This suggests a need for the kind of econometric study well known to many members of the discipline.

In addition, one of the important assumptions of the Banz and Miller model is that the transitions from one state of the economy to another follow a stationary Markov process. Clearly, the marketing expertise in this area could be called upon to assist in tests of this crucial assumption.

Further down the road marketers must focus on efforts to improve the practical application of these emerging financial technologies. Estimating beta coefficients for new marketing projects or forecasting state-contingent cash flows will not be an easy task. Furthermore, the behaviorial implications of employing these new approaches must be considered. For example, what are the consequences of using differential screening rates as performance measurement and reward criteria? It is unlikely that product managers will react favorably if their own required return is higher than that of other product managers. This is particularly true if the managers do not fully understand the basis for the different return standards. Most marketing decision makers are not used to thinking of risk in terms of beta coefficients, state-contingent prices or variability of cash flows. As such, the implementation of this type of system could lead to severe morale problems unless it is preceded by an educational program. It would be extremely useful to study the implementation of such a system in a corporate setting to determine the types of problems which arise and the remedies which are employed.

Indeed, behavioral considerations may be a major constraint in the adoption of equilibrium models as marketing investment tools. For example, the implications of the CAPM or APT for product line diversification may be particularly difficult for many marketing decision makers to accept. The concept of diversification as a risk reduction strategy is fairly well ingrained in American industry. It is doubtful that financial theorists will be able to overturn such a time-honored tradition in a short period of time. Unfortunately, little is known about the adoption of managerial technologies by industry. Perhaps additional research in this area is a necessary antecedent to the full implementation of theoretical finance concepts in marketing.

Finally, an obvious avenue for research involves a comparison of the decisions generated by the newer technologies with those of the existing investment analysis procedures. This could be accomplished by reevaluating the past investment decisions of a firm or a sample of firms using the CAPM, the APT and the state-preference model. The objective would be to determine if these approaches would make a real difference in the kinds of marketing investments undertaken by the firm.

Of course, this would not constitute a test of the models' normative implications. However, it would suggest the magnitude of the impact that these approaches could have on marketing decision making. For example, if it is found that the impact is slight, we can assume that existing technologies and subjective risk adjustments are doing a reasonably good job of allocating marketing resources within the firm. On the other hand, if significant differences emerge, it appears that it will be time for marketers to reevaluate their methods of analyzing investments. Whatever the outcome, more research is clearly needed to resolve the many unanswered questions in this area of marketing.

ACKNOWLEDGMENT

The author benefited from numerous discussions with Professor John Thatcher. Errors and omissions, however, are solely the responsibility of the author.

NOTES

1. Because of the "reinvestment rate" problem and the potential for multiple rates of return, the net present value method is considered to be theoretically superior to the internal rate of return model. See [47,63,98], for example.

2. Additional techniques will be found in [43,44,45,46,64,65,97].

3. A similar approach is suggested by Pessemier [74].

4. The rate of return and variance of a project are estimated subjectively by the decision maker.

5. Capital rationing is generally considered to be a less than optimal investment strategy. See [89] for example.

6. For opposing viewpoints and the middle-ground position on this issue, see [33,98,100].

7. The ultimate objective of the firm is to maximize shareholder utility. As long as capital markets are perfectly competitive, this is equivalent to maximizing shareholder wealth [31].

8. This section draws heavily upon [75,92,98].

9. Of course, market imperfections such as entry barriers can distort this relationship. However, as Solomon points out, the fault is not with the wealth maximization criterion, but rather with those charged with ensuring the competitiveness of American industry [92].

10. For a discussion of the role of social responsibility objectives in the wealth maximizing firm, see [98].

11. Markowitz measures the return on a security in a single-period context as:

$$R = \frac{(P_{t+1} - P_t) + D_t}{P_t} \tag{5}$$

where

$R =$ the single-period return on the security,

$P_t =$ the price of the security at the beginning of the period t,

P_{t+1} = the price of the security at the end of period t, and

D_t = the dividends paid during period t.

12. This proof is adapted from Lev [57] and Fama and Miller [31].

13. The concept of the beta coefficient was developed by Sharpe [88].

14. In the financial literature the raw regression coefficient has come to be known as beta. This is not to be confused with the standardized regression coefficient or beta weight.

15. Weston suggests that the relatively high beta coefficient reflects the fact that Chrysler manufactures a consumer durable with relatively high income elasticity [100].

16. For simplicity, it is assumed that the firm is financed entirely with equity.

17. These issues will be discussed in greater detail in a later section.

18. This is a direct consequence of the fact that all firms are concerned only with systematic risk [98].

19. For an alternative approach to the computation of divisional hurdle rates, see Section V., A.,3.

20. The possibility of improving return by following a harvesting or milking strategy must also be considered [54].

21. Despite the new accounting standards [4], some firms may exclude leased assets from divisional balance sheets.

22. Blume and Friend actually tested a form of the two-factor model proposed by Black, Jensen, and Scholes [10]. This model will be discussed below.

23. Richard W. Roll, "The Capital Asset Pricing Model: Issues and Controversies," Seminar presented at Virginia Polytechnic Institute, May 8, 1979.

24. This illustration is adapted from Haley and Schall [41].

25. This assumes that the economy is currently in a "normal" state.

REFERENCES

1. Abdelsamad, Moustafa H. *A Guide to Capital Expenditure Analysis*. New York: AMACOM, 1973.

2. Alberts, William W. and Segall, Joel E. *The Corporate Merger*. Chicago: University of Chicago Press, 1966.

3. Allen, Chester L., Martin, John D., and Anderson, Paul F. "Debt Capacity and the Lease-Purchase Problem: A Sensitivity Analysis." *Engineering Economist* 24 (Winter 1979): 87–108.

4. Anderson, Paul F. "Accounting Changes Should Benefit Equipment Lease Marketer, Customer." *Marketing News* (17 December 1976): 3.

5. ———. *Financial Aspects of Industrial Leasing Decisions: Implications for Marketing*. East Lansing: Michigan State University Press, 1977.

6. ———. "Distribution Cost Analysis Methodologies, 1901–1941." *The Accounting Historians Journal* 6 (Fall 1979): 39–51.

7. Arditti, Fred. "Risk and the Required Return on Equity." *Journal of Finance* 22 (March 1967): 19–36.

8. Arrow, Kenneth. "The Role of Securities in the Optimal Allocation of Risk Bearing." *Review of Economic Studies* 31 (April 1964): 91–96.

9. Banz, Rolf W. and Miller, Merton H. "Prices for State-Contingent Claims: Some Estimates and Applications." *Journal of Business* 51 (October, 1978): 653–672.

10. Black, F., Jensen, M., and Scholes, M. "The Capital Asset Pricing Model: Some Empirical Tests." In M. Jensen, ed., *Studies in the Theory of Capital Markets*. New York: Praeger, 1972, pp. 79–121.

11. Black, Fischer, and Scholes, Myron. "The Pricing of Options and Corporate Liabilities." *Journal of Political Economy* 81 (May-June, 1975): 637-654.
12. Blume, Marshall, and Friend, Irwin. "A New Look at the Capital Asset Pricing Model." *Journal of Finance* 28 (March 1973): 16-33.
13. Bower, Richard S., and Jenks, Jeffrey M. "Divisional Screening Rates." *Financial Management* 4 (Autumn 1975): 42-49.
14. Bower, Richard S. and Lessard, Donald R. "An Operational Approach to Risk-Screening." *Journal of Finance* 28 (May 1973): 321-337.
15. Breeden, Douglas, and Litzenberger, Robert. "Prices of State Contingent Claims Implicit in Option Prices." *Journal of Business* 51 (October 1978z: 621-51.
16. Burger, Philip C. "A Marketing Model for Selecting Among Interdependent New Product Candidates." Working Paper #75-08, State University of New York at Binghamton, February 1975.
17. Bursk, Edward C. "View Your Customers as Investments." *Harvard Business Review* 44 (May-June 1966): 91-94.
18. Cravens, David W., Hills, Gerald E., and Woodruff, Robert B. *Marketing Decision Making.* Homewood, Ill.: Richard D. Irwin, 1976.
19. Crissy, W. J. E., Fischer, Paul, and Mossman, Frank H. "Segmental Analysis: Key to Marketing Profitability." *MSU Business Topics* 21 (Spring 1973): 42-49.
20. Dean, Joel. "Does Advertising Belong in the Capital Budget?" *Journal of Marketing* 30 (October 1966): 15-21.
21. Dearden, John. "Problem in Decentralized Financial Control." *Harvard Business Review* 39 (May-June 1961): 72-80.
22. ———. "Problem in Decentralized Profit Responsibility." *Harvard Business Review* 38 (May-June 1960): 79-86.
23. Debreu, Gerard. *The Theory of Value.* New York: John Wiley, 1959.
24. Donaldson, Gordon. "Strategic Hurdle Rates for Capital Investment." *Harvard Business Review* 50 (March-April 1972): 50-58.
25. Douglas, George. "Risk in the Equity Markets." *Yale Economic Review* 9 (Spring 1969): 3-45.
26. Duncan, Delbert J., and Hollander, Stanley C. *Modern Retailing Management.* 9th ed. Homewood, Ill.: Richard D. Irwin, 1977.
27. Edmonds, Charles P. III, and Hand, John H. "What Are the Real Long-Run Objectives of Business?" *Business Horizons* 19 (December 1976): 75-81.
28. Etgar, Michael, and Schneller, Meir. "Advertising Budgeting in a Multiproduct Firm." In *Contemporary Marketing Thought,* Barnett A. Greenberg and Danny N. Bellenger (eds.) Chicago: American Marketing association, 1977, p. 527.
29. Fama, Eugene F. "Risk-Adjusted Discount Rates and Capital Budgeting Under Uncertainty." *Journal of Financial Economics* 5 (August 1977): 3-24.
30. Fama, Eugene, and MacBeth, James. "Risk, Return, and Equilibrium: Empirical Tests." *Journal of Political Economy* 81 (May 1973): 607-636.
31. Fama, Eugene, and Miller, Merton H. *The Theory of Finance.* Hinsdale, Ill.: Dryden Press, 1972.
32. Findlay, M. C., and Danan, Alian. "A Free Lunch on the Toronto Stock Exchange." *Journal of Business Administration* 6 (Spring 1975): 31-40.
33. Findlay, M. C., Gooding, Arthur E., and Weaver, Wallace, Q., Jr. "On the Relevant Risk for Determining Capital Expenditure Hurdle Rates." *Financial Management* 5 (Winter 1976): 9-16.
34. Francis, Jack Clark, and Archer, Stephen H. *Portfolio Analysis.* Englewood Cliffs, N.J.: Prentice-Hall, 1971.
35. Frazer, George E. "The Pro-Rating of Distribution Expense to Sales Orders." *Journal of Accountancy* 13 (January 1912): 25-43.

36. Friedman, Milton. "The Methodology of Positive Economics." In *Essays in Positive Economics*. Chicago: University of Chicago Press, 1956, pp. 3–34.
37. Gabor, Andre. "Marketing's Role in Investment Decisions." *Marketing* (September 1970): 44–47.
38. Gregory, R. H. "Cost of Distribution." *NACA Yearbook*. New York: National Association of Cost Accountants, 1922, pp. 116–126.
39. ———. "Recognizing Distribution Costs and Investment in Pricing." *NACA Yearbook*. New York: National Association of Cost Accountants, 1939, pp. 317–351.
40. Gordon, Myron, J., and Halpern, Paul J. "Cost of Capital for a Division of a Firm." *Journal of Finance* 29 (September 1974): 1153–1163.
41. Haley, Charles W., and Schall, Lawrence D. *The Theory of Financial Decisions*. New York: McGraw-Hill, 1979.
42. Henderson, Bruce D., and Dearden, John. "New System for Divisional Control." *Harvard Business Review* 44 (September-October 1966): 144–160.
43. Hertz, David B. "Investment Policies that Pay Off." *Harvard Business Review* 46 (January-February 1968): 96–108.
44. ———. "Risk Analysis in Capital Investment." *Harvard Business Review* 42 (January-February 1964): 95–106.
45. Hillier, Frederick S. "The Derivation of Probabilistic Information for the Evaluation of Risky Investments." *Management Science* 9 (April 1963): 443–457.
46. Hillier, Frederick S., and Heebink, David V. "Evaluating Risky Capital Investments." *California Management Review* 8 (Winter, 1965): 71–80.
47. Hirshleifer, J. "On the Theory of Optimal Investment Decision." *Journal of Political Economy* 66 (August 1958): 95–103.
48. Hopwood, Anthony. *Accounting and Human Behavior*. Englewood Cliffs, N.J.: Prentice-Hall, 1976.
49. Ibbotson, Roger, and Sinquefield, Rex. "Stocks, Bonds, Bills and Inflation: Simulations of the Future (1976–2000)." *Journal of Business* 49 (July 1976): 313–338.
50. Ibbotson, Roger, and Sinquefield, Rex. *Stocks, Bonds, Bills and Inflation: the Past (1926–1976) and the Future (1977–2000)*. Charlottesville, Va.: Financial Analysts Research Foundation, 1977.
51. Jacob, Nancy. "The Measurement of Systematic Risk for Securities and Portfolios: Some Empirical Results." *Journal of Financial and Quantitative Analysis* 6 (March 1971): 814–833.
52. Jensen, Michael C. "Capital Markets: Theory and Evidence," *Bell Journal of Economics and Management Science* 3 (Autumn 1972): 357–398.
53. Kirpalani, V. H., and Shapiro, Stanley S. "Financial Dimensions of Marketing Management." *Journal of Marketing* 37 (July 1973): 40–47.
54. Kotler, Philip. "Harvesting Strategies for Weak Products." *Business Horizons* 21 (August 1978): 15–22.
55. ———. *Marketing Decision Making*. New York: Holt, Rinehart and Winston, 1971.
56. Larner, Robert J. *Management Control and the Large Corporation*. New York: Dunellen Publishing Company, 1970.
57. Lev, Baruch. *Financial Statement Analysis*. Englewood Cliffs, N.J.: Prentice-Hall, 1974.
58. Lewellen, Wilbur G. "Management and Ownership in the Large Firm." *Journal of Finance* 24 (May 1969): 299–322.
59. Lewellen, Wilbur G., and Huntsman, Blaine. "Managerial Pay and Corporate Performance." *American Economic Review* 60 (September 1970): 710–720.
60. Lintner, John. "Optimal Dividends and Corporate Growth Under Uncertainty." *Quarterly Journal of Economics* 77 (February 1964): 49–95.
61. ———. "Security Prices and Risk." Paper presented at Conference on the Economics of Regulated Public Utilities, University of Chicago, June 1965.
62. ———. "The Valuation of Risk Assets and the Selection of Risky Investments in Stock

Portfolios and Capital Budgets." *Review of Economics and Statistics* 47 (February 1965): 13–37.

63. Lorie, James H. and Savage, Leonard J. "Three Problems in Rationing Capital." *Journal of Business* 28 (October 1955): 227–239.

64. Magee, John F. "Decision Trees for Decision Makers." *Harvard Business Review* 42 (July-August 1964): 126–138.

65. ————. "How to Use Decision Trees in Capital Investment." *Harvard Business Review* 42 (September-October 1964): 79–96.

66. Markowitz, Harry M. "Portfolio Selection." *Journal of Finance* 7 (March 1952): 77–91.

67. Miller, Merton, and Scholes, Myron. "Rates of Return in Relation to Risk." In *Studies in the Theory of Capital Markets,* M. Jensen (ed.). New York: Praeger, 1972, pp. 47–78.

68. Modigliani, Franco, and Pogue, Gerald A. "An Introduction to Risk and Return." *Financial Analysts Journal* 30 (March-April 1974): 68–80.

69. Mossin, Jan. "Equilibrium in a Capital Asset Market." *Econometrica* 34 (October 1966): 768–783.

70. Mossman, Frank H., Crissy, W. J. E., and Fischer, Paul M. *Financial Dimensions of Marketing Management.* New York: John Wiley, 1978.

71. Mossman, Frank H., Fischer, Paul M., and Crissy, W. J. E. "New Approaches to Analyzing Marketing Profitability." *Journal of Marketing* 38 (April 1974): 43–48.

72. Myers, Stewart C. "Procedures for Capital Budgeting Under Uncertainty." *Industrial Management Review* (Spring 1968): 1–19.

73. Myers, Stewart C. and Turnbull, Stuart M. "Capital Budgeting and the Captial Asset Pricing Model: Good News and Bad News." *Journal of Finance* 32 (May 1977): 321–333.

74. Pessemier, Edgar A. *Product Management.* Santa Barbara, Calif.: John Wiley, 1977.

75. Porterfield, James T. S. *Investment Decisions and Capital Costs.* Englewood Cliffs, N.J.: Prentice-Hall, 1965.

76. Quirin, G. David. *The Capital Expenditure Decision.* Homewood, Ill. Richard D. Irwin, 1967.

77. Rao, Vithala R., and Smidt, Seymour. "A Model for Multiperiod Evaluation of New Product Investments." *AMA 1975 Combined Proceedings.* Edward M. Mazze (ed). Chicago: American Marketing Association, 1975, pp. 367–372.

78. "Report of the Committee on Cost and Profitability Analysis for Marketing." *Accounting Review Supplement* 47 (1972): 577–615.

79. Robichek, Alexander, and Myers, Stewart C. *Optimal Financing Decisions.* Englewood Cliffs, N.J.: Prentice-Hall, 1965.

80. Roll, Richard. "A Critique of the Asset Pricing Theory's Tests: Part I." *Journal of Financial Economics* 4 (March 1977): 129–176.

81. Ross, Stephen A. "Options and Efficiency." *Quarterly Journal of Economics* 90 (February 1976): 75–89.

82. ————. "The Arbitrage Theory of Capital Asset Pricing." *Journal of Economic Theory* 13 (December 1976): 341–360.

83. ————. "Return, Risk and Arbitrage." In *Risk and Return in Finance,* I. Friend and J. Bicksler (eds). Cambridge, Mass.: Ballinger, 1976, pp. 189–218.

84. ————. "The Current Status of The Capital Asset Pricing Model (CAPM)." *Journal of Finance* 33 (June, 1978): 885–901.

85. Rubinstein, Mark E. "A Mean-Variance Synthesis of Corporate Financial Theory." *Journal of Finance* 28 (March 1973): 167–181.

86. Scheuble, Philip A., Jr. "ROI for New-Product Policy." *Harvard Business Review* 42 (November-December 1964): 110–120.

87. Schiff, J. S., and Schiff, Michael. "New Sales Management Tool: ROAM." *Harvard Business Review* 45 (July-August 1967): 59–66.

88. Sharpe, William F. "Capital Asset Prices: A Theory of Market Equilibrium Under Conditions of Risk." *Journal of Finance* 19 (September 1964): 425–442.

89. _____. *Portfolio Theory and Capital Markets.* New York: McGraw-Hill Book Company, 1970.
90. Simon, Herbert A. "Theories of Decision Making in Economics and Behavioral Science." *American Economic Review* 49 (June 1959): 253-283.
91. Smallwood, John E. "The Product Life Cycle: A Key to Strategic Marketing Planning." *MSU Business Topics* 21 (Winter 1973): 29-35.
92. Solomon, Ezra. *The Theory of Financial Management.* New York: Columbia University Press, 1963.
93. Solomons, David. *Divisional Performance: Measurement and Control.* Homewood, Ill.: Richard D. Irwin, 1965.
94. Spiller, Earl A., Jr. *Financial Accounting.* Rev. ed. Homewood, Ill.: Richard D. Irwin, 1971.
95. "Utility Regiation and the CAPM: A Discussion." *Financial Management* 7 (Autumn 1978): 52-76.
96. Van Horne, James C. "Capital-Budgeting Decisions Involving Combinations of Risky Investments." *Management Science* 13 (October 1966): 884-892.
97. _____. *Financial Management and Policy,* 2nd ed. Englewood Cliffs, N.J.: Prentice-Hall, 1971.
98. _____. *Financial Management and Policy,* 4th ed. Englewood Cliffs, N.J.: Prentice-Hall, 1977.
99. Weingartner, Martin H. "Capital Budgeting of Interrelated Projects: Survey and Synthesis." *Management Science* 12 (March 1966): 485-516.
100. Weston, J. Fred. "Investment Decisions Using the Capital Asset Pricing Model." *Financial Management* 2 (Spring 1973): 25-33.

SIMULATED PRODUCT SALES FORECASTING:

A MODEL FOR SHORT-RANGE FORECASTING AND OPERATIONAL DECISION MAKING

Donald J. Bowersox, David J. Closs, John T. Mentzer, Jr., and Jeffrey R. Sims

I. INTRODUCTION

Since the Industrial Revolution the complexity of business operations has increased significantly. At the turn of the century, management of inventory for most manufacturing firms involved simply the movement and storage of work-in process within the confines of a single building. Similarly, transportation or traffic management concerned only the movement of a few products within a relatively small geographic area. Such small-scale activity required limited coordination and could be understood and controlled by manual observation and

Research in Marketing, Volume 4, pages 39-68

analysis. In contrast, present physical distribution systems have grown to such proportions that they are difficult for an individual to conceptualize or analyze.

In today's operating environment many firms have in-process and storage facilities spread not only throughout the United States but also around the world. In such firms, inventory must be managed at multiple locations and through numerous marketing channels. Additional complexity has been introduced by recent world events which have placed severe constraints upon the energy resources available to accomplish the logistical mission of coordinated movement and storage. For these reasons, the costs of distribution continue to rise and the control of such operation systems requires improved methods of analysis and information processing.

The science of systems analysis, including computer modeling, has developed to the point where it can aid managers in understanding the myriad of system interrelationships involved in logistical planning. Application of the systems concept requires development of models capable of replicating a part or all of a firm's operating structure. These models can be defined as ''a representation of an object, system, or idea in some form other than that of the entity itself [1].'' The research reported in this paper deals with modeling in the areas of demand simulation, statistical forecasting, and dynamic simulation of physical distribution operations.

To date, numerous models have been developed that integrate some aspects of demand simulation, statistical forecasting, and distribution operations simulation [2]. However, the primary deficiency of these models has been their inability to combine the three related areas (forecasting, demand simulation, and dynamic simulation) into a comprehensive decision-making system [3]. A model integrating these components would provide an environment for nonsubjective testing of plans involving the interaction of distribution operations, forecasting, and other aspects of a marketing strategy. A key potential contribution of such an integrated model is its ability to provide a means to incorporate forecasts into the marketing/distribution decision-making process [3].

The need for such a system was the impetus for development of the Simulated Product Sales Forecasting (SPSF) model. This model combines for analysis the logistical system design factors of facility location, transportation, inventory, and materials movement with decisions concerning sales forecasting. All these areas must interact with various marketing strategy decisions which manifest themselves in product demand patterns impacting upon the logistical system.

The SPSF Testing Environment provides a tool and a methodology for analysis of an integrated physical distribution system. Four modules make up the testing environment. The first module replicates market uncertainty by providing a mechanism to create desired demand patterns. This module allows the researcher to test the performance of the physical distribution operating system under different demand environments. The interface between the demand environment and the operating system is provided by the second module in the form of a sales forecast. The logistical system utilizes sales forecasting techniques to anticipate demand. The third module is a dynamic simulator which replicates the operations of the physical distribution system. On a daily basis, the simulator processes customer stock and facility replenishment orders throughout the system. The final module integrates the model performance measures for analysis and management reporting. Thus, through the combined efforts of two types of simulation and statistical forecasting, a time-sequenced record of operational events is captured and documented. Such documentation provides the basis for post-mortem evaluation of forecast deficiency and formulates a basis for sensitivity analysis. Perhaps the most beneficial feature of the SPSF model is that it provides an environment for controlled experimentation.

The major limitation of the SPSF model approach is its scope of analysis. Because the model integrates all the components of a logistical system, the modeling of a large distribution system can become unwieldy in terms of the comprehensive information documented and costly in terms of computer time needed. For these reasons, the applicational scope of the testing environment is limited to what is termed a management decision area (e.g., a trading or warehouse service area). This limitation is not restrictive on the operational planning level. However, when a national plan is desired the solution rests on the capability to generalize area results to those of a national scope. The alternative is extensive duplicate analyses.

The remainder of this article discusses the development of the SPSF Testing Environment for use in the analysis of logistics system [4]. Section II provides an overview of the SPSF model design. Sections III through VI discuss, in detail, the Demand, Forecast, Operations, and Analysis Modules of the SPSF Testing Environment. Sections VII through IX present validation and application of the model.

II. SPSF OVERVIEW

The SPSF Testing Environment consists of four interrelated modules; the Operations Module, the Demand Module, the Forecast Module, and the Analysis Module. Each module provides a specific function in the overall operation of the testing environment. The general design of the SPSF Testing Environment is illustrated in Figure 1.

The Demand Module generates simulated product orders. Orders representing different quantities, levels of business, and patterns of occurence can be developed by the Demand Module. From a design viewpoint, the Demand Module uses four different procedures to generate others. The primary difference between individual procedures is the degree to which marketing and industry factors are included in the order generation process. The significant point about the Demand Module is that it permits the analyst to control the nature of demand confronted by the remainder of the SPSF system. The output of the module is a daily flow of orders that simulate the business situation under analyusis. These orders are transmitted to both the Operations and Analysis Modules. Thus, a record is established regarding what could be sold in the specific business situation.

The Forecast Module generates an estimate of future sales for use in establishing inventory levels at facilities with the distribution system being simulated. The module offers four different exponential smoothing forecasting procedures ranging in complexity from simple to triple adaptive. The data base for the Forecast Module is limited to sales history decomposed into level, trend, and seasonal components. This partial data base contrasts with the comprehensive data that is

Figure 1.   SPSF Testing Environment General Design

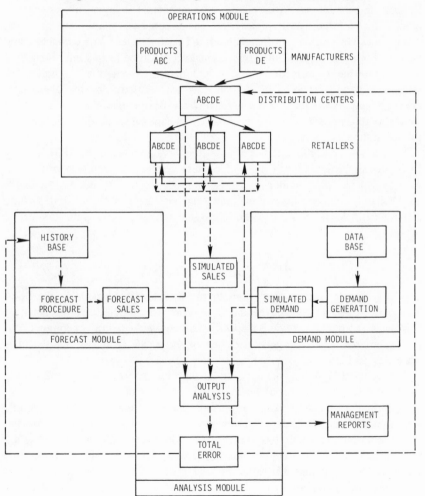

available to the Demand Module. The forecasts generated are input to both the Operations and Analysis Modules.

The Operations Module is a dynamic simulation of the physical distribution system selected for the business situation under study. This model has the capability to perform total physical distribution operations in a multi-echeloned system structure. The uncertainty inherent in typical operations is replicated in the simulator through the use of stochastic lead times. The typical lead-time components are order-processing and transit times. Thus, utilizing input from both the Demand and Forecast Modules, the Operation Module simulates performance of the specified distribution system and its associated policies across the time horizon of the forecast period.

The output of the individual modules is brought together in the Analysis Module. The Demand Module creates a simulated demand environment. Using less information, the Forecast Module produces an estimate of individual product demand at each facility. The forecast is used to establish desired inventory levels. The Operations Module incorporates spatial and temporal uncertainty to simulate the quantity that the system is capable of selling. Using this combination of inputs, the Analysis Module is in a unique position to report system performance. First, the module provides management information describing the activity, performance, and costs of physical distribution operations. This capability provides management with information to evaluate cost and service implications of alternative system designs. Second, the Analysis Module has access to demand (what *could* be sold), the forecast (what was expected *to be* sold), and the simulated operational results (what *was* sold). Thus, the module can isolate why sales do not match demand. Failure to realize all available sales can be categorized as resulting from either forecast or operating deficiencies. The capability to identify factors that cause the business situation under examination to enjoy less than fully available demand is one of the primary contributions of the SPSF Testing Environment.

From this brief overview it should be clear that the main feature of SPSF is its integration of the four modules into a single testing system. The following four sections discuss each of these modules in greater detail. However, keep in mind that the modules themselves are only of importance when combined to create a total testing environment.

III. DEMAND MODULE

The SPSF Testing Environment is initiated by demand generation. Once a physical distribution operating system is defined, an analysis of potential system operating efficiency rests on the capability of satisfying a given demand pattern. If the representation of demand is unrealistic or provides an inadequate approximation of actual demand, the modeling results will have limited, if any, operational validity. Similar relationships exist in all forms of simulation experimentation. The applicability of the experimental results is directly proportional to the validity of the environmental replication.

Four alternative procedures are provided in SPSF to create the demand environment: (1) the direct input of historical orders (Procedure One); (2) the generation of an aggregate sales level through a Monte Carlo process followed by a sampling of orders to create individual orders (Procedure Two); and (3) the estimation of an aggregate sales level via multiple regression followed by the order sampling process (Procedures Three and Four). Two alternative regression applications are included, thus providing the four approaches for creating demand.

Demand Module Procedure One utilizes historical orders. These orders contain a processing date and a list of products and quantities that were requested. When the model begins to simulate the activities of the corresponding processing date, the historical demand is submitted for processing. The use of actual demand history is the most simple method of demand replication and in many cases may be the most realistic. Since actual historical orders are used with no stochastic processes, this method does provide the highest accuracy level with regard to historical performance. However, this method has two serious shortcomings. First, it requires the development of an extensive data base since a record of all historical demand must be maintained. Alternative demand generation methods generally utilize a sample of data. Second, the method is inflexible with regard to its ability to create different experimental test conditions.

Demand Module Procedure Two uses random variate generators for normal, log-normal, erlang, and poisson distributions to create the level of aggregate daily sales. The daily sales level is generated using the specified distribution with selected parameters. Once the aggregate sales level is established individual orders are randomly selected from a sample of orders. The sample may consist of actual historical orders and/or exclusively fabricated orders. The fabricated orders may be structured to simulate experimental conditions such as new product introduction or promotional campaigns. Each order from the sample contains a list of individual products and quantities. Orders are sampled until their combined totals approximate the specified total daily sales. Procedure Two, although easy to use, offers no assurances regarding market reality. The procedure generates orders that are adequate for theoretical experimentation; however, the procedure does not provide adequate environmental control for actual applications.

Demand Generation Procedures Three and Four develop the daily aggregate sales level using regression analysis with economic and strategic variables. For test situations and within limited market areas, it is possible to identify economic indices that can be correlated to sales. Typical factors used in correlation are population, net income, gross national product, housing starts, and selected economic indicators related to the specific products. These factors can also include measures of the firm's operating environment.

When a significant relationship between sales and selected indicators can be identified, the regression procedure for developing demand is more realistic than either Procedures One or Two. In addition to the estimate of current market demand, regression may also be used to project future conditions. The objective of the regression procedures is to estimate aggregate sales. The research did not attempt to establish the regression procedure as a perfect sales predictor. The procedure is used only to approximate the environmental factors that influence sales level. Obviously, the more accurate the representation of the actual market factors, the greater the validity of the results. The following paragraphs discuss the unique features of Procedures Three and Four. Keep in mind that each procedure uses regression to initiate the demand generation process.

Procedure Three uses multiple linear regression to estimate aggregate daily sales. The impact of selected factors upon sales level is measured using least squares regression. The given aggregate daily sales are then decomposed into individual orders through the process described in Procedure Two.

Procedure Four uses a two-step process to arrive at the aggregate sales estimate. The first step estimates industry demand within a specified market area utilizing regression of the following general form:

$$S = a + b_1x_1 + b_2x_2 + \ldots + b_ix_i \tag{1}$$

where

S = industry sales for the period in question;

a = vertical axis intercept;

x_i = independent variable influencing industry sales;

b_i = respective factors of the independent variables.

Equation (1) allows incorporation of any independent variables deemed relevant for the estimate of market area industry sales. It also permits selection of different variables for different environmental situations. For instance, a firm selling household appliances may find housing starts, wholesale price index, and per capita income useful for rendering aggregate forecasts. In contrast, a firm engaged in the marketing of baby products may select different variables.

After industry sales within the market area for the temporal horizon are determined, specific market share for Procedure 4 is approximated using an approach suggested by Kotler [5]. This approach employs a ratio of the subject firm's "marketing effort" to overall industry "marketing effort" to estimate a specific market share. Ideally, such market share formulations should identify the impact that overall marketing strategies have upon a firm's market area demand. However, past and current research has not demonstrated that such a process is either accurate or feasible. Even so, if a moderate relationship can be identified, this procedure may offer the most realistic estimate of total demand

and a given firm's share as expressed in aggregate daily sales. The given aggregate daily sales are then decomposed into individual orders through the process described in Procedure Two.

The purpose of the Demand Module is to provide a controllable mechanism for the creation of daily product orders. Although it would be ideal if one of the procedures could predict actual orders it is not necessary for the purpose of doing meaningful research. The only necessary characteristic is that one or more of the procedures is capable of creating a useful stream of orders for utilization in SPSF operations. The incorporation of multiple individual environmental factors allows for future research investigating the feedback relationships between system performance and the impact of demand environment.

IV. FORECAST MODULE

The Forecast Module provides the interface between the demand environment and the physical distribution operations of the SPSF model. After a careful review of requirements, the forecast techniques that generated the most interest were short-range (one to three months) which required very little, if any, manual intervention.[1] When monthly forecasts are required for thousands of products at numerous facilities it is not practical to conduct a great deal of manual analysis. Although a single forecasting technique could have been used, the incorporation of four procedures was used to add to model flexibility. In addition, multiple procedures created the potential to evaluate alternate techniques within specific operating situations.

Based upon a literature review [6] and discussions with industry users, four forms of exponential smoothing were selected as typical of widely used short-term forecasting procedures. Although other techniques are used in industry and more sophisticated methods are available, a majority of firms have not advanced beyond exponential smoothing in short-range, detailed forecasting [3]. Following a general description of the processes performed by the Forecast Module, the forecast techniques incorporated are discussed.

The module generates forecasts for specific markets or warehouse service areas. The routine develops and maintains data for use in forecasting. When desired, the module selects one of the four available techniques and the necessary data to generate a short-range product sales forecast. The forecast, in turn, is used to compute order points and order quantities for the Operations Module. The routine, when utilizing an adaptive smoothing technique, evaluates simulated results with the forecast and measurement errors. This differential is utilized to update the smoothing factors for use in future forecasts.

The four forecasting techniques selected for use in the SPSF Testing Environment are:

1. Brown's Basic Exponential Smoothing;
2. P. R. Winters' Exponentially Weighted Moving Averages;

3. Trigg and Leach's Adaptive Smoothing;
4. Roberts and Reed's Self-Adaptive Forecasting Technique.

These techniques are representative of levels of exponential smoothing sophistication. Before discussing each technique, the method by which the forecast is incorporated into the SPSF Testing Environment is reviewed.

For a product, two forecast options exist. The first option is to generate independent forecasts for each facility location specified in the Operations Module. Such locations may be on the same echelon level or at various levels within the system structure. The forecast is generated from an analysis of historical patterns of product sales (throughput) at that location. As such, each forecast is developed independently. For example, even though sales at a manufacturing plant may be dependent upon the requirements of a distribution warehouse, forecasts under option one are generated on an independent basis.

The second forecast option concentrates at the locational level in the system that serves the final customer. Using this approach, a forecast is developed for a number of periods in advance. This forecast is then lagged back to all sources that supply the customer. The lead time used in communicating the dependent forecast back to source facilities is based on the expected replenishment cycle times between the locations. Thus, using this option, the system can exploit the fact that demand is dependent between facilities. A factoring methodology (called bleeding) is used to adjust for the fact that facilities operational in a given test area may also be a functional part of other channels of distribution. The bleeding procedure is discussed further in Section V. The remainder of this section discusses the four forecast procedures.

The first forecast technique is the basic exponential smoothing model originally developed by R. G. Brown [8]. Brown's model applies a static smoothing constant (α) to the immediately previous period's sales and forecast using Eq. (2):

$$F_{t+1} = \alpha(S_t) + (1 - \alpha)(F_t) \tag{2}$$

Where:
  F = forecast at time t or t+1
  S = sales at time t

Since the necessary input is limited to a smoothing factor and one period's data for sales and forecasting, the technique is easy to utilize. Since the technique contains no sales forecast error adaptability or provision to incorporate trend or cyclical variation, it would appear to offer limited capability for generating accurate forecasts. For the development of the SPSF Testing Environment, however, simple exponential smoothing provides a control measure by which the benefit of added forecast sophistication and complexity can be evaluated.

The second forecast technique, P. R. Winters' exponential weighted moving averages, incorporates seasonality and trend in addition to sales level [9]. The smoothing constant (α) is also used in this technique. In addition, procedures are included for deriving smoothed estimates of seasonality (β) and of trend (γ). The sales forecast is derived by combining all three factors. Since the Winters technique incorporates trend and seasonal variations, it offers a more sophisticated approach in comparison to basic exponential smoothing. However, computation of a single forecast using this technique requires three calculations and the storage of nine data items.

The third technique used in the Forecast Module was selected from among several techniques available to introduce the adaptability feature. The Trigg and Leach adaptive smoothing procedure functions with a constant (α) set equal to the absolute value of the tracking signal [10]. The tracking signal is a measure of the degree of forecast error. When the error becomes large the tracking signal approaches a value of one. As the value of the tracking signal increases, so does the corresponding value of α. The result is that the smoothing procedure quickly adapts to large differences between sales and forecast. As the error decreases, the tracking signal reduces the value of α, thus adapting the forecast to the new sales level. Although Trigg and Leach offer adaptability, consideration of trend and/or seasonality is not included in their procedure.

The fourth technique includes adaptability plus trend and seasonal components. This is the Self-Adaptive Forecasting Technique (SAFT) developed by Roberts and Reed [11]. SAFT is similar in concept to the Trigg and Leach procedure with the exception that it employs three adaptive constants. SAFT employs the Evolutionary Operations (EVOP) technique of response surface analysis to determine optimal combinations of the values of the three smoothing constants. Using historical data, EVOP systematically adjusts the values of each of the smoothing constants, obtaining a measure of the forecast error for each combination. Each error is squared to form the response surface. This surface is then searched to determine the minimum squared error. The set of smoothing constants which correspond to the minimum squared error is automatically fed into the Winters methodology (Procedure Two). Thus, Roberts and Reed developed what may be termed a closed loop dynamic forecasting technique. Any radical change in the patterns of basic sales, trend, or seasonality which increases forecast error is automatically adjusted for by the establishment of new values for the smoothing constant.

Due to its current popularity, the Box-Jenkins methodology was also considered for integration [7]. However, after analysis it was decided that Box-Jenkins required too much human interaction to be feasible for detailed short-range forecasting of the type required by the SPSF model.

The objective of the Forecast Module is to provide a range of techniques for use in the SPSF Testing Environment. One benefit is that the accuracy of the four procedures can be subjected to cost-benefit analysis under controlled environmental conditions. That is, for any specified market area environment, it is possible to test the relative accuracy of each procedure, the value of the increased accuracy offered by the various procedures, and the cost of achieving such enhancement.

V. OPERATIONS MODULE

The Operations Module is a dynamic simulator that integrates input from the Forecast and Demand Modules in a manner that permits both time- and function-dependent events to be simulated and observed. The Operations Module is designed to model individual events involved in the performance of the physical distribution process. Table 1 lists the events and their basic functions. Each event occurs on an independent basis. The dynamic characteristic of actual operations is achieved through event interaction. As an example, the Inventory Management Event checks the product inventory status at each facility at a specified time. When the inventory-on-hand drops below the specified reorder point, the simulator creates a replenishment order. The order is then held in a queue until the appropriate cycle time has elapsed. When the simulated time has passed, the Replenishment Order Processing and Replenishment Order Shipping Events process the order by deducting the quantities from inventory while incrementing the sales accumulators. The order is then assigned a stochastic transportation time and resubmitted to the queue until the appropriate time passes.

In the linkage of events, the manner in which elapsed performance time is created is critical for the model to capture the dynamic realism of distribution operations. Such realism is achieved through the use of stochastic cycle times. Order cycle components requiring stochastic time variables are communication, order processing, and transportation.

An additional feature of the Operations Module is the capability to incorporate a flexible distribution structure. Specifically, the Operations Module can simulate up to fifteen locations and handle up to ten products or groups of products. Inventory locations may be arranged in any number of echelons, or in any pattern of flow from manufacturing plants to customers. Customer locations can be replicated as specific accounts or demand areas.

Figures 2 and 3 illustrate the structural flexibility inherent in the Operations Module. The simplified distribution structure in Figure 2 illustrates inventory stocking at three locations with product shipment from a manufacturing plant to a distribution center and then to the customer. Although such a simplified distribution structure would seldom be found, the structure provides a useful basis for the analysis of specified policies. Typical policies capable of testing are illustrated on the right side of Figure 2.

Figure 3 provides a more complex example of a distribution structure which consists of twelve locations in four echelons. In addition, this example illustrates multiple source destinations and direct or bypass shipment capabilities from the manufacturer to distribution center locations. It is important to note that the figures illustrate only two typical system configurations which can be simulated within the Operations Module. The illustrations do not include the total SPSF Testing Environment in that the Forecast, Demand, and Analysis Modules are not included.

The flow of the Operations Module is controlled by an event sequencer. All

Table 1.   SPSF Events and Function

Event	Function
Data Read	Accepts parameters and variables, market and warehouse definitions.
Network Configuration	Configures the distribution system by integrating nodes, links, and the geographic market area as managerially specified.
Demand Forecasting	Uses one of the pre-defined forecasting techniques to forecast product sales for the market area. This forecast can either be built up through the system back to the manufacturing facility, or each echelon can be forecasted independently. The forecasts will be offset by the lead times when necessary.
Demand Generation	Generates pseudo customer orders for use in approximating the uncertainty of the demand environment.
Customer Order Processing	Processes the customer demand for each simulation period. The de-

Table 1.   SPSF Events and Function (continued)

Event	Function
	mand is provided via a call to the Demand Module.
Demand Bleed-Off	Due to the fact that all of the locations receiving shipments from a warehouse or manufacturing location may not be included in a desired configuration, this event automatically reduces the inventory available to simulated locations according to the percentage of the total inventory at the stocking location that the simulated locations receive in actuality.
Inventory Management	Accumulates the daily state measurements so that averages may be reported. In addition, this event initiates replenishment orders when the inventory level drops below the designated reorder point.
Production	Simulates the production function by incrementing the product in-

(continued)

Table 1.   SPSF Events and Function (continued)

Event	Function
	ventory at the manufacturing facilities when scheduled or necessary, with or without uncertainty.
Replenishment Order Processing	Initiates the order processing phase for replenishment orders at the source location.
Replenishment Order Picking	Completes the processing of the replenishment order and initiates the shipment of the order.
Shipment Arrival	Simulates the arrival of the replenishment order through adding the quantities into inventory-on-hand.
Back-Order Checking	Reviews the back-order queue after the arrival of additional inventory to determine if any of the back-orders can now be filled.
Report File Generation	Reports the current values of all status and flow variables to a file that is suitable for input to the cost or report modules.

Figure 2.   Example of Simplified Distribution Structure

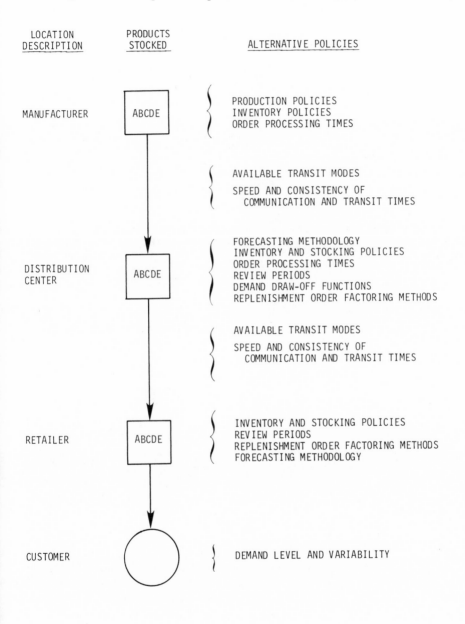

Figure 3.   Example of Complex Distribution Structure

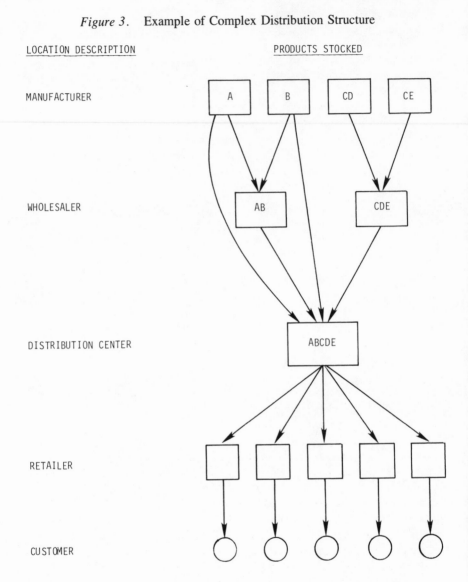

events are initiated by the event sequencer. When events scheduled during a particular operational period are completed, the simulation period counter is incremented by one. The value of this counter "clock" is then checked against the predetermined ending number for the simulation. If time remains in the simulation the model returns to the event sequencer and begins event processing for the next day.

VI. ANALYSIS MODULE

The Analysis Module utilizes the information developed by the simulator to produce management and error reports. This subsystem consists of three independent programs which utilize model results for summarizing system performance. The Cost Generator uses the physical distribution flow and level information to calculate the cost of system operation. The Report Generator formats and prints management reports. These reports provide the details and a summary of system performance. The third program is the Error Analysis Routine which details the reasons for each stockout. This program allows the researcher to identify whether the source of the stockout was the forecast technique or physical distribution operating system. The following sections discuss the details of each program.

A. Cost Generator

The Cost Generator is an independent routine which may be used to compute costs incurred by simulated distribution operations. The independent operation of this routine has two benefits. First, the absence of the cost components in the simulation model provides a more efficient utilization of computer core and thereby reduces run requirements. Second, the use of an independent Cost Generator permits sensitivity analysis of different cost assumptions without incurring the additional time and expense of duplicate simulations.

The individual costs included in the generator are transportation, warehousing, storage, inventory, ordering, and back-order costs. Each includes fixed and variable components as desired. The computation of costs is linear and dependent on either a unit of throughput or an average storage level. Since the operations simulator is a dynamic model, accurate measurement and costing of both status and flow variables are possible. A summary of the cost elements and the method of computation is presented in Table 2.

The Cost Generator obtains inputs from two sources. Data related to distribution operations are obtained as output from the Operations Module. Cost parameters applicable to a specific simulation are provided as direct inputs. Given these two inputs, the Cost Generator creates a data file which contains the simulator output as well as calculated costs. This file is the primary input to the Management Report Generator.

A final aspect of the Cost Generator is a review of the basic characteristics of each cost element. Transportation cost is computed for all replenishment orders on the basis of the weight shipped. In addition to being dependent on the source and destination of the shipment, the rate is also based on the transportation mode. For each pair of linked locations, up to six different weight breaks may be used to represent alternative modes. There is a fixed transportation cost available at each origin location to permit simulation of private fleet operations.

Table 2.   Cost Function Summary

Cost Element:	Can Be Uniquely Defined By:	Is a Function of:	Components:
Transportation	Shipping Source Shipment Destination	Weight Shipped	Variable Fixed
Warehousing (Throughput)	Location Product	Weight, unit, or cube Throughput (In, Out, or In+Out)/2)	Fixed Variable
Warehousing (Storage)	Location Product	Average Inventory Level Elapsed Time	Variable
Inventory Cost (Includes Storage)	Location	Average Inventory Level Elapsed Time	Variable
Order Cost	Location (Shipping)	Number of Orders Number of Lines	Fixed Variable
Back-Order Cost	Location (Shipping)	Number of Orders Back-ordered	Variable

Warehousing cost consists of handling and storage. The handling cost, which is unique by product and facility location, is based on throughput. Handling costs include fixed expenses related to labor, suppliers, and material handling equipment. The variable portion of handling is based on weight, cube, or units, and can be calculated on inbound volume, outbound volume, or an average of the two. The second aspect of warehouse expense is storage. Storage is a variable cost based on average inventory level. The components of storage include building depreciation, utilities, and any other facility-specific charges.

Inventory cost is variable and is calculated as a function of the average inventory level at a facility. The assessment percentage may be varied by product and location if management desires.

The cost for order placement and processing is assessed at the shipping location on both a fixed and variable basis. The variable cost is calculated as a function of the number of orders and the number of lines shipped. The variable cost covers expenditures such as labor and supplies. The fixed cost element, which is assessed on a per order basis, covers such items as computer hardware and supervisory expenses.

The final cost relates to back orders. The variable charge may be assessed against all out-of-stocks. The charge is assigned on a location basis and is based upon a managerial estimate.

The calculation of the cost is based on the activity level experienced in the operations simulator. It provides a basis for managerial review of alternative operating configurations and policies. Reports that are available to management regarding these expense levels are discussed next.

B. Report Generator

This Analysis Module component produces management reports for system performance evaluation. The Report Generator is independent of the remainder of the SPSF Testing Environment in that an intermediate file is used to pass the output from the simulation to the Report Generator. This intermediate file may or may not be passed through the Cost Generator for computation of system costs.

The input to the Report Generator includes simulator output and a small number of parameter cards. The general type of parameter information necessary includes descriptive names of the facility locations, customers, products, run identification information, and report selection parameters. These descriptors make the model output more intelligible to readers. The report selection parameters define the level of report detail desired.

There are twenty-four available reports which detail five information groups. The groups and their reports are illustrated in Table 3. Each report group is discussed below [4].

1. Sales and Physical Levels This group includes both the market area and the interfacility sales for each system location. This information is available by facility or by facility-product detial. The reports summarize sales information by dollars, net weight, and unit, as well as by lines and orders. In addition, this group details average inventory level along with a record of transfers and a count of all open orders. Finally, this group reports the system bleed-off on an individual product basis. Bleed-off is necessary to permit a partial system simulation to function within a total firm operating environment.

Table 3. Report Groups and Records

Groups	Records
Sales and	System Customer Sales
Physical Levels	System Shipments
	System Receipts
	System Inventory Report
	Replenishment Sales
	Replenishment Sales and In-Transit In-
	ventory
	Replenishment Volume: Weight Shipped
	Product Inventory Report
	Product Sales Report (Units)
	System Bleeding Report
	Product Bleeding Report
Costs	System Cost
	Replenishment Volume: Cost of Shipping
Service	System Service Measure
	System Percentage of Orders by Quantity
	Met
	System Back-Order Recovery and Thousands
	of Dollars Filled Within Days
	Replenishment Order Cycle Time Summary
Error	Operating Error Report
	Forecasting Error Report
Managerial Summary	Run Summary: Sales
	Run Summary: Service
	Run Summary: Inventory and Back Orders
	Run Summary: Costs

2. Operating Costs. The second group of reports presents operating costs. The individual functions that are costed include inventory, storage, handling, order processing, and freight. The information for each of these reports is computed by the Cost Generator.

3. Service. The third group of reports present operating results which provide the market area and inter-facility service measurement. The service group contains three types of reports. One series of service reports provides a record of the stockouts for customer demand and replenishment demand. This information is presented by location and product.

The second service measurement report consists of a record of the replenishment order cycle time components and variances. The individual time elements include communication, processing, back-order delay, and transit. Since this information is order oriented rather than product oriented, it is summarized only by facility.

The third service report consists of order cycle time and back-order recovery information. These reports are summaries of order information which are compiled by location. Using a list of service standards as defined through the input parameters, the model adds the dollar value of each order with respect to time and recovery.

4. Error. The fourth category of reports for the operations simulator elaborates two types of error that the SPSF Testing Environment identifies. The first is the forecast error, which is the difference between the quantity forecasted and the quantity demanded. Although the forecast error could be computed without the use of the Operations Module, it is measured as the demand is processed so that the time frames are synchronized for measuring operational error. The second component of the error measurement is the difference between what the inventory level actually is and what it should be, based on the forecast. This form of error is referred to as operational error. Referring back to Figure 1, the combination of forecast error and operational error was identified as total error.

5. Managerial Summary. The final category consists of four reports which provide a managerial summary of the performance of the simulated system. The first report is the summary of both customer and replenishment sales on a report period and year-to-date simulation basis. The system service summary is provided in the second report, detailing both percentage of lines and orders met by the system, as well as the mean and standard deviation of the order cycle time. The third report summarizes beginning and ending inventories for the total system and the quantity, as well as average recovery time of back orders. The fourth and final summary report provides both total operating and inventory costs on an aggregate and per-hundredweight basis.

In total, the SPSF Report Generator provides information which details operations over the length of the simulation run. These reports provide the means whereby logistical operations may be analyzed to isolate and evaluate system characteristics and performance.

VII. VALIDATION

Validation of the SPSF Testing Environment utilized a two phase procedure. The model was first tested using controlled data to establish that the programs performed as desired. The second phase used actual data to determine whether or not the model, as a whole, performed as expected. The following discussion briefly outlines the questions that were investigated and the results obtained when evaluating the testing environment.

A. Initial Model Validity

The first phase of testing model validity addressed the basic question of whether or not the model operates as desired. This phase established that the computer program(s) operated correctly. The performance of four tasks was required to complete this phase of validation. The first task involved a detailed evaluation of the program flow and logic while processing a limited test application. This established that the program flow and logic appeared to operate correctly. The stochastic variable generators were also evaluated for fit and stability as a part of this first task. Task 2 utilized a review board of academicians and distribution practitioners to determine whether the individual simulated activities adequately modeled the desired distribution activities. Task 3 selected a measurement variable and then statistically evaluated the point and dynamic stability of the model. For validating SPSF, the service level was selected as the stability measure. Statistical analysis was performed for both high and low variance conditions. The validation results statistically demonstrated that the model produced stable results. Task 4 evaluated model performance under different sets of environmental and policy conditions. The objective of this task was to determine whether the model, under the controlled conditions, responded to changes in its environment in a manner similar to an actual distribution system. Once again the model was judged valid.

The results obtained from the performance of all four tasks indicated that the basic model was valid. However, tests of true model validity are data dependent and can only be evaluated after repeated applications in actual environments. Strictly speaking, each new application should be subjected to the four tasks discussed to determine situation specific model validity. This, however, is impractical due to economic and temporal constraints. As a compromise a modified procedure was developed to establish the validity for individual applications. The following section describes this procedure.

B. Model Application Validity

Business applications were utilized to further validate the model. This phase of the validation procedure identified three tasks that are recommended for the establishment of the validity of a specific application.

Task one evaluates the historical fit of model results in comparison to past experience. Ideally, the model output should closely match the user's history under similar environmental and operating conditions. Task 2 determines the effect of the random processes and start-up conditions on the model results. Although this task has often been overlooked in past distribution modeling research, the results clearly indicate that such random processes may significantly influence model response. As an example, one application produced stable results almost immediately after the simulation began. In contrast, another required a forty-day simulation period before stable results were obtained. Task 3 compared the model results with the intuition and knowledge of planning managers to determine whether the model performed as they anticipated.

In conclusion, the model was found to produce results which passed the validity requirements for both the controlled and actual applications. On the basis of the two-phase procedure followed, the SPSF Testing Environment was judged valid.

VIII. MODEL APPLICATIONS

The SPSF Testing Environment provides a broad-based tool for the analysis of theoretical and applied situations. The results of existing research utilizing the model are discussed first, followed by some suggestions concerning future possibilities.

A. Existing Research

To date, the SPSF Testing Environment has been used for research in numerous areas. The initial four applications considered problems in demand generation, forecasting techniques, safety stock policy, and system planning with industrial firms. A brief description of each application and the results follows.

1. Demand Generation. The initial research conducted with the SPSF Testing Environment addressed the capabilities and accuracy of the alternative demand generation procedures. Therefore, the objective of this research was to measure the accuracy of various procedures under different environmental conditions.

To accomplish this objective, the research compared the fit of demand patterns obtained from the three stochastic demand generation procedures of the model (Procedures Two, Three, and Four) against corresponding historical demand patterns. The first stochastic procedure approximates daily sales levels for the firm using standard probability distributions. The second procedure approximates daily demand for the firm through the use of a single regression analysis. The third procedure approximates daily demand for the industry and firm market share through the use of regression analysis.

These three procedures were combined to yield seven different approaches to demand generation. These demand approaches were tested for accuracy under ten environmental conditions. The environmental conditions were determined by various changes in the trend, seasonality, and variation of the demand patterns. Seventy experimental simulations runs were conducted for a test period of 200 simulated days each. The following conclusions were drawn from the research:

1. The simplest method of demand generation, the stochastic procedure, was by far the most accurate under any environmental condition where seasonality did not exist.
2. With little or no seasonlity, the stochastic procedure was superior to the firm regression and industry regression procedures. However, at high levels of seasonality, the stochastic method became less accurate than either the firm regression or industry regression procedures.
3. Comparison of the accuracy of the regression approaches developed from the firm regression and industry regression procedures revealed the level of correlation in the regression analysis had a negligible effect on the accuracy of demand generation.

A number of implications for the use of demand generation in simulation research follow from the conclusions of this research. Previous simulation research has primarily utilized the stochastic method. However, this research suggests that the stochastic procedure would be preferred only for simulations in which seasonality is either nonexistent or at a low level. If seasonal fluctuations exist which represent a significant percentage of business, a regression procedure should be utilized.

For further discussion of the research design and results see "Simulated Product Sales Forecasting—Analysis of Market Area Demand Simulation Alternatives [12]."

2. *Forecasting Technique.*   The forecasting research utilized the SPSF Testing Environment to evaluate the impacts of the two types of uncertainty while using different levels of forecasting technique sophistication. The first, demand uncertainty, deals with the rate at which a product is demanded. The second, operating uncertainty, deals with the channel's ability to replenish inventories as they are depleted. The combination of these factors affects system performance. The objective of this research was to measure the combined impacts of variations in demand and operating uncertainty on the performance of a channel system.

Measures to reduce the effects of demand and operating uncertainty are generally considered independently. However, when management seeks to implement an improved forecasting technique, two factors must be considered: 1) the accuracy of the proposed technique in comparison to that presently in use: and 2) whether the distribution system can effectively support the sales as forecast by the improved technique. Using the SPSF Testing Environment, the performance of a distribution system was analyzed under four time series forecasting techniques in combination with varying levels of demand and operating uncertainty. Twenty-four test combinations were simulated for a period of 240 days. Channel performance was tested in terms of sales, service, and cost to identify the effects of changes in forecasting accuracy and demand and operating uncertainty. The total discrepancy between sales and demand was separated into forecasting and operating error.

Three general hypotheses were tested using analysis of variance.

1. Different levels of each uncertainty (demand and operating) have different impacts on channel performance.
2. Variations in forecasting accuracy have significant impacts on channel performance.
3. Different combinations of demand uncertainty, and operating and forecasting accuracy have different impacts on channel performance.

The major conclusions, as they correspond to the hypotheses, were:

1a. Increases in the variation of demand result in increased stockouts and reduced profit regardless of the level of operating uncertainty or the forecasting technique employed. The more complex the forecasting technique, the smaller the decreases in performance resulting from increased demand uncertainty.
1b. Increases in operating uncertainty result in increased stockouts and reduced profit. This result was consistent for all combinations of forecasting techniques and demand patterns except one. However, changes in system performance varied across the forecasting techniques. The less complex the technique, the smaller the decrease in channel performance.
2. Variations in forecasting accuracy lead to variations in channel performance. This result was consistent across demand patterns and levels of operating uncertainty. The complexity of the forecasting technique was inversely related to accuracy when considered across all demand patterns and levels of operating uncertainty. Considered only across demand patterns, the more complex techniques were better able to adapt to increased demand variation.
3. There is an interaction between demand and operating uncertainty in their effects on channel performance. Any discrepancy between demand and sales is the result of the combined effects of these factors and may be

separated into forecasting and operating discrepancy. The effects of increases in demand and operating uncertainty tend to cancel each other. The total discrepancy between demand and sales is less than the sum of forecasting and operating discrepancy.

A number of observations follow from this research. First, defining forecasting error as the difference between sales and forecast is incorrect. Such a procedure generates future forecasts based upon past levels of operating as well as forecast discrepancy. Second, more consistent system performance is achieved using simple forecasting techniques. Complex techniques, although more able to track highly variable demand patterns, are also more affected by variations in operating uncertainty. Finally, the performance of the channel must be monitored and analyzed from a system's perspective to separate forecasting and operating discrepancies.

For a complete discussion of the research design and results regarding the forecasting applications, see "Simulated Product Sales Forecasting—Analysis of Forecasting Discrepancies in the Physical Distribution System [6]."

3. Inventory. Current model research is focusing upon the interaction of the physical distribution echelon structure and safety stock. In particular, the need and effectiveness of safety stock at different system locations is being evaluted under different environments of demand and lead time. The specific research questions are:

1. To determine the relative accuracy of current probabilistic techniques for determining safety stock requirements in physical distribution system;
2. To evaluate the relative impact of different levels of safety stock on the customer service levels of a multi-echeloned physical distribution system under varying conditions of demand and lead time uncertainty; and
3. To evaluate the relative impact of safety stock echelon positioning on the customer service levels of a multi-echeloned physical distribution system under varying conditions of demand and lead time uncertainty.

This research is still in progress so final results are not available.

4. Industry. Initial model research included the analysis of data provided by two firms. Their use of the model focused on the performance evaluation of alternative distribution systems and policies. The first application evaluated the distribution system of a consumer products firm while the second considered consumer durables. This application diversity provides some basis for model generalization. The model analysis for both firms involved three phases.

The first phase established the historical or fit model validation. For this phase, the model output based upon historical demand, was compared to the actual operating experience of the firm. The essential test was whether the model simulated acceptable results when given the same environmental conditions. The model results both at a detailed and aggregate level were validated to within five percent of the actual experience of both firms.

The second analysis phase evaluated the relative model stability for each firm. As previously, model stability refers to the model's capability to adjust to initial starting conditions and to accurately simulate system performance. This analysis identifies performance differences due to policy changes with those that result from the stochastic processes of the model. The results illustrate the need to evaluate stability. The first firm realized accurate estimates of system performance within ten simulation days. The second firm, which operated under a more uncertain environment, required a forty simulation day warm-up period. Although the model did perform differently for the two firms, the consensus of both managements was that it produced credible results.

The third phase used the model to evaluate alternative distribution structures and policies. Although the firms were essentially evaluating operational alternatives in this phase, the model was still under scrutiny. The results offered a basis for comparisons of model results and management intuition. The failure to realize a reasonable match would have resulted in a decrease in model credibility. After an analysis of ten runs for each firm, management felt the results matched their expectations.

As a result of each use of the model with industry data, managers of the firms felt the SPSF Testing Environment offered both an accurate and useful tool.

B. Potential Research

Given the availability of the SPSF Testing Environment, many opportunities exist for future research and industrial application. The following examples illustrate some planned and potential research areas.

1. Analysis of System Discrepancies. As previously discussed, any discrepancy between the actual and potential levels of sales in a single period may be the result of an inaccurate forecast or the inability of the physical distribution system to support demand levels. The SPSF Testing Environment provides the capability to analyze the relative and absolute impact of each such discrepancy. Each type of error results from a distinct type of uncertainty. Forecast discrepancy results from uncertainty about the level of future demand. Operating discrepancy results from uncertainty relating to the performance of the distribution system. On an experimental basis, each form of discrepancy may be identified and measured to formulate improved forecasting procedures and operating policies.

2. Customer Service Standards. Research in the area of customer service deals with one of the most timely problems facing management. Customer service is the focal point of all logistical activity. Working to achieve a given service level is difficult in itself; identifying the effective or desired service level is even more difficult. Using the SPSF Testing Environment, a controlled analysis of the relationship between levels of customer service, system sales, and total operating cost can be simulated. In addition, the impact of selected policy changes on system performance can be evaluated. For example, changes in transportation costs, inventory costs, and corresponding service levels resulting from a decrease in order cycle times may be quantified. Likewise, the response of service and cost to changes in base and/or safety inventories may be analyzed. The SPSF Testing Environment may also be adapted to test customer service policies under conditions of scarcity.

3. Channel Cost Revenue Analysis   An additional area for research is the comparative evaluation of alternative channel designs. The structure of existing distribution systems has often evolved in response to changing conditions. The evolution has been painful economically because of the inability to create complex system designs in anticipation of such changes. The SPSF Testing Environment provides the means to reduce uncertainty accompanying any planned change. For example, the actual performance of the firm's channel system over a period of time may be compared to simulated performance of an alternative or modified structure. Modifications could be in the form of structure or operating policies. For example, the system concentration of inventories might be simulated systematically and analyzed from one echelon to another to determine the structure offering the highest degree of efficiency. On a system basis, repeated simulation may be employed to investigate the relative cost-benefit relationship of alternative systems. Once a valid replication of an actual operation is achieved, the testing environment offers a way to evaluate modified distribution structures and/or policies.

4. Market Share Analysis.   An interesting area of potential research is analysis of the effect of various marketing strategies on corporate market share. Procedure Four of the Demand Module incorporates a model developed by Kotler to estimate a firm's market share. Such marketing strategy inputs as price, product quality index, customer service, and level of promotional expenditures for the firm and the competition can be included in this model. These inputs can be analyzed against market share over time via regression analysis to estimate and forecast market share. Further, through a log transformation of the data and further regression analysis, the elasticities of each of the marketing strategy inputs can be estimated. Thus, the potential exists not only for estimating market share, but for estimating the degree to which market share will fluctuate with any change in marketing strategy.

5. Contingency Planning.   A final broad area for potential research is contingency planning and evaluation. The response of an operating system to environmental change and acts of nature may be simulated under specific experimental situations. For example, the performance of the distribution system under varying degrees of recession and/or economic boom may be analyzed in conjunction with the Demand Module. Another form of contingency planning could evaluate the impact of supply restrictions on inventory availability and services using the Operations Module. Likewise, the impact and potential of a given restructure to perform "reverse logistics" can be predetermined. The above examples represent just a few of the wide variety of contingency planning situations that can be evaluated using the SPSF Testing Environment.

IX. CONCLUSION

It is estimated that the nation's logistics expenditure accounts for approximately 20 percent of the Gross National Product. Since such a significant expenditure is involved, it is absolutely necessary that resources be used as efficiently and effectively as possible in providing the required marketing services. It is only through a complete and accurate analysis of the integrated distribution process that we can evaluate overall system performance. The Simulated Product Sales Forecasting Testing Environment and the associated application methodology provides a proven tool to assist in such integrated analysis.

NOTES

1. Since logistical systems generally include multiple locations and products which each require short-range forecasts, it is necessary to utilize forecasting techniques which can be automated with a minimal amount of manual interaction. After investigating the alternatives available and some discussion with the industry sponsors, it was concluded that the exponential smoothing time series models best satisifed this criteria. It was felt that this model class was most representative of that used by industry for short-range operational planning. Further research could incorporate other specific types of models.

REFERENCES

1. Shannon, R. E. "Systems Simulation—The Art and Science." New York: Prentice-Hall, 1975.
2. Closs, D. J. "Simulated Product Sales Forecasting: Mathematical Model, Computer Implementation, and Validation." Unpublished dissertation, Michigan State University, 1978.
3. Spyros, M., and Wheelwright, S. *Journal of Marketing* 24 (October 1977).
4. Bowersox, D. J., et al. "Simulated Product Sales Forecasting." Michigan State University Bureau of Business Research, East Lansing, Michigan, 1979.
5. Kotler, P. "Marketing Decision Making: A Model Building Approach." New York: Holt, Rinehart & Winston, 1971.
6. Sims, J. R. "Simulated Product Sales Forecasting: Analysis of Forecasting Discrepancies in the Physical Distribution System." Unpublished dissertation, Michigan State University, 1978.
7. Box G. E. P., and Jenkins, G. M. "Time Series Analysis—Forecasting and Control." San Francisco: Holden-Day, 1970.

8. Brown, R. G. and Meyer, R. F. *Operations Research* 673 (September-October 1961).

9. Winters, P. R. *Management Science* 324 (April 1960).

10. Trigg, D. W., and Leach, A. G. *Operational Research Quarterly* 53 (March 1967).

11. Roberts S. D., and Reed, R., Jr. *AIIE Transactions* 314 (December 1969).

12. Mentzer, J. T. "Simulated Product Sales Forecasting: Analysis of Market Area Demand Simulation Alternatives." Unpublished dissertation, Michigan State University, 1978.

INNOVATION DIFFUSION AND ENTREPRENEURIAL ACTIVITY IN A SPATIAL CONTEXT:
CONCEPTUAL MODELS AND RELATED CASE STUDIES[1]

Lawrence A. Brown, Marilyn A. Brown, and
C. Samuel Craig

INTRODUCTION

Diffusion of innovation has traditionally been viewed by marketers as an area of inquiry related to consumer behavior. Reflecting this, most research on innovation diffusion has concentrated upon variables related to the individual or household adoption decision and has emphasized the role of social networks, information flows, consumer demographics, and psychological variables such as innova-

Research in Marketing, Volume 4, pages 69–115
ISBN: 0–89232–169–5

tiveness and resistance to adoption.[2] More recent research indicates that this perspective alone does not provide sufficient explanation if, as in the case for most contemporary innovations, the innovation is propagated by an entity motivated to bring about rapid and complete diffusion [9,11,12,15,16]. In this context, the mechanisms through which innovations are made available to potential adopters are of equal if not greater importance. Consequently, understanding innovation diffusion involves more than treating it simply as a consumer behavior phenomenon; that is, product distribution and logistics or, more specifically, channel structure, policy, and strategy also must be considered. Stated alternatively, the topic is one for which both *supply* and *demand* factors are relevant.

This paper complements the traditional innovation diffusion literature by presenting a supply oriented framework which focuses upon the mechanisms through which innovations are made available to potential adopters. This views the diffusion process in terms of three stages (Figure 1).

The *first stage* is the establishment of diffusion agencies, the public or private sector entities through which an innovation is distributed or made available to the population at large. Examples of entities that might perform such a function include retail and wholesale outlets, government agencies (for example, Cooperative Extension Service county offices), or nonprofit organizations (for example, Planned Parenthood affiliates). Important to this aspect of diffusion is the locus of decision making with respect to agency establishment. Specifically, these decisions may be made solely by the propagator of the innovation (*centralized*), by a number of disparate entities acting independently (*decentralized*), or by a number of disparate entities acting independently but under the direction of the propagator of the innovation (*decentralized with a coordinating propagator*).

In the *second stage* of the diffusion process, each diffusion agency conceives and implements a strategy to promote adoption among the population in its market or service area. From a spatial perspective, an important distinction in this step is whether the diffusion of an innovation depends heavily upon the simultaneous establishment, either by the diffusion agency or some other entity, of a suitable infrastructure. If so, the diffusion is *infrastructure constrained,* and formulation of an effective diffusion strategy involves considerations pertaining to infrastructure accretion. Alternatively, the diffusion may be *infrastructure independent* if there is no infrastructure requirement or the relevant infrastructure is ubiquitous and does not act as a limiting factor. In either case, however, diffusion agency strategy also involves the development of *organizational capabilities* to facilitate rapid diffusion, the establishment of a *price* for the innovation, the *selection of an appropriate market (market selection and segmentation),* and the design of *promotional programs* to provide information to potential adopters.

The diffusion agency establishment and strategy formulation stages, operating

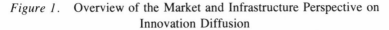

Figure 1. Overview of the Market and Infrastructure Perspective on Innovation Diffusion

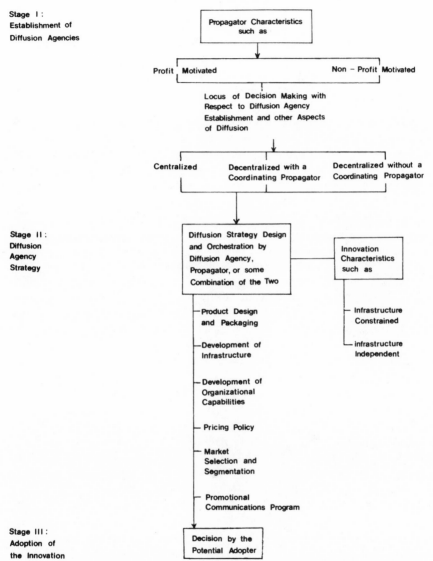

in conjunction with other private and public entities providing, for example, complementary goods and infrastructure, comprise the *supply* side of diffusion. Together, these *market and infrastructure* factors permit and influence *adoption* of the innovation, which constitutes the *demand* side of diffusion and the third stage of the sequence.

Viewed in another way, conceptually recognizing the supply side of diffusion shifts attention to the diffusion agency instead of the adopter. The locations of these agencies and the temporal sequencing of their establishment determine where and when the innovation will be available. This provides the general outline of the spatial pattern of diffusion. Further detail is contributed by the operating procedures of each agency. These create differing levels of access to the innovation depending upon a potential adopter's economic, locational, and social characteristics. The establishment of diffusion agencies and the operating procedures of each agency are, more generally, aspects of marketing the innovation. This marketing involves both the creation of infrastructure and its utilization. Thus, the characteristics of the relevant public and private infrastructure, such as service, delivery, information, transportation, electricity, or water systems, also have an important influence upon the rate and spatial patterning of diffusion. Accordingly, both within the agency service area and within the larger region of which it is a part, the diffusion process is shaped by what has been termed the *market and infrastructure context of innovation adoption and diffusion*.

The steps of this framework—diffusion agency establishment, diffusion agency strategy, and adoption—are presented sequentially for heuristic purposes. In reality, however, they may not occur in order and may not be mutually exclusive. For instance, while existing diffusion agencies are implementing marketing strategies to induce adoption of a particular innovation, other agencies may be being created. Alternatively, the agencies may themselves be the innovation, for example, the fast-food outlet, the planned regional shopping center [33], and the department store in Japan [122].

This brings up the question of exactly what we mean by innovation and to which kinds of innovations this framework pertains. The examples above indicate that an innovation may either be a new product or service, such as quadraphonic stereo systems or credit card services, or it may be a new way of providing an old product or service, such as 24-hour banking or the planned regional shopping center. Furthermore, each of these types of innovation may be *continuous*, involving alteration of an existing product such that consumers need not develop new consumption patterns; *dynamically continuous*, involving the creation of a new product or service or the alteration of an existing one such that consumption patterns are somewhat disrupted; or *discontinuous*, involving the creation of previously unknown products or services such that new consumption patterns must be established [101:4–7]. The framework presented in this paper applies to any of these innovations in so far as they manifest spatial tendencies, but may be more applicable to dynamically and discontinuous innovations.

The remainder of this paper is divided into three major sections. The first deals with diffusion agency establishment and the second with diffusion agency strategy, corresponding with the first two stages of innovation diffusion. The third section addresses the ways in which the framework presented here fits in with the marketer's concern with new product growth models. Throughout the discussion, the spatial patterning of diffusion is given particular emphasis, and case studies are used to illustrate the validity of the market and infrastructure framework and its translation into a real world setting.

DIFFUSION AGENCY ESTABLISHMENT

The majority of innovations, and particularly those of interest to marketing professionals, are *propagated* by profit or nonprofit motivated organizations or government agencies seeking to induce a rapid and complete diffusion. A critical aspect of their effort is the choice of market area for distributing the innovation, a part of a broader *market penetration* strategy. This is treated in the present framework in terms of the decision of where and when to establish a diffusion agency. Other aspects of market penetration such as the selection of a specific site within the market area, size of outlet, design of outlet, or inventory will, at most, be only briefly discussed.[3]

An important consideration is the locus of *decision making* with respect to diffusion agency establishment. At one extreme is a *centralized structure* where a single propagator (or several propagators acting together as one) determines the number of outlets to be established at any given time and their location, size, and other characteristics. Thus, the gross pattern of diffusion is centrally controlled. At the opposite extreme is a *decentralized structure* in which each diffusion agency is established independently by a different entrepreneurial or non profit motivated entity, so that the gross pattern of diffusion comes about solely through the aggregation of individual actions and decentralized decision making.

In between these two extremes is diffusion in a *decentralized structure with a coordinating propagator*. In this, each agency is established by a different entrepreneurial or nonprofit motivated entity, but some aspects of this are controlled and orchestrated by the coordinating propagator. Thus, the pattern of diffusion is *influenced, but not determined by,* the coordinating propagator. The degree of coordination may vary considerably, as indicated by the variety of francise arrangements, so that this latter case really represents a continuum depending upon the extent of propagator control and orchestration of the diffusion. One thing that cannot be controlled, however, is the decision to establish an agency in the first place since, by definition, this must be done by the local individual entrepreneur.[4]

In general, diffusion patterns and the relative importance of different variables varies according to the organizational structure of the diffusion. Market potential, profitability, or economic factors, for example, are of paramount importance in the case of a centralized decision-making structure, operating to order the spatial sequencing of diffusion, but these only serve as threshold conditions in the decentralized situation where information flow factors (among entrepreneurs) take on a greater importance. If the diffusion is in a decentralized structure with a coordinating propagator, the most common case, the relative importance of economic as opposed to information factors varies according to the arrangement between the propagator and the entities establishing diffusion agencies.

Empirically observed diffusions are not necessarily characterized by only one of these three prototypes. For instance, centralized and decentralized structures may occur simultaneously, as in the spread of Coca-Cola in Ontario, which resulted from the actions of one key firm, Coca-Cola, Ltd., and numerous independent bottlers [87]. Similarly, a diffusion may evolve from one type of structure to another. In fast food operations, for example, there was initially only one firm, MacDonalds, operating in a centralized fashion, which was later joined by other firms after success became apparent.

From the perspective of one concerned with the spatial patterns of innovation diffusion, one of the important decisions in agency establishment is *whether to create a new network of diffusion agencies or to utilize an existing one*. If an *existing distribution network* is utilized, there are two basic possibilities which reflect the organizational characteristics of the existing network. On the one hand, the existing network might consist of a series of outlets that are linked together organizationally. Thus, a decision to utilize that network, aside from test marketing considerations, generally results in the innovation's simultaneous availability over a wide range of locations or markets. For decentralized diffusion with a coordinating propagator, an example is a large package goods manufacturer using a number of supermarket chains to introduce a new brand. For centralized diffusion, that existing network would, by definition, be controlled by the propagator. An example is an automobile manufacturer introducing a new model through its existing dealer network.

An alternative to a distribution system that is organizationally linked is diffusion through independently owned outlets such as mom and pop stores. This type of system would characterize decentralized diffusion without a coordinating propagator. The establishment of cable television systems in Ohio provides an example [25]. However, such a system also might be utilized by a coordinating propagator. For example, the bank credit card in Ohio was made available through local banks, each of which is independently owned [18].

If an existing network of diffusion agencies is utilized, whether it is organizationally linked to the propagator or made up of independently owned outlets, the spatial patterns of diffusion will be constrained by and reflect the spatial pattern of the existing network. Suppose, for example, that Federated Department stores were the sole outlets through which an innovation was distributed. These are found in only some regions of the country and only in some cities within those regions, and accordingly, the spatial patterns of diffusion would be constrained to those locations irrespective of the actual distribution of potential adopters. Alternatively, there could be a close correlation between the spatial distribution of the existing network and of the population of potential adopters. Examples of this would be an outlet network of supermarkets or local banks. In this case, then, the diffusion pattern would closely approximate the distribution of potential adopters (*ceteris paribus*).

If a *new network* is established, whatever the prototype situation, diffusion agencies are typically located sequentially in time and space. Thus, there is a more marked geographical problem. Attention now turns to elaborating this problem in terms of the three situations of diffusion agency establishment: through a centralized decision making structure, through a decentralized structure without a coordinating propagator, and through a decentralized structure with a coordinating propagator. These are discussed here only for a profit motivated setting. With respect to their applicability in a nonprofit motivated setting, see Brown [15].

Profit-Motivated Diffusion Under a Centralized Decision-Making Structure

The most important single consideration for agency location in a centralized setting is the expected profitability associated with alternative urban areas [16].[5] Optimally, the markets would be ranked and then sequentially exploited; the most profitable first and the less profitable later, if at all. This occurs because of limited supplies of the innovation, the business uncertainty associated with the introduction of an innovation, limited capital, and the consequent importance of obtaining maximum levels of performance from established diffusion agencies.

One critical factor in the profitability estimate is revenues. These can be estimated in terms of market potential, and (*ceteris paribus*) those areas with larger potential ought to be preferred. For many innovations market potential will vary directly with the number of persons in each urban area and its hinterland. That is not always the case, however. The market potential for agricultural innovations provides an obvious example.

Expenses also enter into the calculation of profitability. These would include the unit cost of the innovation, the costs of transporting it to the diffusion agency and of distributing it to adopters, the costs of advertising and otherwise promoting the innovation, and the costs of establishing, maintaining, and operating each diffusion agency.

From a spatial perspective, the most important expenses are those related to the accessibility of a potential agency location to the parent entity.[6] This is primarily relevant to *logistics* aspects of propagation, such as servicing the agency and transporting the innovation to it. Accessibility also enters in other ways, particularly because of the risk and uncertainty associated with innovation diffusion. Given limited resources for market research, nearby locations, especially those that are personally known to the propagator, can be better evaluated in terms of sales potential, the means of tapping that potential, and the extent of various costs. Even without severe resource limitations, however, it is likely that more will be known about accessible locations, and further, it is reasonable to suppose that what is known will be perceived as more reliable. Finally, there are accessibility related economies in innovation promotion and in agency maintenance and operating costs. With regard to the latter, accessible locations can be easily supervised by the propagator, thus reducing expanses and increasing control and the likelihood of success.

One conclusion of this discussion of market selection under a centralized decision making structure is that *market potential* and *accessibility* or *logistics* will be important factors underlying the locational priorities established by the propagator. These provide, respectively, *hierarchy* and *neighborhood effect* tendencies in the pattern of diffusion.[7]

However, the degree to which either of these patterns actually appear would depend upon whether the centralized propagator was operating to minimize costs, maximize profits, or maximize sales, and that in turn would depend in part upon the *capital available* to the propagator. Specifically, sales maximization is a viable option for the capital rich propagator, whereas the capital poor propagator would be more likely to follow a strategy of cost minimization until expansion capital is available.[8] In either case, after a level of success has been attained, mixed strategies are likely. For example, sales maximization might be pursued in new markets at the same time that profit maximization is pursued in older markets.

Also of significance to the spatial pattern of diffusion is the relative importance of each of the logistics variables. To illustrate, if transportation costs are high relative to other costs, a strong neighborhood effect tendency is provided; a lesser effect is obtained if spatially variant elements of maintenance and operating costs dominate; and if neither of these are important there may be no neighborhood effect whatsoever.

Whether neighborhood, hierarchy, or both tendencies are present, diffusion agency establishment will be limited to places with sales potential sufficient to support at least one agency. Thus, for a higher order compared to a lower order (of good) innovation, fewer places will have agencies and there will be fewer agencies in any given place.[9] With regard to the patterns of establishment, if agencies are identical, operate at full capacity, and are taken as independent units rather than entities in a system, all places surpassing the threshold will provide the same sales and profit potential for the individual agency. The result would be locational indifference. Why then, is there an impetus for hierarchically ordered locational priorities? One factor introducing a hierarchical tendency is the spatial agglomeration economies accruing to the diffusion agency that is part of an integrated system. A second factor devolves from the difference between the sales (profit) threshold required to operate an agency and its sales (profit) capacity, an index of the utility to the individual agency of areas with larger sales potential. The value of these factors would differ by innovation. It seems reasonable to hypothesize that higher order innovations feature a higher *elasticity of agency profitability with regard to urban area sales potential*, and therefore a greater impetus towards hierarchically ordered locational priorities. However,

Figure 2. Expected Patterns of Diffusion under a Centralized Decision-Making Structure[a]

Characteristics of the Firm	Characteristics of the Innovation							
	Market or Sales Potential Related to the Number of Persons in an Urban Area				Market or Sales Potential Not Related to the Number of Persons in an Urban Area			
	Logistics Effect							
	Significant		Minimal		Significant		Minimal	
	Elasticity of Agency Profitability							
	Sig	Min	Sig	Min	Sig	Min	Sig	Min
Low Capital Availability	Hierarchy Effect Constrained by a Neighborhood Effect	Neighborhood Effect	Hierarchy Effect Slightly Constrained by a Neighborhood Effect	Slight Neighborhood Effect	Neighborhood Effect with Random Element	Neighborhood Effect	Random Element Slightly Constrained by a Neighborhood Effect	Slight Neighborhood Effect
High Capital Availability	Hierarchy Effect Constrained by a Neighborhood Effect	Neighborhood Effect with Slight Hierarchy Effect	Hierarchy Effect	Slight Neighborhood and Hierarchy Effects	Neighborhood Effect with Random Element	Neighborhood Effect	Random Element	Slight Neighborhood Effect with Random Element

[a]If a propagator used an existing network of diffusion agencies, it would channel the diffusion accordingly, but within that constraint, the same tendencies in pattern would be expected.

the argument in this paragraph also implies that the hierarchical tendency should always be less than that expected by considering only place-to-place differences in sales potential.

To sum up, the critical factors for diffusion in a centralized decision making setting are *capital availability, sales potential, logistics,* and the *elasticity of agency profitability with regard to sales potential.* Although the expected pattern of diffusion would vary according to the mix of these characteristics in a given situation, the discussion provides little support for the hierarchy effect as a dominant tendency. To illustrate this further, Figure 2 considers situations comprised of idealized levels (for example, high-low capital availability) of these four characteristics. The hierarchy effect is a tendency in only six of the sixteen situations and is a singular force in only one, whereas the neighborhood effect appears thirteen times. Without knowing the frequency of occurrence of each characteristic, projective statements are tenuous, but there clearly is strong support for expecting neighborhood effects or no marked spatial bias in diffusion patterns in a centralized setting.

The Case of Friendly Ice Cream[10]

An example of diffusion agency establishment under a centralized decision-making structure is the spread of Friendly Ice Cream shops, where the innovation or new product is largely the image presented by the Friendly shop. The Friendly organization is highly centralized. The manufacture of ice cream and the processing of other foods sold in Friendly shops is carried on at Friendly's central processing plant in Wilbraham, Massachusetts, just outside of Springfield, the home of the founders of the *Friendly Concept*. Further, all market penetration and site selection decisions are controlled by corporate headquarters, as are decisions pertaining to product promotion and managerial training. Friendly also owns the land on which most of its shops stand, builds most of its free-standing shops, and operates a fleet of trucks to supply all the shops from the central commissary. Virtually the only decisions made at the local shop level are how much to order from the central commissary, where to obtain fresh produce and milk locally, and whom to hire as service personnel.

The conceptual model presented above suggests that the key determinants of the pattern of diffusion of Friendly shops ought to be the logistics of service, supply, and control; market potential; the elasticity of outlet profitability with regard to market potential; and capital availability. Attention now turns to each of these factors.

With respect to *logistics* effects, the trucks delivering to Friendly shops from the central commissary have an overnight range of about 400 miles, creating a barrier to spread beyond that distance. Also, even within the 400-mile range, increased distances mean increased costs. Another logistical consideration is the relatively high degree of involvement of headquarters personnel in all aspects of the corporation's activity pertaining to individual shops. Thus, distance to the commissary or home office has been a critical consideration in the locational strategy for individual shops, suggesting that a neighborhood effect will be in evidence in the timing and location of shop openings.

The accuracy of this expectation is illustrated by a map portraying the spatial dispersion of Friendly shops at selected years from 1936 through 1974 (Figure 3). The first shop was opened in Springfield in 1935; by 1951 there were ten shops in western Massachusetts and Connecticut; in 1965 the first Friendly shop was opened outside New England; and by 1974 Friendly Ice Cream had ex-

Figure 3. The Spatial Dispersion of Friendly Ice Cream Shops for Selected
Years, 1936 through 1974

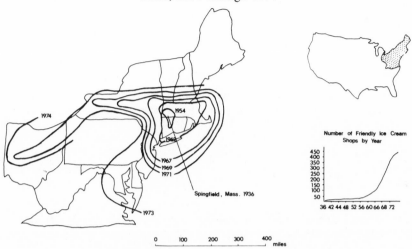

Number of Friendly Ice Cream
Shops by Year

450
400
350
300
250
200
150
100
50

36 42 44 48 52 56 60 66 68 72

Spingfield , Mass. 1936

0   100   200   300   400
                              miles

panded as far west as Ohio. Further evidence of a neighborhood effect in the
diffusion of Friendly Ice Cream is provided by a regression analysis in which
logged distance to Springfield explains 44 percent of the variance in the year each
of the Friendly shops was established.

Sales potential also is an important element in Friendly's locational strategy.
While most of the variables used by Friendly to estimate this pertain to the site of
the shop, and thus are not of interest in the present analysis, some are significant
in choosing the urban place in which the shop is located. These are not *ordering*
criteria, however, but *threshold* criteria of population size (more than 12,000),
disposable family income (above average), and community growth (above average). In actuality, only 32.2 percent of the urban places with Friendly shops meet
all three of the threshold requirements. Yet, 85.6 percent meet the population
requirement, 59.2 percent the income requirement, and 49.6 percent meet the
growth-rate requirement. More significantly, only 1.7 percent, or six of the
urban places, meet *none* of the threshold requirements.

One apparent reason why sales potential operates in a threshold fashion rather
than controlling the time order of Friendly shop establishment is because the
shops have a *low elasticity of profitability with respect to urban size.* Each
Friendly shop provides essentially the same services, the same format, and has
approximately the same capacity of ninety seats. While there is variation in their
success, some operating at maximum capacity more often than others, this appears to be dependent upon site related differences rather than upon differences
among urban areas. Thus, locating the first shops in larger or faster growing
cities would not be expected to provide significantly higher levels of profit.

Together with the fact that Friendly stresses a solid, traditional, middle-class image which favors suburbs and smaller towns, these factors suggest that the pattern of Friendly shop openings will not exhibit a strong hierarchy effect, if any.

This expectation is confirmed by a stepwise regression analysis in which the year each Friendly shop was established is related to logged distance from Springfield, to control for logistics effects, and the three sales potential variables of logged population, logged median income, and population growth. In general, the sales potential variables only relate minimally to the time order of shop opening. This—together with the fact that 98.3 percent of towns with Friendly shops meet at least one of the basic requirements of population, disposable income, or community growth—indicates that sales potential does function as a threshold, rather than as an ordering condition.

The last factor to be considered is *capital availability*. The theoretical discussion indicates that sales maximization is a viable policy for capital-rich propagators, whereas capital poor propagators would be more likely to follow cost minimization until expansion capital is available.

Like many economic ventures, the Friendly Ice Cream Corporation began with limited capital and a significant infusion of entrepreneurial labor. Minimizing operating expenses was therefore important. Costs of delivery, supervision, control, and market information had to be kept low in locating Friendly shops. It was important, therefore, to keep distance to the home office in Springfield at a minimum. As the corporation grew and capital availability improved, distance to Springfield became a less limiting factor. Even though logistical considerations still remained, decision making and control were in part delegated to regional managers, and specialists in real estate took the responsibility for the development and siting of new shops.

The implication is that over time, as more capital becomes available, there should be a shift in the factors controlling the diffusion pattern. To test this, the regressions reported above were rerun for two separate time periods, 1936–1964, the period prior to incorporation, and 1965–1974. A very dramatic shift is in the role of logistics, which drops to explaining only 21 percent of the variance in the second phase, less than half its importance in the first phase of Friendly's existence. There also is evidence of a shift toward sales maximization in recent years, although it doesn't show up in the regression analyses, in Friendly's explanation for their policy of spreading in a wave like or neighborhood effect pattern (by *osmosis* is their description of it). Whereas this policy was initially justified only in terms of logistics costs, it is now justified in terms of market saturation and advertising benefits as well.

In summary, the logistics of service, supply, and control are critical factors in the market penetration behavior of Friendly Ice Cream, leading to a pattern of diffusion agency establishment with marked neighborhood effects. Sales potential differences among urban places act as a threshold for diffusion agency establishment, but do not affect the sequencing of establishment because there is a low elasticity of Friendly shop profitability with regard to urban area size (or sales potential). Thus, a hierarchical component in the diffusion pattern is not evident. Capital availability also plays a role. A comparison of the years 1936 through 1964, preceding incorporation, with the years 1965 through 1974 indicates that diffusion in the earlier period occurred at a slower rate and in a more highly constrained neighborhood effect pattern. This is consistent with the expectation that cost factors would exert more control in a period of relatively scarce capital and that sales potential would become more important when capital was less scarce.

These findings are essentially those which would be hypothesized by considering the conceptual framework of diffusion agency establishment in a centralized decision making setting together with the particular characteristics of the Friendly situation. Thus, support is provided for this portion of the market and infrastructure model of innovation diffusion. The case study also provides a qualitative sense of how the various relevant factors interact and play off with one another.

Profit-Motivated Diffusion Under a Decentralized Decision-Making Structure

The previous discussion dealt with the single propagator who establishes a network of diffusion agencies. In the decentralized situation, on the other hand, each diffusion agency is established independently by a different entrepreneurial or economic entity, and it rather than a central propagator carries the burdens of risk, capital provision, and decision making responsibility. One implication is that the degree of success (or failure) of a single agency generally will be of limited concern to other agencies or to the coordinating propagator (if there is one), a fact reflected in the decentralization of decision making responsibility.[11]

Thus, the agency location process in a decentralized setting will differ from the centralized. The profitability associated with a particular urban center will be important, but should operate primarily as a *threshold* for agency establishment rather than as a basis for ranking alternative locations. At most, a local entrepreneur will evaluate a small number of nearby centers; other locations will not usually be considered even though they may be more suitable for the diffusion agency.

The profitability threshold condition will be met by numerous locations. Within this set, where and when agencies are established will depend upon the entrepreneur learning about the innovation and about establishing an agency from which it may be propagated. In the diffusion of rural purchasing cooperatives in Britain [117,118], for example, individuals starting a new cooperative were previously in contact with one or more leaders of existing cooperatives. From these contacts they obtained evidence of the effectiveness and likely success of a cooperative, knowledge of how to establish and successfully operate a cooperative, and moral support for the venture.

Characteristics of the entrepreneur also are important.[12] The entrepreneur must, for example, have sufficient capital to establish an agency, be capable of seeing the potential of the innovation, be willing to take the required risks and to expend the required effort, and possess certain promotional and management skills. The congruence of the innovation with the ongoing activities of the entrepreneur also may be important. Cable television systems, for example, frequently were established by store owners selling television receivers [25]. In terms of a place characteristic, then, those with human resources capable of being aware of and exploiting the innovation are more likely to receive diffusion agencies [32].

The preceding discussion indicates that a critical element in decentralized diffusion is information linkages among urban places and related means of exposure to the innovation. If there is a coordinating propagator, a conscious strategy may underlie the information flow pattern. If there is not a central propagator, and often when there is, the information flow system is less explicit.

Perhaps relevant in this context is Hagerstrand's [54] suggestion that flows may occur via a hierarchy of networks of social communication, although they should be seen to involve several types of communication, not just the social. Empirical work on regional contact systems is reported in Hagerstrand and Kuklinski [56], Thorngren [125], and Tornqvist [127], but these works are primarily concerned with contacts between established businesses. More relevant is the work of Gould and Tornqvist [49], Pred [92–99], and Warneryd [129], which are concerned with contact systems more applicable to the establishment of diffusion agencies. Nevertheless, our knowledge of regional contact systems is not sufficient to permit specification aside from crude surrogates such as the gravity model [Pedersen, 88, 89; Pred, 93: 229–238] or distance to a diffusion node. Clearly then, more work must be done to identify which contact systems are relevant to diffusion in a decentralized setting and to determine their spatial characteristics.

Another important question concerns the strategy employed by a coordinating propagator in meting out information flows and incentives to prospective diffusion agents (agencies). Evidence indicates that expected profitability or gain would be the ordering criteria [18, 21, 24, 86]. Thus, many of the points made above with respect to diffusion under a centralized decision making structure also apply to a coordinating propagator. One important difference, however, is that profitability for the coordinating propagator could well be defined on a narrower basis reflecting only that aspect upon which its return is calculated. For instance, franchisers typically profit from a one-time-only fee paid by each franchisee and from a percentage of the gross sales of each franchisee. Thus, their agency establishment strategy would *not* be based upon maximizing the profits of the agency system as a whole as in diffusion under a centralized decision making structure [134].

Another important aspect of the strategy employed by the coordinating propagator is its variability from situation to situation. At one extreme, almost identical to the decentralized case, the coordinating propagator may not in any way narrate information flows with regard to the innovation and agency establishment. Alternatively, moving further along the continuum, the coordinating propagator might provide this kind of input as well as support packages such as training programs for diffusion agency personnel or designed systems to be used by the diffusion agency in disseminating the innovation. The coordinating propagator's role may even extend to selecting locations for diffusion agencies, and at the extreme, there might be so much control that the diffusion can be viewed as centralized!

With regard to the spatial patterns of diffusion under a decentralized decision-making structure, the historical evidence of Pred [93: 227-238], Pedersen [88, 89], and Robson [102: 131-185] indicates that diffusion agencies generally would be found in larger cities and their environs before smaller cities.[13] Similarly, Hagerstrand's [51] study of the diffusion of the radio and motor car in southern Sweden indicates that a combination of hierarchy and neighborhood effects is likely to occur. Studies of more recent diffusions, however, indicate that patterns dominated by neighborhood and/or random effects also are extremely common. These latter examples include the diffusion of planned regional shopping centers in the United States [33], Planned Parenthood affiliates in the United States [21], the Department store in Japan [122], rural purchasing cooperatives in Britain [117, 118], cable television systems in Ohio [25], and BankAmericard-Master Charge in Ohio and West Virginia [18].

To illustrate the above observations, attention now turns to the diffusion of cable television systems in Ohio. This represents diffusion under a decentralized decision-making structure without a coordinating propagator. For an example of diffusion under a decentralized decision making structure with a coordinating propagator, the reader is referred to Brown and Malecki's [18] study of the spread of BankAmericard-Master Charge in Ohio and West Virginia, a profit-motivated situation, and to Brown and Philliber's [21] study of the spread of Planned Parenthood affiliates in the United States, a nonprofit motivated situation.

The Case of Cable Television[14]

In the early 1950's, cable primarily existed where broadcast reception was marginal and where there was sufficient population to support a system. Particularly significant development in this era occurred in the populated, mountainous areas of the eastern United States where terrain obstructed broadcast signals [135: 39]. After 1956, when microwave relay equipment became more readily available, cable service was extended to more remote locations, notably to populated pockets in the West [70: 93]. In the late 1950's, cable also entered the larger cities, impelled by the increasing demand for diversity in programming, and the increasingly poor quality of reception in growing urban places.[15] The 1970 distribution of cable systems in the United States reflects these trends of early development in eastern mountain areas and of more recent growth in the Southwest, West, and larger cities.[16]

The diffusion of cable systems has occurred primarily under a decentralized decision-making structure. Early cable systems were established locally by a single entrepreneur or group of residents [120: 9–10]. Thus, their decision primarily pertained only to the construction of such a system, not to the community in which it would be located. Multiple system operating companies that engage in a centralized type of decision process have emerged. To date, however, they have grown primarily by buying out existing systems, rather than establishing systems in new areas.

The stages of development of cable television in the United States are mirrored in Ohio. Its temporal sequence of diffusion is parallel to those of the United States overall and generally conform to the traditional S-curve trend. Development began in Ohio in 1950 at a relatively brisk pace. In 1954 it leveled off, reflecting a plateau in the industry's overall growth nation-wide. This plateau gave way to very rapid expansion in 1965 that still continues.

This temporal pattern suggests that division into two phases—before and after 1965—is appropriate. Support for this division also is to be found in the development of the cable industry. The year 1965 marks the beginning of extensive FCC regulation of the cable television industry. In addition, none of the top one hundred market cities in Ohio had cable service prior to 1965, an indication of a difference in market focus. Another difference lies in the role of cable television. Initially, cable was seen as a means of providing some television reception to remote communities. Later the role shifted to providing improved reception and a greater variety of programming than that provided by broadcast television.

These aspects of the development of cable television also are seen in the spatial pattern of diffusion in Ohio (Figure 4). Early development occurred in two areas of the Appalachian Plateau portion of Ohio, areas of rather rugged terrain. In central eastern Ohio a system was established at Glenmont in 1950, followed the next year by systems at nearby Millersburg, Dover, and New Philadelphia. In the same year, 1951, systems were established in southeastern Ohio at Athens, The Plains, and Murray City. Through 1964, the termination of Phase I, the location of new systems generally follows a neighborhood effect pattern nucleated around these two areas, resulting in a broad zone of cable service across the Appalachian Plateau section of eastern and southeastern Ohio.

In 1965, the beginning of Phase II, more systems were established than in any previous year, and they are located in new and widely separated areas. The shift to northwestern Ohio is particularly noticeable, occurring in the towns of Kenton, Piqua, Fostoria, Bowling Green, Findlay, Tiffin, and Wauseon. However, this shift is not accompanied by the spatial clustering that characterized the initiation of Phase I.

Figure 4. Spread of Cable Television Systems in Ohio for Selected Years

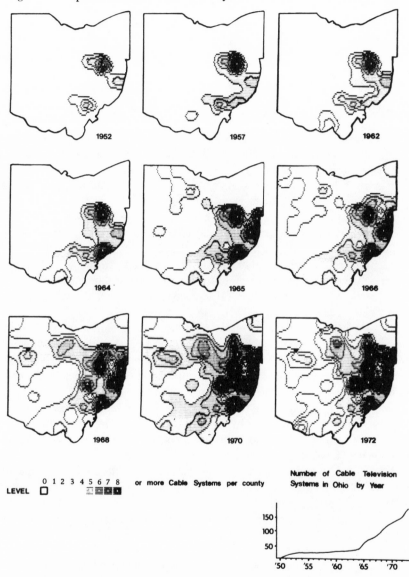

These trends continue for the whole of Phase II. By 1972, cable systems were located throughout the entire state with the exception of the large metropolitan centers, but density of service remained greatest in the Appalachian Plateau areas. Further, although some medium-size cities in the top one hundred market areas received cable during Phase II—Steubenville in 1965, Toledo and Canton in 1966, and Akron in 1969—development in the state's largest metropolitan areas such as Cincinnati, Cleveland, and Columbus is only currently taking place.

To further evaluate the spatial pattern of cable system establishment in Ohio, statistical analyses were carried out using independent variables pertaining to market potential and exposure to cable television whereby entrepreneurs learn that a system may be established, how that is accomplished, and that doing so may be profitable or advantageous in some other way. Variables employed to measure market potential primarily pertain to the quality of television reception without cable; those employed to measure exposure were distances from Glenmont in eastern Ohio, Athens in southeastern Ohio, and Kenton in northwest Ohio. These represent the earliest established cable systems in each area and were taken to be diffusion nodes.

In general, both market potential and exposure are significantly related to the year in which a cable system is established, but the exposure variables are somewhat less important in Phase II. There also are some interesting differences in distinguishing between towns that established a cable system in Phase I, those in Phase II, and towns that had not established such a system at all. Phase I adopter towns have significantly higher levels of market potential and are located closer to the original nodes of the diffusion in eastern Ohio than are Phase II adopter towns. In comparing Phase II with nonadopter towns the differences are not as marked and are even inconclusive for several variables.

Taken together, these analyses support the conceptualization of diffusion agency establishment under a decentralized decision making structure without a coordinating propagator. Both *market potential* and *exposure* were important factors. That Phase II adopter towns were not so different from nonadopter towns underlies the additional importance of a factor akin to *firm characteristics pertaining to management aggressiveness and innovativeness.* Cable television systems were generally established by single entrepreneurs. Thus, the variable(s) to capture this factor should pertain to the local pool of entrepreneurial ability or the level of individual innovativeness.

Another interesting comparison is in the random pattern characterizing the diffusion of the bank credit card [18], which involved a coordinating propagator, and the neighborhood effect pattern characterizing cable television. It seems that this difference occurs because of the different mechanisms of exposure in the two cases. A central element of the strategy for diffusing the bank credit card was the use of a formal communications network, the correspondent banking system of the propagator, and this network had no marked spatial characteristics.[17] By contrast, cable television spread *naturally,* without the orchestration of a coordinating propagator, through a grass roots system of interpersonal contact and local spatial interaction among towns. Thus, we can see how the *organizational structure* of the diffusion directly affected the diffusion pattern and who had access to the innovation at any given time.

Finally, there is the role of *institutional* factors. These operated both in the establishment of cable television systems and in the bank credit card case. In the latter instance, these factors pertained to the relationship between the bank propagating the credit card and other banks. Specifically, since the propagating bank was of modest size, its efforts were resisted by larger banks of greater institutional stature that were more conservative and more oriented toward business and real estate clienteles than toward individual or household consumers. By contrast, the institutional factors operating in the diffusion of cable television were external to the establishment decision itself, that is, they pertained to creating the conditions for diffusion rather than to the interactions between the various actors in the system.[18]

DIFFUSION AGENCY STRATEGY

Once the diffusion agency is established, whether through centralized or decentralized decision making, it becomes a vehicle for establishing the innovation in the surrounding area. To accomplish this, each agency implements a strategy designed to induce adoption. This strategy may originate with the diffusion agency itself, in which case it probably would differ from agency to agency. Alternatively, all or part of the strategy may be product or service wide and, thus, more or less similar among diffusion agencies. The latter is most common if there is a coordinating or centralized propagator. Whether the diffusion strategy is different or similar from agency to agency, however, its general dimensions remain the same. These dimensions constitute another portion of the market and infrastructure perspective, which is elaborated in this section of the paper.

While diffusion agency strategy involves a variety of activities, four are particularly relevant to the spatial pattern of diffusion. One of these is the *development of infrastructure and organizational capabilities*. This permits the diffusion process to be implemented, maintained, and expanded and often channels its spatial form. A second element of strategy is the *price* charged for the innovation, which is likely to change over time and to vary over space according to the location of the potential adopter. As such, price affects the density of adoption in a given population at a given time and may influence its spatial variation. Third, *promotional communications* are employed to provide individuals with information about the innovation and to persuade them to adopt. The fourth element of diffusion agency strategy is *market selection and segmentation*, that is, identification of the clientele for the innovation and targeting in differential ways upon segments of that clientele. In many instances, both promotional communications and market segmentation procedures have explicit effects upon the spatial pattern of diffusion.

Another consideration is how these elements *interact* with each other in the articulation of diffusion agency strategy, that is, the way the strategy elements are orchestrated to bring about an efficient manipulation of the diffusion process. One aspect of this is the affect of the details of one element of diffusion strategy upon other elements. The placing of infrastructure in certain locales and not others, for example, would also influence the spatial placement and effects of promotional communications. Second, there will be joint effects from various combinations of the strategy elements that will exceed the effects of each considered singly, as in a diffusion strategy involving both infrastructure development and associated promotional communications. A third aspect is that one or more of the strategy elements might originate from entities other than the diffusion agency, and this would affect the latter's strategy. For example, a new energy efficient electrical appliance would employ an infrastructure provided by public utility companies. Further, while promotion of the appliance would be handled directly by the firm propagating it, that firm also would benefit from promotion by the utilities and by environmental agencies of the government stressing energy conservation. Finally, the actions of the potential adopter's social network also will have a direct impact on the temporal and spatial patterns of diffusion, and this is sometimes taken account of in designing diffusion agency strategy.

In order to understand better the influence of diffusion agency activities upon adoption, it is useful to separately consider the objective and subjective attributes of an innovation [27]. In particular, infrastructure provision and pricing affect the objective attributes of the innovation, while market selection and segmentation and promotional communications primarily affect the potential adopter's beliefs about and evaluation of these attributes, or the subjective attributes of the innovation. Figure 5 illustrates this as well as the manner in which the diffusion agency strategy interfaces with adoption behavior. Thus, one point incorporated in Figure 5 is that each element of diffusion agency strategy and the activities of related entities affect different aspects of the adoption decision.

It also is useful to consider Figure 5 in light of previous studies of innovation diffusion. In particular, the traditional *adoption or consumer behavior* oriented perspective concentrates almost exclusively upon the right, shaded side of the diagram and neglects the actions of diffusion agencies and their effects. Thus, there are many studies which examine the relationship between adoption and the social, psychological, economic, and locational characteristics of the potential adopter as well as the role of information and influence from a potential adopter's social network [107]. In general, the only diffusion agency actions given attention under the traditional perspective are extension agent influences, examined by rural sociologists for agricultural settings, and promotional communication influences, particularly advertising, examined by marketing professionals [81, 101, 107]. Even when these elements are examined, however, they tend to be treated as exogenous, or given conditions, and evaluated in terms of their influence upon adoption relative to personal, *innovativeness* related characteristics; that is, they are not treated as a manipulable variable with differential effects resulting from alternative strategies.[19]

One proviso is necessary before going on. For the practitioner the diffusion agency strategy portion of the market and infrastructure framework may seem

Figure 5. A Portrayal of the Interface Between Diffusion Agency Actions and Adoption Behavior

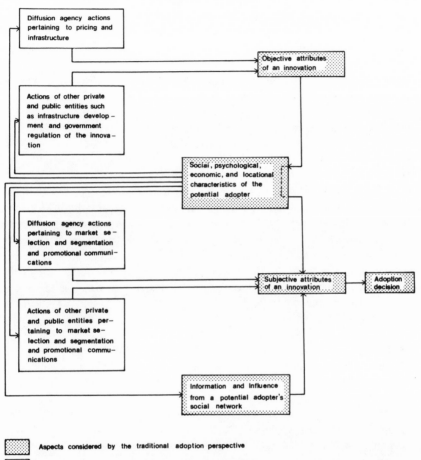

elemental. Surely, for example, the entrepreneur already knows about the role of pricing in new product diffusion, and marketing texts recount a variety of options in pricing policies, when each ought to be used, and anticipated effects. Nevertheless, this knowledge has *not* been incorporated into the academic study of innovation diffusion, not even in marketing, and even less attention has been given to the spatial dimensions of these actions. Further, government or public programs seldom utilize the sophisticated and more effective strategies developed and employed in entrepreneurial settings. A contention in developing this framework, then, is that we must formulate paradigms to reflect reality, and in doing this, that we have a great deal to learn from the practicing entrepreneur.

In return, however, it is anticipated that our work eventually will lead to significantly increased capabilities for the community of practitioners.

Attention now turns to elaborating each of the elements of diffusion agency strategy. This is followed by an illustrative case study.

The Development of Infrastructure and Organizational Capabilities

This diffusion agency strategy element is one means of enabling or enhancing the use or adoption of an innovation. In the diffusion of BankAmericard among households in the United States, for instance, the utility of adoption depended upon the infrastructure of merchants willing to accept the card [18, 29]. Likewise, Nestle's promotion of commercial dairying in Mexico was enhanced by its provision of a collection system whereby the farmer's milk product was shipped to the market (Nestle's warehouse) [17].

The diffusion agency may develop its own infrastructure and organizational capabilities or it may utilize the existing capabilities of other public and private entities [43, 46, 48, 115, 116]. Such existing or *generally available* infrastructures may have been created (1) in conjunction with the diffusion of a specific innovation and later made available to others; (2) as an innovation in its own right; or (3) as a generally available good intended to improve the overall conditions for economic and social development, one aspect of which is innovation diffusion. Examples include, respectively, service and repair stations, electricity infrastructure, and transportation infrastructure.

Use of such generally available infrastructure is a necessity for some infrastructure needs, such as adequate rural roads, a rural public water system, or a rural electrification system. If these are not present, then, the agency might have to await their development in order for innovation diffusion to be feasible. However, for other organizational or infrastructure needs the agency will have a choice, at least in part, of developing its own or utilizing existing capabilities. Examples include collection or distribution services; processing, marketing, warehouse, inventory, and retail facilities; sales, market research, management, and control systems; and personnel training and development programs.

In some situations, potential adopters are able to utilize an innovation only in proximity to the infrastructure, as in the case of cable television [119]. In other situations, an innovation may be used anywhere, but must be serviced frequently, as in the adoption of computer equipment where access to maintenance and repair services are critical. Both of these situations would be *infrastructure constrained* in that adoption will in general occur only *where* there is the required infrastructure and not elsewhere. Where access to such infrastructures does not play an important role, a diffusion process is *infrastructure independent* [12].

That there is some infrastructure which increases the utility of an innovation is not in itself a sufficient condition for classifying a given diffusion situation as infrastructure constrained, however. Other critical elements include the degree to which the innovation's utility increases as a result of access to the infrastructure, the relative cost to the potential adopter of providing the infrastructure his/herself, and the spatial distribution or ubiquity of the infrastructure.

To illustrate, the operation of innovations such as the electric light, telephone, or television require an energy infrastructure that had to be developed as these innovations were being introduced, so that the locations of adopters were dependent upon the location of the infrastructure. While this continues to be the case today in Third World nations, it is not so in the United States where the relevant energy infrastructure is for the most part ubiquitous. Yet, the diffusion of computer innovations in the United States in the 1970's has been constrained by the required service infrastructure; the diffusion of liquid propane gas and oil heating in rural areas is constrained by the required delivery infrastructure; and the diffusion of water-using appliances is constrained by the lack of public water systems in rural areas. Similarly, there is infrastructure constraint in the diffusion of many agricultural innovations that are enhanced by special marketing facilities and collection systems permitting cheap movement to market.

In terms of spatial patterns, we have already noted that adoption will in general occur where the infrastructure is and not elsewhere if the diffusion is infrastructure constrained. Further, there is generally a spatial order in the development of infrastructure which is mirrored in the diffusion of related innovations. More specifically, the economics associated with management, control, promotional, and service infrastructures often militate towards a spatially restricted pattern, and the expansion of such infrastructures tends to be in a nearest neighbor fashion leading to wavelike or contagion patterns of diffusion.

Pricing

The monetary value associated with an innovation is to some degree intrinsic. The color television, for example, is moderately expensive, whereas the electric toothbrush is inexpensive. Within the range of feasible prices, however, the diffusion agency retains considerable discretion over the actual price charged, and in general, higher prices within the range will result in a lower density of adoption among the target population and vice versa [65: 334–339; 66: 515–516]. Accordingly, the actual price charged ought to reflect the diffusion objectives of the agency. Over the long run, for example, the entrepreneurial agency probably would seek to maximize profits, while the public agency might seek to minimize costs or maximize the number of clients served.

Whatever the price charged by the agency, the total cost to the potential adopter generally will vary according to his/her location. For example, if the agency provides no delivery, service, or other infrastructure and charges a *uniform price at the outlet*, the potential adopter will incur a transportation cost in getting to the outlet. Traditional spatial economic theory states that such transportation costs would vary directly with the buyer's distance from the diffusion agency, that the buyer would add these costs to the price of the innovation, and that the level of demand for the innovation would decrease accordingly. This, then, would affect the spatial extent of the market area for the innovation and lead to a distance decay distribution of adoption within it [6: 29–58].

Alternatively, the diffusion agency or some other entity may provide some relevant infrastructure and charge either a *uniform price at the outlet*, a *uniform delivered price*, or a *distance related price*.[20] Whatever the pricing policy, the significance of the infrastructure would itself render the situation infrastructure constrained since adoption will in general be limited to the area served by the infrastructure. Applying traditional economic theory leads to the further conclusion that uniform delivered pricing produces a tendency towards a uniform density of adopters *within* the area served by the infrastructure since access costs are equal across adopters. By similar reasoning, distance related pricing or a uniform price at the outlet produces a tendency towards a distance decay pattern of adoption *within* the area served by the infrastructure.

It is questionable, however, whether distance decay diffusion patterns would in fact occur under the conditions specified above, even if pricing is explicitly distance related. One reason is that the demand for most modern products appears to be relatively inelastic with regard to price [66: 515–516]. Second, when the buyer incurs the transportation costs by traveling to the diffusion agency, as is most commonly the case, it is doubtful that he/she directly associates those costs with those of the innovation, either because the trip is multiple purpose or because it is common place.[21] Finally, Getis [47] provides evidence that one's own transportation costs are perceived as a stepped function of distanced instead of a linear function, and are not markedly differentiated except at extreme distances.

To sum up, when the diffusion agency provides *no* delivery, service, or other infrastructure and charges a uniform price at the outlet, the spatial pattern of adoption will depend upon the price elasticity of demand for the innovation and the degree to which potential adopters perceive accessibility to the diffusion agency as a significant cost. If price elasticity and access costs are significant, a distance decay pattern of adoption would occur and the situation would be infrastructure constrained; otherwise, a uniform density of adopters would be expected, ceteris paribus, and the situation would be infrastructure independent. Alternatively, while the diffusion pattern would be infrastructure constrained if the agency *did* provide delivery, service, or other infrastructure, the spatial pattern within that constraint, whether the pricing policy is uniform at the outlet, uniform delivered or distance related, also would depend upon the price elasticity of demand for the innovation and the degree to which potential adopters perceive accessibility to the diffusion agency as a significant cost. Thus, we see that pricing policy is one of the determinants of infrastructure effects upon adoption.

Promotional Communications

The diffusion agency generates information of various sorts, or utilizes information from other sources, in order to create awareness of the innovation and its characteristics. The impact of this information on the adoption decision and the resulting patterns of diffusion varies, however, according to its *channel, source, content, and motivation*. Each of these dimensions is briefly discussed.

The *channel* or the medium conveying the information may be personal or impersonal. The former involves a one to one correspondence between sender and receiver and enables the sender to custom tailor the message and react to sender feedback. Thus, personal communications channels tend to be more effective than impersonal ones in transmitting a complex information and thereby altering attitudes [1: 35-37, 59: 368-370]. However, impersonal communications, which include mass media, reach a larger number of people per message over a greater spatial range than personal channels [54: 138-139].

Thus, when deciding upon a mixture of personal and impersonal information channels, diffusion agencies must trade off effectiveness with spatial range and number of recipients. If, for example, the agency wishes to maintain a spatial facet in the diffusion, such as confining adoption to the vicinity of a service or delivery infrastructure in order to minimize the cost of maintaining the infrastructure, channels with a small, controllable spatial range and high effectiveness, such as personal selling, might be favored.

In general, channels vary greatly in terms of spatial characteristics. For example, impersonal channels usually reach a more spatially dispersed audience than personal ones, even though audiences may range from a neighborhood for a local newspaper to a nation for a metropolitan daily. Furthermore, within that audience radius, rates of contact may vary considerably. Subscriber and viewer ratios, for example, show much local variation both among neighborhoods within an urban area and among rural areas and small towns surrounding the origin of the newspaper or television station (the latter often in a distance decay fashion). A great deal of variation also occurs with personal promotional communications. The door-to-door salesperson, such as the Avon, Fuller Brush, or encyclopedia representative, would utilize a definite spatial strategy with high focus upon certain areas that may be widely dispersed from one another. The market area of a store salesperson, on the other hand, would depend upon whether the store was neighborhood or city wide in its orientation. Finally, social channels are highly local in their focus, often involving a distance decay pattern of contacts [19, 20, 77, 83, 84].

The *source* of information may be a diffusion agency, another type of agency (for instance, an agency marketing competing or complementary goods, a government agency, or a consumer interest group), or a member of the potential adopter's social system. The first two of these three categories can be further classified as either private or public (the latter including governmental and nonprofit organizations).

These various sources differ in their impact upon attitudes [107: 250-266]. For instance, diffusion agencies tend to be most important in exposing individuals to an innovation and in providing them with information about its attributes [59: 294-321]. Information about the innovation is also obtained from an individual's social system, once news of the innovation has spread. In evaluating the innovation in terms of adoption, however, individuals tend to rely less upon diffusion or other agencies, and more upon information from their social system [44: 412-431, 59: 294-321].[22]

The role of information sources also differs across adopter subgroups. Rogers and Shoemaker [107: 250-266] conclude that innovators and early adopters have more diffusion agency and social system interaction than later adopters, and tend to use a greater variety of information sources. Later adopters, on the other hand, use fewer sources—relying, in particular, upon social interaction and adopting primarily as the result of favorable information from one or more existing adopters.

In terms of the spatial patterns of diffusion, communication levels are greater between individuals who are both geographically and socially proximate to one another [52-55, 62: 32-36]. Thus, because of the distance constrained nature of social networks, diffusion processes which are highly influenced by social system interaction will tend to exhibit a neighborhood effect and a clustering of adopters. This pattern would not, however, characterize innovators and early adopters, who would instead be randomly located because of their greater reliance upon impersonal information sources. Later adopters, on the other hand, should be located in physical proximity to previous adopters because of their dependence on social interaction.

Information also varies in *content* and may be promotional, neutral, or counter promotional. Typically, there is a mixture of these although the existence of counter promotional information might depend upon the structure of the market. Too often, the impact of the communications process upon spatial diffusion patterns is described only in terms of sources providing favorable information. Obviously, the location of other sources providing unfavorable information will have an analogous, but deterring impact on diffusion, and the location of neutral sources may also have spatial implications.

Finally, one can distinguish between types of information according to the *motivation* which initiates its transmission. In general, potential adopters may obtain information by seeking it or by merely receiving it without solicitation. This rarely made distinction is useful in comparing the relative importance of competing explanations of adoption behavior [27]. For example, are innovators and early adopters particularly motivated to seek information about innovations, or are these market segments simply the targets of effective marketing campaigns? Addressing such questions should provide insight into the various ways that diffusion agencies manipulate diffusion patterns through promotional communications.[23]

Market Selection and Segmentation

This involves identification of the characteristics of potential adopters and division into *homogeneous* subgroups on the basis of those characteristics.[24] The result is a partitioning that permits the diffusion agency to focus upon particular submarkets in preference to others and to customize its infrastructure development, pricing, and promotional communications.

Segmentation strategies are frequently based on socioeconomic or demographic characteristics.[25] Examples of such submarkets include senior citizens, black youths, young married couples, or housewives.

Alternatively, a segmentation policy may be explicitly locational. This is reflected in the existence of sales territories and regional development strategies or segments such as urbanites, suburbanites, or New Englanders. An example at a local scale is the service station, hardware, or drug store manager who differentiates the service provided to regular neighborhood customers from the service provided to transients, and who accordingly beams promotional efforts to nearby households rather than to the urban area as a whole. In part, such strategies related to spatial scale occur because the market is spatially limited in accordance with the order of the good, that is, lower order innovations have smaller market areas than do higher order ones [7: 169–249, 131: 124–152, 274–301]. However, such strategies also occur because distribution and client oriented service costs are important factors in any marketing strategy [121].

Even if a market segmentation strategy is not explicitly locational, however, it often is implicitly so. Socioeconomic segments such as upwardly mobile middle-class households, for example, frequently are associated with distinct spatial patterns as evidenced by urban neighborhood typologies [7: 306–394, 61, 126]. New product promotional efforts based on such segments, then, would render distinct spatial patterns of innovation diffusion.

There also are other kinds of *implicit market segmentation strategies* that are important to consider. A diffusion agency, for example, may not consciously attempt to reach potential adopters differentially but may nonetheless do so by employing information channels used by subsets of the market, as discussed above under promotional communications. Implicit segmentation policies are particularly typical of government agency change efforts which rarely use sophisticated marketing techniques [30, 133].

An example of implicit market segmentation is the use of the *two step flow model of communications* in conjunction with measures of *innovativeness*, which is particularly prevalent in the diffusion efforts of government agencies. This is a *least resistance ordered* communications strategy in which the more motivated segment(s) of the market receives information first and the less motivated later [100: 22–23]. The initial segment is contacted directly by the diffusion agency and is expected to provide opinion leadership by transmitting the information via interpersonal communications to the lesser motivated segments [38: 378, 91: 102–105, 107: 198–225, 110: 118]. Measures of innovativeness are used with this strategy to identify the more motivated, progressive elements of the potential adopter pool. This is generally done on the basis of socioeconomic characteristics (such as income and education) and/or the amount and timing of adoption of other innovations. There is implicit segmentation in this strategy for two reasons.

First, there is considerable evidence that the second step of the communications chain, involving interpersonal communications from opinion leaders to others, does not consistently occur [30]. Second, differences in adoption time, the traditional measure of innovativeness [81], may be the result of the marketing strategy of public or private propagators of innovations rather than the result of actual innovativeness differences [23]. Thus, a focus upon one particular segment of the market is reinforced.

The Orchestration of Diffusion Agency Strategies

Utilization of the diffusion agency strategy elements discussed above generally involves integrating them into an effective package. There is little choice in some aspects of this because of the interdependence among individual elements of the strategy. For example, infrastructure development involves an implicit segmentation of the market by increasing the utility of adoption for those reached by the infrastructure. It therefore may affect both where promotional communications are directed and the types of channels employed. Conversely, if a particular market segment, as identified by some characteristics such as income, has distinct locational characteristics, infrastructure provision and promotional communications ought to reflect that. Similarly, since pricing policies affect the spatial distribution of adoption costs, they embody an implicit market selection and segmentation policy which may be reflected in the promotional communications strategy.

In addition, diffusion agency strategy will be interdependent with other characteristics of the diffusion. One of these is the nature and technical complexity of the innovation. To illustrate, an innovation that is more a speciality than a convenience good might well be propagated (1) by a careful segmentation of the market, (2) through agencies that are designed to appeal to the market segment of interest and located accordingly, (3) by means of promotional communications that carry a customized message with a relatively high information content, (4) by establishing an extensive service and information providing infrastructure, and (5) by a price reflecting market skimming or satisficing objectives [65: 336–337, 66: 519–521].

Another diffusion characteristic that will affect diffusion agency strategy is the type of agency and its relationship to corporate or institutional propagators. Thus, the convenience or low order function diffusion agency might employ neighborhood focused newspapers and handbills, whereas the specialty or high order function outlet might employ a newspaper with regional readership and topically focused journals. Similarly, creation and maintenance of a delivery infrastructure is a more likely strategy for high order function agencies than for lower order ones, and the order of outlet chosen as a distribution point for an innovation carries with it an implicit spatial segmentation of the market. Further, a strong linkage between diffusion agency and propagator introduces the possibility of diffusion strategies that are more uniform among agencies, propagator provided strategies designed by persons more expert than those the single agency could afford, and economies in the overall diffusion strategy.

Finally, diffusion agency strategy will be affected by the extent of market penetration, spatial proliferation, and competitor imitation, all reflections of the progress of the innovation in its life cycle. To illustrate, diffusion strategy in the introductory stages might well concentrate upon a particular market segment(s) owing to the limits of capital resources, and as demand grows, leading to competition, responses might include identifying new and unexploited needs in the market, product or service modification, increased advertising and promotion, more extensive segmentation schemes, or simply increased price competition. Further, as the life cycle progresses and the spatial extent of the diffusion increases, the market will become more heterogeneous, and this, along with the exigencies of organizational control, might lead to the use of sales territories and local market customization. Finally, as adoption expands into more peripheral areas, the agency may employ price discrimination and allocate resources for infrastructure development and product promotion in a manner such that the core provides support, while the innovation gains a foothold in the periphery.

Empirical Examples of the Diffusion Agency/ Potential Adopter Interface

The previous sections examined the various elements of diffusion agency strategy and provided a theoretical perspective pertaining to the spatial patterns of diffusion. Attention now turns to two empirical examples which illustrate the operation of the strategy portion of the market and infrastructure perspective in a real world setting. Specifically, the introductions of the cattle feed supplement *pro-las* and of *custom-blended fertilizer* into four counties of eastern Ohio (Figure 6) provide an example of two infrastructure constrained diffusions with contrasting pricing policies. This case study first describes the innovations; their propagation structure; and the infrastructure, pricing, promotional communications, and market segmentation strategies undertaken to market them. These factors then are related to the temporal and spatial diffusion patterns of the two innovations. A unique aspect of this study, which is critical to the elaboration of our theoretical framework (Figure 1, Figure 5), is the consideration of diffusion agency actions, their interface with adoption, and the resulting spatial patterns of diffusion.[26]

Pro-las and custom-blended fertilizer were introduced into four counties of Eastern Ohio in 1971 by the Belmont County Farm Bureau. This diffusion agency is a product distribution franchise of Landmark, Inc., the nationwide umbrella organization for Ohio's farm cooperatives. The two innovations were distributed under monopoly conditions, in part because Ohio farm bureaus honor each other's trade areas.

Figure 6.   The Four County Study Area

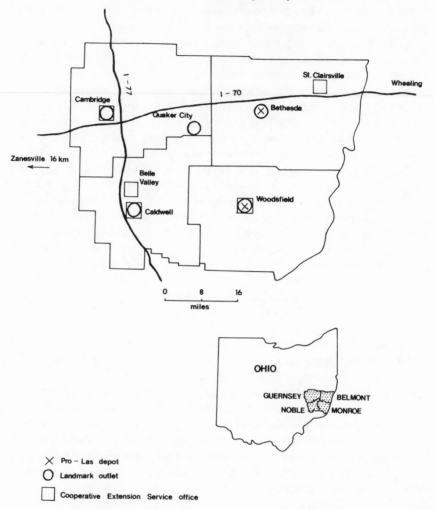

Pro-las is a liqueified feed supplement containing protein, minerals, vitamins, and molasses which involves the creation of a new consumption pattern in the use of liquid as well as dry cattle feed. Custom-blended fertilizer is fertilizer mixed individually to match the soil characteristics of each farm. This is a modification of a well-established product, prepackaged fertilizer, and involves only a slight alteration to the established consumption pattern. Accordingly, both innovations may be viewed as dynamically continuous, with pro-las being closer to discontinuous.

Both pro-las and custom-blended fertilizer are dependent upon a transportation infrastructure. Pro-las is stored in a tank in the farmer's pasture and filled period-ically at a frequency dependent upon the tank's size and the number of cattle using it. Four delivery routes were developed to provide this service. Each serves one of the four counties in the Farm Bureau's market area and originates at a pro-las storage depot, two from Woodsfield and two from Bethesda (Figure 6). A uni-form delivered price was established, thereby distributing transportation costs equally among all customers.

Custom-blended fertilizer is distributed from the Farm Bureau's blend plant in Quaker City, a location central to its market area (Figure 6). The farmer takes one or more soil samples to this plant, where fertilizer is mixed from bulk supplies. The fertilizer is then either transported by the purchaser or delivered by the Farm Bureau at a fee per ton mile. Thus, the total cost of the custom-blended fertilizer varies according to the location of the farmer.

The different pricing policies associated with the pro-las and custom-blended fertilizer infrastructures appear to account for different market segmentation and promotional communication policies. Pro-las, with a uniform delivered price, employed personal contact between Farm Bureau employees and potential adop-ters located in proximity to the delivery routes or to the storage depots at Woodsfield and Bethesda.[27] Further, the spatial segmentation of the market shifted over time since the Farm Bureau sequentially developed its delivery routes as each reached a threshold level of customers. Monroe County (Figure 6) was the first area developed. This county contains its own depot, thereby allow-ing for initially minimal delivery costs. It was also where the employee in charge of the pro-las program lived, where he consequently knew many farmers, and where promotional activities were therefore more economical and effective. In 1972 and 1973 the promotional campaign was extended to Belmont County where the second depot is located. More recently Guernsey and Noble counties have been developed, but not as fully as the first two.

In contrast, the Farm Bureau had little incentive to spatially segment its market for custom blended fertilizer. With a uniform price at the outlet and a distance-related delivered price, the spatial distribution of adopters did not affect profits associated with the innovation. Thus, the Farm Bureau vigorously promoted its product throughout the four county market area, with no spatial bias and predom-inantly relying upon mass media. Ads were placed in one or more newspapers in each county, mailers were enclosed with bills to all Farm Bureau credit custom-ers, radio advertising was undertaken, and some farmers were visited by Farm Bureau employees.

Figure 7A illustrates the temporal trend of pro-las adoption from January 1971, when it was first made available. Most striking are the two periods of rapid growth in usage: first during the spring and summer of 1971 and again in the autumn, winter, and spring of 1973-1974. These spurts coincide with the Farm Bureau's most active months of promotional activities and demonstrate the dra-matic effect of agency efforts upon the temporal pattern of adoption.[28]

Figure 7. Temporal Trends of Adoption and Spatial Diffusion Patterns for Two Agricultural Innovations

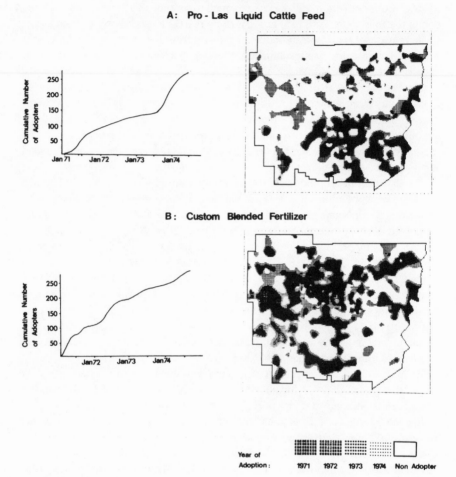

A: Pro - Las Liquid Cattle Feed

B: Custom Blended Fertilizer

Year of Adoption: 1971   1972   1973   1974   Non Adopter

Custom-blended fertilizer presents a different temporal trend (Figure 7B). Starting in March 1971, the date of the blend plant's completion, this is approximately linear with periodic fluctuations corresponding to the seasonal need for fertilizer. The extent of diffusion exceeds that for pro-las until July 1973, at least in part because custom-blended fertilizer is more of a continuous innovation and was more widely promoted.

Figure 7A also illustrates the spatial pattern of pro-las adoption, which decreases in density with distance from Bethesda and Woodsfield, the locations of the two pro-las depots. Over time, however, the pattern expands outward in a wavelike fashion, mirroring the Farm Bureau's intention to promote the new cattle feed first in Monroe County, next in Belmont County, and finally, in Guernsey and Noble counties. This interpretation of Figure 7A is supported by a quadrat analysis of the distribution of adopters in the years 1971 through 1974. The R statistics of .252, .273, .385, and .405, respectively, indicate a markedly clustered distribution overall, but one which becomes less so over time.[29]

The spatial distribution of custom blended fertilizer adopters also is clustered, but around the Quaker City blend plant (Figure 7B). Further, there is a scattering of adopters in peripheral areas. Since the cost to the adopter of obtaining the fertilizer increases with distance from the blend plant, and assuming the demand for custom blended fertilizer is price elastic, such a decay in adoption with distance from Quaker City is predictable. Over time, however, it appears that earlier adopters were more scattered throughout the study area and that the clustering noted above occurred later. This observation is supported by a quadrat analysis of the distribution of adopters in the years 1971 through 1974. These R statistics of .455, .408, .369, and .325, respectively, indicate a trend toward greater clustering, a marked contrast from the pro-las diffusion patterns.

This difference in the evolution of the spatial pattern of diffusion for pro-las and custom-blended fertilizer provides an interesting observation about the consequences of diffusion agency strategy. The pricing policy for pro-las provided an incentive to develop the required delivery and service infrastructure in a spatially sequential and distance decay fashion and to undertake highly personalized promotional communications utilizing a parallel spatial segmentation of the market. The resulting gradual expansion of delivery and service routes accounts for the outward spread of pro-las adopters over time.

Alternatively, the pricing policy for custom blended fertilizer provided little incentive to spatially segment the market or personalize promotional communications. Instead, the potential adopter bore the greater concern for discerning the real costs of adoption, and the contraction of the diffusion pattern over time would seem to reflect increased awareness of these costs, leading to a more *rational* distribution of adopters. For these reasons, then, the distribution of adopters for pro-las and custom blended fertilizer are similar by 1974, but the evolution of the patterns over time follows opposite courses.

Case studies also were carried out for two agricultural innovations that were *infrastructure independent* and diffused over the same four-county area. Although these are not reported here, it is useful to consider the conclusions derived from a comparison with the diffusions of pro-las and custom blended fertilizer. First, it appears that the temporal trend of diffusion is not predictably influenced by whether the diffusion is infrastructure constrained or independent.[30] More important are characteristics of the innovation, such as its degree of continuity with ongoing practices, and characteristics of the diffusion agency such as the vigor and skill with which promotion is pursued. However, the infrastructure constrained/independent distinction is an important influence on the spatial pattern of diffusion. Both custom-blended fertilizer and pro-las showed marked clustering overall, centering on the focal points of the infrastructure and shifting over time in a manner coincident with the development of the infrastructure. By contrast, the spatial patterns of diffusion for the infrastructure independent innovations, from their inception, were spread throughout the study area in a random fashion. Finally, our evidence strongly supports the conclusion that diffusion agency actions such as promotional communications and market selection and segmentation, which pertain to subjective attributes of the innovation, are in general as, if not more, influential in determining adoption behavior than are innovativeness differences.

THE MARKET AND INFRASTRUCTURE PERSPECTIVE AND NEW PRODUCT GROWTH MODELS

An intriguing aspect of marketing research is the search for predictive models that enable the practitioner to determine the likely extent of diffusion. One set of these *new product growth models* primarily involves extrapolating a curve fit to the levels of diffusion over time. The logistic is most commonly used, although other functions also are found [14, 42, 65: 519-563, 71, 72, 81: 248-277]. These models do not take into account alternative diffusion strategies, but simply predict likely sales given a particular strategy. Another set of new product growth models, which are more appropriately termed *product management models,* are more ambitious in their conceptualization and explicitly consider the likely effect of alternative diffusion strategies. TRACKER, for example, includes an actual component for establishing the effects of advertising, price, distribution, and product attributes [8]. In implementation, however, consideration generally is given only to advertising and price, and even in that, extrapolation constitutes an important basis of the prediction. Further, these models are generally oriented towards continuous innovations in a modern society, such as supermarket goods, and do not include the majority of the diffusion considerations discussed in this paper. They also do not provide predictions with a spatial component.

The quandary, then, is that the extrapolation models generally are not suitable for evaluating the likely effects of different diffusion strategies, because of their lack of substantive detail, but our knowledge of diffusion processes is not sufficiently extensive to enable the design and implementation of a predictive model with more substantive content. Nevertheless, the design and partial implementation of models such as TRACKER or SPRINTER [128] are worthwhile tasks in that they illuminate parts of the relationship between diffusion strategy and outcomes of which we know little; point out data and knowledge needs; and provide a forum for adapting operations research, management analysis, and related techniques to the study of innovation diffusion as broadly conceived in this paper. Such tasks, then, define a research agenda which, when completed, allows modification, further articulation, and calibration of the predictive model.[31]

Given our beliefs on this point, it is noteworthy that the market and infrastructure perspective is consistent with the new product growth models that are conceived in the spirit of TRACKER and SPRINTER. This is illustrated by considering the following model for the establishment of diffusion agencies under a centralized decision making structure. This model has been operationalized in a game simulation mode as PROMAR, The New Product Marketing Game [22, 40, 41].

A Model

The establishment of diffusion agencies in a centralized decision-making structure is essentially a multiple facility location problem. The extensive literature on this problem [68, 69] provides many models that may be adapted or directly applied to the innovation diffusion setting [for example, 26, 58, 63, 64, 111, 112, 113, 123, 124]. Generally, however, these models do not portray the complexities of the substantive problem. More appropriate are the models presented in Kotler [65: 302–323) or Craig and Brown [39]. These provide the basis for the following discussion.

The model presented below provides a criterion for evaluating alternative locations over time. In doing so it incorporates elements of the propagator's diffusion strategy. Where it differs from existing models is in the explicit consideration of the spatial aspects of the diffusion strategy, specifically the capacity and effectiveness of the diffusion agency and the fact that the profitability of alternative areas is evaluated.

The propagator in a centralized structure is assumed to evaluate alternative location in terms of establishing a single diffusion agency in each in time t.[32] A criterion for this can be provided by

$$\bar{Z}_{it} = \sum_{k=t}^{t+h} \frac{Z_{ik} - I_{ik}}{(1 + r)^k} \tag{1}$$

where

$\bar{Z}_{it}$ is the net present value in time t of anticipated profit from place i over the planning horizon h

Z_{ik} is the anticipated profit from place i in time k

I_{it} is the out of pocket cost in time k related to establishing a diffusion agency in place i at time t, which would include debt service payments (principal and interest) as well as other out of pocket costs, if any

r is the discount rate per time interval k

In this

$$Z_{ik} = (P_{ik} - c_{ik} - d_{ik})q_{ik} - m_{ik} - a_{ik} \tag{2}$$

where

P_{ik} is the unit sales price of the innovation in place i at time k

c_{ik} is the unit cost of the innovation in place i at time k

d_{ik} is the unit cost of transporting the innovation from the point of production or warehousing to the diffusion agency(ies) in place i at time k

q_{ik} is the estimated unit sales of the innovation in place i at time k

m_{ik} is the cost of maintaining and operating the diffusion agency(ies) in place i at time k

a_{ik} is the advertising expenditure in place i at time k

The estimated unit sales variable in equation (2) q_{ik}, requires further attention. For each place i there is a market potential for the innovation, Q_i.[33] The portion of this realized at a given time, however, will be limited by the degree of market penetration in place i. This effect may be traced by employing the cumulative first time sales of the innovation in a functional form such as the logistic, for example,

$$w_{ik} = \frac{Q_i}{1 + e^{-(a+b \sum_{j=1}^{k-1} N_{ij})}} \tag{3}$$

where w_{ik} is an estimate of unit sales in place i at time k on the basis of market potential (Q_i) and the degree of market penetration (N_{ij}).[34] Equation (3) also may be viewed as portraying the market response or the growth in demand for the innovation in place i.[35]

There are other factors in addition to the innovation's market potential and market penetration that affect its diffusion. Thus,

$$q_{ik} = f(w_{ik}, g_{ik}, p_{ik}, a_{ik}, h_{ik}, e_{ik}) \tag{4}$$

where

g_{ik} is the general economic conditions in place i at time k, perhaps indicated by a surrogate such as unemployment

p_{ik} is the price of the innovation in place i at time k

a_{ik} is the advertising expenditure for the innovation in place i at time k

h_{ik} is the diffusion agency capacity in place i at time k

e_{ik} is the diffusion agency effectiveness in place i at time k

General economic conditions would be taken account of in the planning of the propagator, but would not be in it control. However, decisions are made with regard to price, advertising expenditures, and those diffusion agency characteristics that affect agency capacity and effectiveness.[36]

Given an estimate of sales in location i for each time period k (q_{ik}, equation 4) and estimates of other variables in the profit equation (2), the net present value of anticipated profit from place i over the planning horizon h ($\bar{Z}_{it}$) may be estimated by equation (1). Then, locating a given number and size of diffusion agencies, determined by capital or other constraints, simply consists of successively choosing the locations with the highest values of $\bar{Z}_{it}$. Similar models have been developed for diffusion under a decentralized decision-making structure, with and without a coordinating propagator [15, 134].

CONCLUDING OBSERVATIONS

Diffusion of innovation has traditionally been viewed by marketers as an area of inquiry related to consumer behavior. Consistent with this perspective the focus of most research on the diffusion of innovation has been on the characteristics of individuals or households adopting new products or ideas. While this coincides with the traditional social science research focus upon adoption, the market and infrastructure framework fits more within the areas of distribution and logistics or channel structure, policy, and strategy. This paper thus represents an attempt to broaden the consumer oriented perspective to include these other aspects of the process that weigh heavily in the eventual diffusion of a new product or idea.

In developing this perspective a framework was established which incorporates the three major stages in the diffusion process: (1) diffusion agency establishment, (2) strategy formulation and implementation, and (3) adoption. The first two deal with the supply side of the process while the third deals with the demand side. Marketing professionals have implicitly acknowledged the role of the first two stages in the spread of new products and ideas, but they have given them little, if any, formal attention.

The shift in focus from an emphasis on diffusion as consumer behavior to an emphasis on diffusion as marketing strategy provides a more thorough understanding of diffusion phenomena. The case studies presented provide considerable insight into the operation of entrepreneurial, government, and other institutional elements in innovation or new product diffusion. A distinction was made between situations that are infrastructure constrained and those that are not. Attention was also given to the various options in diffusion agency strategy such as pricing, infrastructure and organizational development, promotional communications, market selection, and segmentation. Likewise, in the area of diffusion agency establishment a distinction was made between diffusion under a centralized decision making structure, and diffusion under a decentralized decision making structure (with and without a coordinating propagator). Further, the processes associated with each have been studied. These situations were documented by empirical case studies and other evidence which illustrated how the various processes are manifest and how the interaction of other factors brings about diffusion.

This broader perspective from which to view the diffusion of innovation has considerable potential for providing new insights and knowledge about the process. For example, taking on a different focus and asking a different set of questions leads the way to adapting operations research, management analysis, and related techniques to the study of innovation diffusion. An example of this is Brown's [12: 187-190] use of location allocation principles from geography and operations research together with marketing models pertaining to market penetration to design an algorithm for determining the optimal location of diffusion agencies and the time in which each should be established. Another example is found in Roberto's [100] marketing oriented strategies for the diffusion of family planning practices.

It is posited here that the extension of efforts such as these and a more explicit consideration of the market and infrastructure perspective in applied contexts, including those pertaining to new product growth or product management models, will greatly enhance our understanding of innovation diffusion. It is our hope that this paper will serve as a catalyst to the end of a broader understanding of diffusion phenomenon.

One general point remains. The orientation of research on diffusion has been towards adoption behavior, but as indicated here, the diffusion strategies actually used have been quite different. In the case of any diffusion involving a central propagator, for example, it appears that the effort is likely to utilize existing societal levers, organizations, and networks from the top down, instead of from the bottom up as the demand based adoption paradigm would suggest. That this pattern has been practiced in profit motivated settings may not be surprising, but it also has been practiced in pragmatically oriented nonprofit settings, as indicated by the diffusion of Planned Parenthood and of Montessori education [78]. As academics, however, we are only beginning to examine this phenomenon, and we know relatively little about the organizational structure and other aspects of diffusion by which innovations are made available to potential adopters, particularly in nonprofit motivated settings [67]. Clearly, then, our research priorities must be broadened and policy relevant findings will be more likely.

NOTES

1. This paper is a partial summary of research on a diffusion of innovation supported by the National Science Foundation (Grant G-36829). This support is appreciated. For a more extensive treatment of that work, see Brown [15].

2. For a review of the literature, see Rogers and Shoemaker [107], Robertson [101], Midgley [81], Brown and Moore [19], and L. A. Brown [13].

3. For a broad review of these and related decisions, we have found Kotler [65, 66] to be useful, although he gives little explicit attention to the situation of innovation or new product diffusion. The decisions of particular interest here pertain to what Kotler terms *distribution lcoation* [65: 302-323]. Our neglect of the selection of a specific site within the designated market area reflects the geographical scale examined in this paper. On a more local scale, the site selection decision is clearly relevant and should be considered. For a discussion, see Kotler [65: 312-320].

4. In earlier papers developing the diffusion agency establishment framework [12] the terminology used was, respectively, *diffusion in a mononuclear propagation structure, diffusion in a polynuclear propagation structure (without central propagator support)*, and *diffusion in a polynuclear propagation structure with central propagator support*. Irrespective of the terminology, however, whether there is or is not a coordinating propagator, establishment of the agency is itself an adoption process in a decentralized setting whereas this is not so in a centralized setting. Finally, the ensuing discussion on these organizaitonal structures is concerned with their relevance for diffusion to entities *outside of* the organization itself. A related literature that might provide some guidelines for further development of this topic deals with the effects of organizational structure on adoption *within* the organization. For an introduction to this literature, see Zaltman, Ducan, and Holbeck [132], Rogers and Agarwala-Rogers [106] and Havelock [57].

5. Griliches[50] also makes this point with regard to rural settings. Other objectives may guide the propagator such as cost minimization or sales maximization, but these appear to operate on a short term basis. For a discussion of firm objectives in general, see Baumol [5: 310-334].

6. Accessibility generally varies inversely with distance, but not always. For example, air service renders many distant locations more accessible than nearby ones, and the locational patterns of some agency systems reflect this.

7. A hierarchy effect is characterized by the location of diffusion agencies in order of decreasing urban size. The neighborhood effect is characterized by agencies being located at ever increasing distances from the initial location in a wave-like fashion.

8. Although expansion capital may be generated internally, financial institutions are a more important source. Thus, the credibility of the propagator and the innovation are critical, and the demonstration of credibility should be a goal of the initial efforts of the propagator. An important aspect of this is the market response with regard to the innovation.

9. There is a correspondence between the order of a good and the more common marketing scale of convenience, shopping, and specialty goods. Specifically, higher order goods correspond with specialty goods and lower order goods with convenience goods.

10. This is a synopsis of research reported more fully in Meyer, Brown, and Camarco [80] and Meyer and Brown [79]. Most of this material is based upon information and data provided by the advertising and real estate divisions of Friendly Ice Cream and upon personal interview with Ronald Erickson, their real estate director.

11. This can be rationalized as follows. In the centralized case all aspects of the agency system affect propagator profit, so the propagator will want to maximize each agency's profit (one factor in which will be its location). In the decentralized case where there is a coordinating propagator, its profit will be related only to some aspects of agency experience, such as sales volume. Any intervention with regard to this aspect would depend upon the required commitment of resources compared to the potential gain. In general, however, there could be little incentive for intervention, particularly since adequate agency performance may consist only of meeting some threshold level. Likewise, an agency has little incentive to intervene in the affairs of another agency since the profits of each generally would be viewed as independent of one another. Thus, the failure or marginal success of a small number of agencies in a decentralized setting should not significantly affect the overall diffusion of the innovation, and only when the experience is pervasive will the diffusion be in jeopardy.

12. There is a correspondence between these characteristics and those noted as important in firm adoption behavior where the innovation is for the firm's own use [75: 99-133; 76: 133-194; 84]. The

diffusion problem treated in this section, that is of consumer innovations in a decentralized setting, also involves adoption by firms, but as an intermediary rather than as a final user. This similarity provides a link between the diffusion of consumer good and service innovations and the diffusion of technological innovations, which for the most part have been studied as distinct and unrelated phenomena. For an elaboration of this point, see Malecki [73, 74] or Brown [15: Chapter 5].

13. Pred's examples are from the United States in 1790–1840: banking, horse drawn omnibuses and intra urban street railways, the suspension of specie payments during the panic of 1837, daily newspapers and the penny press, and steam-engine usage. Pedersen's are from Chile in the nineteenth and twentieth centuries: newspapers, fire brigades, Rotary Clubs, radio stations, and supermarkets. Robson's examples are from nineteenth-century England: building societies, telephone exchanges, gas works, and street lighting.

14. This is a synopsis of work reported more fully in Brown et al. [25].

15. The latter results from an increase both in the spatial extent of urban areas and in the number of signal blocking buildings and various generators of electrical noise.

16. J. Foley of the Ohio State University Department of Speech Communications points out that another factor is the regulatory climate of a state. Such regulations greatly influence the ease with which cable systems may be started. Connecticut, for instance, has had very strict laws and, consequently, lags in the establishment of cable systems. For an elaboration of these issues, see Seiden [114: 79–84].

17. The fact that the correspondent banking network had no noticeable spatial characteristics may be typical of organizaitonal structures that might be employed for diffusion purposes. On this point, see Pred [94–99].

18. A further discussion of the role of condition creating institutional factors in innovation diffusion can be found in Rosenberg [108, 109] and Brown [14, 15: Chapters 6 and 9].

19. An exception to this observation is the product management literature [90], but generally, this has not been associated with innovation diffusion, even by members of the marketing discipline. The congruence between product management models and the market and infrastructure perspective is given further attention in the penultimate section of this paper.

20. Some combination of these also may be charged. For example, an agency may charge a uniform delivered price for the purchase of an innovation, but a uniform price at its outlet for service and repairs.

21. Note, however, that even if travel costs are not directly associated with acquisition of the innovation they may be a significant consideration. An example is when the innovation requires frequent service which must take place at the agency.

22. Accordingly, the use of communication from a potential adopter's social system can be an explicit part of the diffusion strategy. This is termed *indirect marketing* [59: 296–299].

23. Of all the tools available to the diffusion agency, communciations has received the most attention by social scientists modeling social processes. For reviews of the multitude of efforts in this area, see Karlsson [62], Hudson [60], Coleman [34], Brown [10], Bartholomew [2], and Bartos [3].

24. For a more complete discussion of market selection and segmentation and related strategies, see Kotler [66: 165–191], Roberto [100], and Frank, Massy, and Wind [45].

25. A more behavioralistic approach has been advocated [130] in which markets are scrutinized for important differences in potential adopter attitudes, motivations, values, usage patterns, aesthetic preferences, or degree of susceptibility, but it has not been widely employed.

26. The material reported here is a synopsis of work reported more fully in M. A. Brown [27] and M. A. Brown and Brown [28]. Data sources for this material include a comprehensive survey of 597 farm operators and 26 public and private diffusion agents in the four county area, related diffusion agency records, and informal interviews with Herman Preston, manager of the Belmont County Farm Bureau Coperative, and Joe Pittman, Bill Shaw, Loren Sanford, Weldell Little, Don Pollack, Ken Simeral, and Richard Smith of the Cooperative Extension Service.

27. A variety of personal contact strategies were used to develop each route. The employee in charge of the promotional program spoke about pro-las at farm meetings and followed through with visits to interested persons located near developed or developing delivery routes. Brochures were also sent to a sample of farmers who raised cattle and were good Farm Bureau customers; many of these farmers were subsequently visited by salesmen. Newspaper advertisements with testimonials from satisfied customers were placed in several newspapers, but there was no radio or television advertising.

28. In this context one could well argue that the rapid growth traditionally associated with the middle phase of diffusion has less to do with the innovativeness characteristics of adopters or their level of interpersonal interaction than with the extent and timing of diffusion agency promotional efforts. For an elaboration of this point with regard to innovativeness, see Brown, Malecki, and Spector [23]. This observation also has relevance to S-curve models such as logistic, which often are formulated on the assumption that interpersonal communications are the critical factor in innovation diffusion [10, 31].

29. The study area was divided into 176 cells for the quadrat analyses, and the number of adopters per quadrat was determined. From this data an R Statistic was calculated as the ratio of the mean number of adopters per quadrat to the variance. In general, an R value of 1 indicates a random distribution, values higher than 1 indicate a tendency toward uniformity and values less than 1 indicate a tendency toward clustering [103–105]. These inferences are based upon the assumption that the population of potential adopters is randomly distributed. However, a randomly selected sample of 345 farm operators from the four county area yields an R value of .741 indicating that the distribution of the base population of potential adopters is more clustered than random. Therefore, the R statistics pertaining to adoption patterns are evaluated by comparison to the R statistics for the base population rather than the value of 1.0.

30. In the infrastructure constrained situation, the rate at which relevant infrastructure is developed would affect the temporal trend of diffusion, but the exact nature of this is not predictable within the framework articulated in this paper. In infrastructure independent diffusion, however, this influence would not be an issue.

31. For a comprehensive discussion of new product growth or product management models in marketing see Kotler [65:119–163], Midgley [81:248–277], Robertson [101:249–294], and Pessemier [90].

32. The model is described in terms of establishing a single diffusion agency, but this is not a limiting assumption since the agency could be of any size and/or represent several agencies.

33. This could be estimated in several ways. Very common is to derive a sales potential index on the basis of the population of place i relative to all other places being considered. The *Sales Management Magazine's: Survey of Buying Power* recommends deriving such an index on the basis of place i's percent of buying power, retail sales, and population, weighted at .5, .3 and .2 respectively. This index then would be applied to an estimate of unit sales potential overall to derive the unit sales potential for place i. One is still faced with the problem of estimating overall sales potential. In a locational context, however, this is of minimal significance because the major concern is the potential return of each place i relative to others.

34. At initiation of the diffusion there will be no competitive activity, and w_{ik} would be estimated as in (3). As the diffusion continues, however, competition may enter, and in locations where this occurs the market share of the initial propagator will be eroded. The single firm, then, would be concerned with its market share as well as the market potential and market penetration of the innovation. This could be incorporated into the model by

$$w_{ik} = (1 - v_{ik})w_{ik}$$

where V_{ik} is the degree of competition in location i at time k, $o \leq V_{ik} \leq 1$.

35. An important aspect of demand not explicitly considered in equation (3) is the frequency of repurchase of the innovation. If repurchase occurs in each time period after initial adoption, for

example, w_{ik} would never be less than the cumulative first time sales of the innovation, whereas this is unlikely if repurchase is less frequent. Incidently, the estimation equation for market share suggested in footnote 34 implies that competition takes away existing customers of a firm in the same proportion as it takes new customers. A formulation that applied full competitive effects only to new customers and lesser effects to old customers would be more realistic. For a review of the state of the art in models portraying the market response or growth in demand for the innovation, see Mahajan and Peterson [71, 72].

36. Equation (4) is stated generally because no single way of stating it explicitly is clearly preferable to alternatives. Craig and Brown [39] employ a multiplicative format in which the variables p, a, h, and e are indices, each taking on the value of one if price, advertising and outlet decisions, respectively, are optimal. Thus, the net effect under optimal decision making by the propagator would be sales (q_{ik}) equivalent to expectations on the basis of market potential, market penetration, market share (w_{ik}), and general economic conditions (g_{ik}); but if propagator decisions are otherwise, sales less than or greater than $w_{ik}g_{ik}$ are possible.

REFERENCES

1. Arndt, J. *Word of Mouth Advertising.* New York: Advertising Research Foundation, 1967.
2. Bartholomew, D. J. *Stochastic Models for Social Processes, Second Edition.* New York: John Wiley, 1973.
3. Bartos, O. J. *Simple Models of Group Behavior.* New York: Columbia University Press, 1967.
4. Bass, F. M. "A New Product Growth Model for Consumer Durables." *Management Science,* 15: 215–227, 1969.
5. Baumol, W. J. *Economic Theory and Operations Analysis, Third Edition.* Englewood Cliffs, N.J.: Prentice-Hall, 1972.
6. Beckmann, M. *Location Theory.* New York: Random House, 1968.
7. Berry, B. J. L., and Horton, F. E. *Geographic Perspectives in Urban Systems.* Englewood Cliffs, N.J.: Prentice Hall, 1970.
8. Blattberg, R., and Golanty, J. "TRACKER: An Early Test Market Forecasting and Diagnostic Model for New Product Planning." *Journal of Marketing Research* 15: 192–202, 1978.
9. Brown, L. A. *Diffusion Dynamics: A Review and Revision of the Quantitative Theory of the Spatial Diffusion of Innovation.* Lund, Sweden: Gleerup, Lund Studies in Geography, 1968a.
10. ——— *Diffusion Processes and Location: A Conceptual Framework and Bibliography.* Philadelphia: Regional Science Research Institute, 1968b.
11. ——— "Diffusion of Innovation: A Macroview." *Economic Development and Cultural Change* 17: 189–211, 1969.
12. ———. "The Market and Infrastructure Context of Adoption: A Spatial Perspective on the Diffusion of Innovation." *Economic Geography* 51: 185–216, 1975.
13. ———. "Diffusion Research in Geography: A Thematic Account." Studies in the Diffusion of Innovation Discussion Paper Series, Department of Geography, Ohio State University, 1977.
14. ———. "The Innovation Diffusion Process in a Public Policy Context." In M. Radnor, I. Feller, and E. M. Rogers (eds.), *The Diffusion of Innovations: An Assessment.* Evanston,Ill.: Center for the Interdisciplinary Study of Science and Technology, Northwestern University. Also in Studies in the Diffusion of Innovation Discussion Paper Series, Department of Geography, Ohio State University, 1978.
15. ———. *Innovation Diffusion: A New Perspective.* London and New York: Methuen, 1981.
16. Brown, L. A., and Cox K. R. "Empirical Regularities in the Diffusion of Innovation." *Annuals of the Association of American Geographers* 61: 551–559, 1971.
17. Brown, L. A., and Lentnek, B. "Innovation Diffusion in a Developing Economy: A Mesoscale View." *Economic Development and Cultural Change* 21: 274–292, 1973.
18. Brown, L. A., and Malecki, E. J. "Comments on Landscape Evolution and Diffusion Processes." *Regional Studies* 11: 211–223, 1977.

19. Brown, L. A., and Moore, E. G. "Diffusion Research in Geography: A Perspective." In C. Board, R. J. Chorley, P. Haggett, and D. R. Stoddart (eds.), *Progress in Geography, Vol. 1*. London: Edward Arnold, 1969.

20. Brown, L. A., and Moore, E. G. "The Intra Urban Migration Process: A Perspective," *Geografiska Annaler*, Series B 52: 1–13. Also in *Yearbook of the Society for General Systems Research* 15: 109–122, 1970.

21. Brown, L. A., and Philliber, S. G. "The Diffusion of a Population-Related Innovation: The Planned Parenthood Affiliate." *Social Science Quarterly* 58: 215–228, 1977.

22. Brown, L. A., Craig, C. S. and Zeller, R. E. "PROMAR: The New Product Marketing Game." *Computer Applications* 4: 677–768, 1977.

23. Brown, L. A., Malecki, E. J., and Spector, A. N. "Adopter Categories in a Spatial Context: Alternative Explanations for an Empirical Regularity." *Rural Sociology* 41: 99–118, 1976.

24. Brown, L. A., Schneider, R., Harvey, M. E., and Riddell, J. B. "Innovation Diffusion and Development in a Third World Setting: The Case of the Cooperative Movement in Sierra Leone," *Social Science Quarterly* 60: 249–268, 1979.

25. Brown, L. A., Malecki, E. J., Gross, S. R., Shrestha, M. N., and Semple, R. K. "The Diffusion of Cable Television in Ohio: A Case Study of Diffusion Agency Location Processes of the Polynuclear Type." *Economic Geography* 50: 285–299, 1974.

26. Brown, L. A., Williams, F. B., Youngmann, C. E., Holmes, J., and Walby, K. "The Location of Urban Population Service Facilities: A Strategy and Its Application." *Social Science Quarterly* 54: 784–799, 1974

27. Brown, M. A. *The Role of Diffusion Agencies in Innovation Diffusion: A Behavioral Approach*. Ph.D. Dissertation, Ohio State University, Department of Geography. Also in Studies in the Diffusion of Innovation Discussion Paper Series, Department of Geography, Ohio State University, 1977.

28. Brown, M. A., and Brown, L. A. "Innovation Establishment in a Rural Setting: Four Case Studies with Reference to a Theoretical Framework," Studies in the Diffusion of Innovation Discussion Paper Series, Department of Geography, Ohio State University, 1976a.

29. Brown, M. A., and Brown, L. A. "The Diffusion of Bank Americard in a Rural Setting: Supply and Infrastructure Considerations." *Proceedings of the Association of American Geographers* 8: 74–78, 1976b.

30. Brown, M. A., Maxson, G. E., and Brown, L. A. "Diffusion Agency Strategies and Innovation Diffusion: A Case Study of the Eastern Ohio Resource Development Center." *Regional Science Perspectives* 7: 1–26, 1977.

31. Casetti, E. "Why Do Diffusion Processes Conform to Logistic Trends?" *Geographical Analysis* 1: 101–105, 1969.

32. Cochran, T. C. "The Entrepreneur in Economic Change," *Explorations in Entrepreneurial History*, Second series 4: 25–38, 1966.

33. Cohen, Y. S. *Diffusion of an Innovation in an Urban System: The Spread of Planned Regional Shopping Centers in the United States 1949–1968*. Chicago: University of Chicago: Department of Geography Research Paper Series, 1972.

34. Coleman, J. S. *Introduction to Mathematical Sociology*. New York: The Free Press, 1964.

35. Coleman, J. S., Katz, E., and Menzel H. "The Diffusion of an Innovation Among Physicians." *Sociometry* 20: 253–270, 1957.

36. Coleman, J. S., Katz, E., and Menzel, H. "Social Processes in Physicians' Adoption of a New Drug." *Journal of Chronic Diseases* 9: 1–19, 1959

37. Coleman, J. S., Katz, E., and Menzel, H. *Medical Innovation: A Diffusion Study*. Indianpolis: Bobbs-Merrill, 1966.

38. Copeland, O. B. "Public Relations." In H. C. Sanders (ed.), *The Cooperative Extension Service*. Englewood Cliffs, N.J.: Prentice-Hall, 1966.

39. Craig, C. S., and Brown, L. A. "An Experimental Approach to the Study of Diffusion Agency Establishment Processes." Studies in the Diffusion of Innovation Discussion Paper Series, Department of Geography, Ohio State University, 1974.

40. Craig, C. S., and Brown, L. A. "Spatial Diffusion of Innovation: A Gaming Approach." *Simulation and Games* 9: 29–52, 1978.
41. Craig, C. S., and Brown, L. A. "Simulating the Spatial Diffusion of Innovation: A Gaming Experimental Approach." *Socio-Economic Planning Sciences* 14, 1980.
42. Dodson, J. A., and Muller, E. "Models of New Product Diffusion Through Advertising and Word-of-Mouth." *Management Science* 24: 1568–1578, 1978.
43. Drucker, P. F. "Marketing and Economic Development." *Journal of Marketing* 22: 252–259, 1958.
44. Engel, J. F., Blackwell, R. D.,and Kollat, D. T. *Consumer Behavior, Third Edition.* Hinsdale: Dryden Press, 1978.
45. Frank, R. E., Massy, W. E., and Wind, Y. *Market Segmentation.* Englewood Cliffs, N.J.: Prentice-Hall, 1972.
46. Garst, R. D. "Spatial Diffusion in Rural Kenya: The Impact of Infrastructure and Centralized Decision Making." Studies in the Diffusion of Innovation Discussion Paper Series, Department of Geography, Ohio State University, 1974.
47. Getis, A. "Residential Location and the Journey from Work." *Proceedings of the Association of American Geographers* 1: 55–59, 1969.
48. Glade, W. P., Strang, W. A., Udell, J. G., and Littlefield, J. E. 1970. *Marketing in a Developing Nation: The Competitive Behavior of Peruvian Industry.* Lexington, Mass.: Heath-Lexington, 1970.
49. Gould, P. R., and Tornqvist, G. "Information, Innovation, and Acceptance." In T. Hagerstrand and A. R. Kuklinski (eds.), *Information Systems for Regional Development: A Seminar.* Lund, Sweden: Gleerup, Lund Studies in Geography, 1971.
50. Griliches, Z. "Hybrid Corn: An Exploration in the Economics of Technological Change." *Econometrica* 25: 501–522, 1957.
51. Hagerstrand, T. *The Propagation of Innovation Waves.* Lund, Sweden: Gleerup, Lund Studies in Geography, 1952.
52. ———. "A Monte Carlo Approach to Diffusion." *Archives Europeennes de Sociologie* 6: 43–67, 1965a.
53. ———. "Quantitative Techniques for Analysis of the Spread of Information and Technology." In C. A. Anderson and M. J. Bowman (eds.), *Education and Economic Development.* Chicago: Aldine, 1965b.
54. ———. *Innovation Diffusion as a Spatial Process.* Chicago, Ill.: University of Chicago Press, 1967a.
55. ———. "On the Monte Carlo Simulation of Diffusion." In W. L. Garrison and D. F. Marble (eds.), *Quantitative Geography, Part I, Economic and Cultural Topics.* Evanston, Ill.: Northwestern University Press, Studies in Geography, 1967b.
56. Hagerstrand, T., and Kuklinski, A. R. (eds.). *Information Systems for Regional Development: A Seminar.* Lund, Sweden: Gleerup, Lund Studies in Geography, 1971.
57. Havelock, R. G. *Planning for Innovation: Through Dissemination and Utilization of Knowledge.* Ann Arbor: University of Michigan, Institute for Social Research, 1969.
58. Holmes, J., Williams, F. B., and Brown, L. A. "Facility Location Under a Maximum Travel Restriction: An Example Using Day Care Facilities." *Geographical Analysis* 4: 258–266, 1972.
59. Howard, J. A., and Sheth, J. N. *The Theory of Buyer Behavior.* New York: John Wiley, 1969.
60. Hudson, J. C. *Geographical Diffusion Theory.* Evanston, Ill.: Northwestern University Press, Studies in Geography, 1972.
61. Johnston, J. R. *Urban Residential Patterns: An Introductory Review.* New York: Praeger, 1972.
62. Karlsson, G. *Social Mechanisms: Studies in Sociological Theory.* New York: Free Press, 1958.
63. Kochen, M., and Deutsch, K. W. "Toward a Rational Theory of Decentralization: Some Implications of a Mathematical Approach." *American Political Science Review* 63: 734–749, 1969.

64. Kochen, M., and Deutsch, K. W. "Pluralization: A Mathematical Model." *Operations Research* 20: 276-292, 1972.
65. Kotler, P. *Marketing Decision Making: A Model Building Approach.* New York: Holt, Rinehart, and Winston, 1971.
66. ———. *Marketing Management: Analysis, Planning and Control.* Englewood Cliffs, N.J.: Prentice-Hall, 1972.
67. ———. *Marketing for Nonprofit Organizations.* Englewood Cliffs, N.J.: Prentice-Hall, 1975.
68. Lea, A. C. "Location-Allocation Models: A Review." M.A. Thesis, Department of Geography, University of Toronto, 1973a.
69. ———. "Location-Allocation Systems: An Annotated Bibliography." Discussion Paper Series, Department of Geography, University of Toronto, 1973b.
70. LeDuc, D. R. "Community Antenna Television as a Challenger of Broadcast Regulatory Policy." Ph.D. Dissertation, University of Wisconsin, 1970.
71. Mahajan, V., and Peterson, R. A. "Innovation Diffusion in a Dynamic Potential Adopter Population." *Management Science* 24: 1589-1597, 1978.
72. Mahajan, V., and Peterson, R. A. "First Purchase Diffusion Models of New Product Acceptance." *Technological Forecasting and Social Change* 15: 127-146, 1979.
73. Malecki, E. J. "Innovation Diffusion Among Firms." Ph.D. Dissertation, Ohio State University, Department of Geography. Also in Studies in the Diffusion of Innovation Discussion Paper Series, Department of Geography, Ohio State University, 1975.
74. ———. "Firms and Innovation Diffusion: Examples from Banking." *Environment and Planning* 9: 1291-1305, 1977.
75. Mansfield, E. *Industrial Research and Technological Innovation: An Econometric Analysis.* New York: W. W. Norton, 1968a.
76. ———. *The Economics of Technological Change.* New York: W. W. Norton, 1968b.
77. Marble, D. F., and Nystuen, J. D. "An Approach to the Direct Measurement of Community Mean Information Fields." *Papers of the Regional Science Association* 11: 99-109, 1963.
78. Meyer, J. W. *Diffusion of an American Montessori Education.* Chicago: University of Chicago, Department of Geography, Research Paper Series, 1975.
79. Meyer, J. W., and Brown, L. A. "Diffusion Agency Establishment: The Case of Friendly Ice Cream and Public Sector Diffusion Processes." *Socio Economic Planning Sciences* 13: 241-249, 1979.
80. Meyer, J. W., Brown, L. A., and Camarco, T. J. "Diffusion Agency Establishment in a Mononuclear Setting: The Case of Friendly Ice Cream and Related Considerations." Studies in the Diffusion of Innovation Discussion Paper Series, Department of Geogrpahy, Ohio State University, 1977.
81. Midgley, D. F. *Innovation and New Product Marketing.* New York: John Wiley, 1977.
82. Moore, E. G. "Some Spatial Properties of Urban Contact Fields." *Geographical Analysis* 2: 376-386, 1970.
83. Moore, E. G., and Brown, L. A. "Urban Acquaintance Fields: An Evaluation of a Spatial Model." *Environment and Planning* 2: 443-454, 1970
84. Morrill, R. L., and Pitts, F. R. "Marriage, Migration, and the Mean Information Field." *Annals of the Association of American Geographers* 57: 401-422, 1967.
85. Nabseth, L., and Ray, G. F. (eds.). *The Diffusion of New Industrial Processes: An International Study.* Cambridge: Cambridge University Press, 1974.
86. Nartowitz, F. "The Diffusion of Zero Population Growth Chapters Within the United States." Studies in the Diffusion of Innovation Discussion Paper Series, Department of Geography, Ohio State University, 1977.
87. Osleeb, J. P. "The Optimum Size of Plant for the Uniform Delivered Price Manufacturer." *Proceedings of the Association of American Geographers* 6: 102-105, 1974.
88. Pedersen, P. O. "Innovation Diffusion Within and Between National Urban Systems." *Geographical Analysis* 2: 203-254, 1970.

89. ———. *Urban-Regional Development in South America: A Process of Diffusion and Integration.* The Hague: Mouton, 1975.

90. Pessemier, E. A. *Product Management: Strategy and Organization.* New York: John Wiley, 1977.

91. Pesson, L. L. "Extension Program Planning with Participation of Clientele." In H. C. Sanders (ed.), *The Cooperative Extension Service.* Englewood Cliffs, N.J.: Prentice-Hall, 1966.

92. Pred, A. R. "The Growth and Development of Systems of Cities in Advanced Economies." In *Systems of Cities and Information Flows: Two Essays by A. R. Pred and G. E. Tornqvist.* Lund, Sweden: Gleerup, Lund Studies in Geography, 1973a.

93. ———. *Urban Growth and the Circulation of Information: The United States System of Cities, 1790-1840.* Cambridge: Harvard University Press, 1973b.

94. ———. "Industry, Information, and City System Interdependencies." In F. E. Hamilton (ed.), *Spatial Perspectives on Industrial Organization and Decision Making.* New York: John Wiley, 1974a.

95. ———. *Major Job Providing Organizations and Systems of Cities.* Washington, D. C.: Association of American Geographers, Resource Paper Series, 1974b.

96. ———. "Diffusion, Organizational Spatial Structure, and City System Development." *Economic Geography* 51: 252–268, 1975a.

97. ———. "On the Spatial Structure of Organizations and the Complexity of Metropolitan Interdependence." *Papers of the Regional Science Association* 35: 115–142, 1975b.

98. ———. "The Interurban Transmission of Growth in Advanced Economies: Empirical Findings Versus Regional Planning Assumptions." *Regional Studies* 10: 151–171, 1976.

99. ———. *City Systems in Advanced Economies: Past Growth, Present Processes and Future Development Options.* New York: Halstead, 1977.

100. Roberto, E. L. *Strategic Decision Making in a Social Program: The Case of Family Planning Diffusion.* Lexington, Mass.: Lexington Books, 1975.

101. Robertson, T. S. *Innovative Behavior and Communications.* New York: Holt, Rinehart, and Winston, 1971.

102. Robson, B. T. *Urban Growth: An Approach.* London: Methuen, 1973.

103. Rogers, A. "Quadrat Analysis of Urban Dispersion: 1. Theoretical Techniques." *Environment and Planning* 1: 47–80, 1969a.

104. ———. "Quadrat Analysis of Urban Dispersion: 2. Case Studies of Urban Retail Systems." *Environment and Planning* 1: 155–172, 1969b.

105. ———. *Statistical Analysis of Spatial Dispersion: The Quadrat Method.* New York: Academic Press, 1974.

106. Rogers, E. M., and Agarwala-Rogers, R. *Communication in Organizations.* New York: The Free Press, 1976.

107. Rogers, E. M., and Shoemaker, F. F. *Communication of Innovations: A Cross Cultural Approach.* New York: The Free Press, 1971.

108. Rosenberg, N. "On Technological Expectations." *Economic Journal* 86: 523–535, 1976a.

109. ———. *Perspectives on Technology.* Cambridge: Cambridge University Press, 1976b.

110. Sanders, H. C. "The Legal Base, Scope, Functions, and General Objectives of Extension Work." In H. C. Sanders (ed.), *The Cooperative Extension Service.* Englewood Cliffs, N.J.: Prentice-Hall, 1976.

111. Schneider, J. B., and Symons, J. G. "Locating Ambulance Dispatch Centers in an Urban Region: A Man-Computer Interactive Problem-Solving Approach." Discussion Paper Series, Regional Science Research Institute, University of Pennsylvania, 1971a.

112. Schneider, J. B., and Symons, J. G. "Regional Health Facility System Planning: An Access Opportunity Approach." Discussion Paper Series, Regional Science Research Institute, University of Pennsylvania, 1971b.

113. Scott, A. J. "Dynamic Location-Allocation Systems: Some Basic Planning Strategies." *Environment and Planning* 3: 73–82, 1971.

114. Seiden, M. H. *Cable Television U.S.A.: An Analysis of Government Policy.* New York: Praeger, 1972.
115. Semple, R. K., Brown, L. A. and Brown, M. A. "Propagator Supported Diffusion Processes: Agency Strategies and the Innovation Establishment Interface." Studies in the Diffusion of Innovation Discussion Paper Series, Department of Geography, Ohio State University, 1975.
116. Semple, R. K., Brown, L. A., and Brown, M. A. "Strategies for the Promotion and Diffusion of Consumer Goods and Services: An Overview." *International Regional Science Review* 2: 91-102, 1977.
117. Shawyer, A. J. "Diffusion: An Appraisal." Ph.D. Dissertation, University of Nottingham, Department of Geography, 1970.
118. ———. "Diffusion: Social Process and Spatial Pattern." Working Paper, Annual Conference of the European Society of Rural Sociology, 1974.
119. Sieling, R., Malecki, E. J., and Brown, L. A. "Infrastructure Growth and Adoption: The Diffusion of Cable Television Within a Community." Studies in the Diffusion of Innovation Discussion Paper Series, Department of Geography, Ohio State University, 1975.
120. Steiner, R. L. *Visions of Cablevision.* Cincinnati: Stephen H. Wilder Foundation, 1973.
121. Stewart, W. M. "Physical Distribution: Key to Improved Volume and Profits." *Journal of Marketing* 29: 65-70, 1965.
122. Tanaka, H. "The Japanese Department Store: Spatial Patterns as Related to Cultural Change." M.A. Thesis, Department of Geography, University of Western Ontario, 1971.
123. Teitz, M. B. "Location Strategies for Competitive Systems." *Journal of Regional Science* 8: 135-148, 1968a.
124. ———. "Toward a Theory of Urban Public Facility Location." *Papers of the Regional Science Association* 21: 35-51, 1968b.
125. Thorngren, B. "How Do Contact Systems Affect Regional Development?" *Environment and Planning* 2: 409-427, 1970.
126. Timms, D. *The Urban Mosaic: Towards a Theory of Residential Differentiation.* Cambridge: Cambridge University Press, 1971.
127. Tornqvist, G. *Contact Systems and Regional Development.* Lund, Sweden: Gleerup, Lund Studies in Geography, 1971.
128. Urban, G. L. "SPRINTER Mod III: A Model for the Analysis of New Frequently Purchased Consumer Products." *Operations Research* 18: 805-854, 1970.
129. Warneryd, O. *Interdependence in Urban Systems.* Goteborg: Regionkunsult Aktiebolag, 1968.
130. Yankelovich, D. "New Criteria for Market Segmentation." *Harvard Business Review,* March-April: 83-90, 1964.
131. Yeates, M. H., and Garner, B. J. *The North American City, Second Edition.* New York: Harper and Row, 1976.
132. Zaltman, G., Duncan, R., and Holbeck, J. *Innovations and Organizations.* New York: John Wiley, 1973.
133. Zaltman, G., Kotler, P., and Kaufman, I. (eds.). *Creating Social Change.* New York: Holt, Rinehart, and Winston, 1972.
134. Zeller, R. E. "A Study of the Selection of Multiple Locations for Consumer Oriented Facilities." Ph.D. Dissertation, Department of Geography, Ohio State University. Also in Studies in the Diffusion of Innovation Discussion Paper Series, Department of Geography, Ohio State University, 1978.
135. Zoerner, C. E. "The Development of American Community Antenna Television." Ph.D. Dissertation, University of Illinois, 1966.

REGULATION IN ADVERTISING

S. Watson Dunn

Practitioners in advertising and marketing today are forced to operate under much more stringent regulations than their counterparts of but a few years ago. The proliferation of controls has caused some business people to complain that government regulators and such nongovernmental bodies as consumer groups are trying to take over the advertising industry. Certain critics, however, complain that the controls are still too lenient and too easy to circumvent. Researchers generally claim that both the regulators and the regulated make all too little use of modern research methodology.

In this chapter we shall look first at what problems are most subject to control in advertising, then at the methods which are used to cope with those problems, some of them informal and voluntary, others strictly legal or administrative. We shall then attempt to determine what the proper role of research should be in today's highly charged regulatory climate.

I. TYPES OF PROBLEMS WHICH ARE REGULATED

Most of the regulatory activity in advertising involves problems of the content of the advertising message, the type of product or service which is to be promoted,

Research in Marketing, Volume 4, pages 117–141
Copyright © 1981 by JAI Press Inc.
All rights of reproduction in any form reserved.
ISBN: 0–89232–169–5

the proportion of advertising vs. nonadvertising material to be accepted by the media, fairness of advertising allowances, labeling, and the "fairness" of presenting all sides of a controversial matter (especially in the broadcast media).

A. Content of the Advertising Message

1. Deception   Much of the attention of those who regulate advertising focuses on what is communicated either intentionally or unintentionally in an advertisement. The problem of defining what is and what is not deceptive has long been a troublesome one for both advertising practitioners and for regulators. Yet it is a problem which must be faced realistically if advertising is to enjoy the confidence of consumers so that it can perform its communication job effectively.

To determine what such terms as "deception" and "truth" really mean we must look at what the Federal Trade Commission (the principal U.S. agency involved in regulation of advertising) and the various courts have to say about deception. According to Dunn and Barban [1] the following are the principal FTC criteria:

1. It is necessary only to establish the tendency or capacity of an advertisement to deceive, not actually deception itself.
2. Misrepresentation of fact is considered deceptive.
3. A totally false statement cannot be qualified or modified.
4. A statement may be deceptive even though, literally or technically, it is not construed to be misrepresentation.
5. In making product performance claims, substantial test data are needed to support claims.
6. Products must be "reasonably related" to the size of the containers in which they are needed to support claims.
7. There must be a "reasonable basis" for making product claims.
8. Ambiguous statements that are susceptible to both misleading and truthful interpretations will be construed against the advertiser.
9. Failure to disclose material fact where the effect is to deceive a substantial segment of the public is equivalent to deception.

Judged by these criteria most of the advertisements checked each year by the FTC are not deceptive. In a normal year the FTC issues about 270 complaints against "deceptive practices" in labeling and advertising. Less than one fourth of these require action. Both the courts and the FTC change their interpretation of when an advertisement is deceptive from time to time.

Some critics of advertising would include "puffery" as a part of deception. This is a description of a product or service which exaggerates its good qualities but is not necessarily deceptive under present interpretations of that word. For example, Preston [2] calls puffery ''soft-core'' deception; and comments on it as follows is one of his books:

> Puffery affects people's purchasing decisions by burdening them with untrue beliefs, but our regulators say it does no such thing except to the out-of-step individual who acts unreasonably and therefore deserves no protection. Puffery deceives, and regulations which have made it legal are thoroughly unjustified. There are many varieties of puffery and they account for a huge proportion of the claims made by sellers and advertisers in the marketplace.

Some critics regard as deceptive any advertisement that claims a brand contains a particular ingredient unless that ingredient was unique or unless the advertisement contains a statement disclosing the fact that it was *not* unique. However, Levitt [3] contends that advertising involves expected benefits rather than a literal interpretation of the truth. He notes the following:

> In a world where so many things are either commonplace or standardized, it makes no sense to refer to the rest as false, fraudulent, frivolous or immaterial. The world works according to the aspirations and needs of its actors, not according to the arcane or moralizing logic of detached critics who pine for another age.

Cunningham and Cunningham [4] presented a series of advertising statements (e.g., ''A radial tire has at least eight belts of steel radial cord'' and ''Micro-encapsulated means that the particles in a pill are separately encapsulated'') to a sample of 2,200 residents of a medium-sized Texas city. The percentage of incorrect responses ranged from a low of more than 19 percent to a high of more than 80 percent. They suggest that it is not possible for the government to attempt to protect the citizenry by requiring that all commercials be understood by ''the least reasonable man.'' They suggest that only the ''reasonable man'' and not the ''unreasonable man'' should be protected by the FTC. For example, words like ''micro-encapsulated'' would not be permitted since they are not understood by vast numbers of the public. They suggest also that the FTC be given funds to establish a mechanism to test terms for their comprehension by the public. They believe that the latter mechanism would be particularly useful to firms which use technical words or expressions in their advertising copy.

Another suggestion comes from Gardner [5] who recommends that norms be set for each class of product. These would state what the average consumer believed about the product class. Extensive research among prospective consumers would be needed to determine whether an advertisement was or was not deceptive. This leads to serious difficulty, however, when one attempts to define both ''class of product'' and ''average consumer.'' With the changing uses people make of products and the continuing avalanche of new products coming on the market, research in this area would be exceptionally complex.

Some practitioners contend that deception will be self-regulating in that consumers will turn against a product or service that does not live up to its claims. This is often true in the case of advertisements which contain information which is easily verifiable by consumers, such as price or physical characteristics of the product. However, we have all too little research on just how often such verifiable situations occur and how likely consumers are to check performance against advertising claims. We also do not know under what conditions deceptive advertising is any more effective than nondescriptive advertising in stimulating sales of a product. It is assumed by many critics of advertising that consumers take quite literally what they see or hear in advertising messages, and we know this is not necessarily the case.

The effect of advertising on children has been a special worry to many consumer groups. Although the areas of advertising's influence on children has been widely researched, the findings tend to contradict each other in certain important respects. For example, Scott Ward [6] provides the following summary of the effect of television advertising on children:

1. Between second and fourth grades children not only begin to descriminate between programs and commercials but also begin to understand the intent of the commercials.
2. By the sixth grade, children have relatively well-developed attitudes toward commercials.
3. Children do not "tune-in" to commercials (i.e., increase their attention to them relative to program fare).
4. Children do form positive and negative attitudes toward advertisements (i.e., adolescents are generally quite cynical toward advertising claims).
5. Television advertising is neither the sole nor necessarily the most influential determinant of children's wants and purchasing behavior.
6. Adolescents acquire consumer attitudes and skills from television advertising.
7. Black and white adolescents do not differ markedly in their responses to television advertising.
8. Intelligence is a better predictor of recall of commercial themes and slogans than exposure to television advertising (i.e., the higher the intelligence the greater the recall).

A somewhat contrary view has been presented by the FTC staff which has requested rulemaking hearings to consider serious reform of children's television advertising. In a document entitled *FTC Staff Report on Television Advertising to Children* [7] and released in February 1978, the staff attempted to summarize the result of research studies it has examined and make suggestions for correction of what it viewed as abuses. The staff was convinced that younger children are helpless before commercials directed to them. They were also convinced that there is danger in promoting heavily sugared foods to children on television. The proposed remedies included the curtailing of all advertising in children's programming for "sugar-laden" foods and all commercials aimed at young children. The FTC, as well as the business representatives, was seriously concerned about the welfare of children. They differed seriously in how children can best be protected—in the case of business much confidence was vested in the play of competitive forces, in the case of the FTC much more confidence in the power of the government to regulate competition.

The first director of the National Advertising Division of the Council of Better Business Bureaus, Emilie Griffin [8], cites the difficulty her unit—the first business-sponsored unit set up for regulation of children's advertising—has had in determining standards of deception among children. She contends that research should be directed more at what children perceive in advertisements, less on what they think about different types of advertising and advertised products.

2. Obscentiy and Bad Taste. A second area in which problems of content arise is that of obscenity and bad taste. These terms cause considerable trouble for regulators since both involve subjective standards and concepts of each have changed drastically over time. The U.S. Supreme Court, for example, has tried to apply "community standards" to the interpretation of obscenity (which is illegal) and to bad taste (which is not) [1, p. 103]:

1. whether the average person applying contemporary community standards would find that the work, taken as a whole, appeals to prurient interests;
2. whether the work depicts or describes in a patently offensive way sexual conduct specifically defined by the applicable standards; and
3. whether the work—if it appeals to prurient interest and is patently offensive—lacks serious literary, artistic, political or scientific value.

Standards may change drastically over time. Within a few years nude pictures were accepted as not offensive in many leading magazines as standards changed. In many cases advertising which is acceptable in magazine advertising (e.g., live models demonstrating the virtues of women's underwear) is not deemed acceptable by those who regulate television advertising. An advertising message or illustration which is not considered offensive by the publishers of *Playboy* or *Penthouse* may be turned down by *Reader's Digest*.

3. Lotteries Although more and more states now allow lotteries and other forms of gambling within their borders, these are still illegal in *interstate* commerce. This is an important distinction since most advertisements are considered illegal if three elements are present in the offer: prize, consideration, and chance. If any one of these is absent the offer does not constitute a lottery. For example, the matter of "consideration" is often a nebulous one and a frequent cause of confusion. In some states a contest that requires one to visit a certain store to qualify for a contest is illegal, because this requirement constitutes a "consideration."

4. Right of Privacy An increasingly troublesome area in advertising is the extent to which a person has the right to be left alone. In the case of advertising the legal doctrine of right of privacy prohibits the use of the name or picture of a living person without consent and thus makes it necessary to get a signed release even from a professional model. It is sometimes argued that professional actors or celebrities of any kind are so much in the public eye that they have no real right of privacy. However, the courts have generally ruled that they cannot be featured in any commercial publicity without their consent. Nor can one use a "look-alike" model which the public might confuse with the celebrity.

With the increased focus on people's right to be left alone and the post-Watergate fears of too much government surveillance, privacy questions are likely to increase. At the same time both straight testimonial advertisements and advertising featuring celebrity spokesmen or spokeswomen have been on the increase. According to trade magazine reports, those firms using such celebrities as Joe Namath and Farrah Fawcett-Majors have enjoyed sizable sales increases. There is, however, little research to indicate whether it is the attention value of the celebrity which accounts for the impact of the advertisements or whether the consumer believes that the celebrity actually uses and endorses the product. We also do not know how soon the effect of such celebrity ads wears out.

5. *Trademarks and Copyrights*   According to the Lanham Trademark Act the term "trademark" includes "any word, name, symbol or device or any combination thereof adopted and used by a manufacturer or merchant to identify his goods or distinguish them from those manufactured or sold by others." In earlier times trademarks were used as means of policing the output of guilds or other organizations. Today the trademark is the symbol the advertiser uses to identify his products and make it easier for consumers to select them. Consequently the trademark is an important company asset and the seller will make great effort to protect it. Under present law not only a distinctive mark but names, symbols, titles, designations, slogans, character names and distinctive features emphasized in advertising are specifically protected. Such slogans as the Schlitz "The beer that made Milwaukee Famous" and Colonel Sanders (as spokesman for fried chicken) are protected.

Copyright protection, on the other hand, is used to cover creative works. For example, one may not copyright an idea but one may be protected on the way that idea is expressed in an advertisement. Copyright protection was extended through a new U.S. law which went into effect at the beginning of 1978.

B. Type of Product Advertised

Since January 1, 1971, it has been illegal in the United States to advertise cigarettes on the broadcast media. Many other countries of the world also prohibit such advertising, often in print as well as broadcast media. However, cigarettes can still be sold legally in most countries. This is a particularly interesting case of a product that can be sold legally being prohibited from being promoted, regardless of the type of advertising used. This has established a precedent which may well be extended to other products which many people consider harmful. For example, some countries prohibit advertising of alcoholic liquor although there is no such legal prohibition in the United States. On the other hand, the broadcast media have attempted to prevent members of their association from accepting liquor advertising on the basis that it might bring on great public pressure to curtail independence of broadcasting stations. Other groups would like to prohibit advertising of any product which might pollute the air, patent medicines, certain types of breakfast cereals, pornographic films, and many other types of products.

C. Excessive Amounts of Advertising

A troublesome problem for the advertisers and the managers of the advertising media is the decision as to how much advertising is too much (i.e., at what point do people rebel at the overuse of advertising). Most people have objected at one time to the pyramiding of commercials on radio or television programs. A great many people have protested at the excessive numbers of billboards on certain highways. Most newspapers and magazines contain more advertising than nonadvertising material but the managers of these media normally try for a certain ratio between the two which they attempt to maintain over time. Only in the case of the broadcast media have specific amounts of allowable advertising time been set, and these have been determined by the industry itself, rather than by law or administrative fiat. The broadcasting industry has long felt that excessive amounts of advertising need to be controlled more during the prime evening television hours when people presumably devote closer attention to what they are seeing on their television screen. Even in the case of television, however, research evidence regarding the threshold at which people rebel at advertising excesses is sadly lacking.

D. Advertising Allowances

This is a problem with which both business and government regulators have struggled for many years. The problem is that advertising allowances provided by manufacturers to dealers often constitute a hidden discount, particularly when they are offered to very large buyers, such as the chain stores. As such, they are considered illegal under the Robinson-Patman Act, since they constitute price discrimination. If, on the other hand, such advertising allowances are offered on an equitable basis to all dealers and they are actually used as an encouragement for advertising at the local level, there is not necessarily any legal problem. In cases such as these, the only problem is one of control by the manufacturer so that he makes sure the quality is consistent with his national advertising and that the products which he wants featured in the advertising are actually featured by the local dealer.

An additional problem comes up in the case of collusion between the local advertising medium and the local retailer. In several cases the practice of "double billing" has resulted in action taken against media and loss of licenses by some radio stations. Under this practice, one bill is submitted to the retailer which he will in turn submit to the national manufacturer to collect his share of the space or time which he bought. Another bill (much lower) is submitted to the local retailer for actual payment.

E. Labeling

If we consider labeling as a form of advertising we run into another whole group of problems regarding what may or may not be said about products. This is a particularly troublesome problem in the case of the marketing of foods, drugs and cosmetics, for which specifications are set forth in the Food, Drug and Cosmetic Act. In the eyes of the regulatory bodies such products are worthy of special attention because of the danger that misuse of them may pose to the health of consumers. What is *not* included on a label, such as instructions on when to use or not to use the product, may be just as important as what is included. The regulatory authorities have in the late 1970's been giving considerably more attention to labeling than in previous years.

F. Fairness of Presentation

This is a problem that is of special importance to the managers of radio and television stations who are required under the First Amendment to give equal time to all sides of any controversial issue. Political and public relations ads are the ones that advertisers and stations must police with particular care. These are usually about services and people rather than products. For example, much advertising around election time involves the promotion of one candidate as compared with another. However, advertising for products may also fall under the "Fairness Doctrine." In 1967, before cigarette advertising was banned on television, the Federal Communications Commission decided that such advertising was controversial and that stations carrying it must give opponents of cigarette smoking the chance to air their views. Like truth, "fairness" is a nebulous concept and its exact interpretation by consumers is not particularly clear. For example, certain groups feel that radio and television stations should once again be required to include anti-cigarette-smoking commercials even though they are not allowed by law to carry those promoting smoking. This would seem, however, to be a dubious application of the fairness doctrine, since it would mean that only the opponents would have a chance to get their viewpoints across to the public. This is especially dubious in view of the fact that several state courts and the U.S. Supreme Court both reaffirmed in late 1976 that advertising is covered by the First Amendment to the Constitution. Up to this time, the exact nature of its coverage had been somewhat in doubt. The case which brought this to a head was one in Virginia involving rights of lawyers to advertise when a state statute prohibited such advertising [1]. In several states, laws have been passed to prohibit such professionals from advertising their wares in the public media. It remains to be seen whether people will be better informed about the comparative costs of such services as the proponents have claimed. The opponents had justified such curtailment of advertising on the basis that allowing professionals to advertise would denigrate the quality of service and lead to cutthroat price competition. There is no evidence at this point that such is the case.

II. TYPES OF CONTROL OVER ADVERTISING

Consumers often think of controls only in terms of those who are given specific statutory power over advertising. In practice, controls come in many forms, some direct, some indirect, some long range, some short range. In general it is perhaps best to consider controls in two broad categories—those which are informal or voluntary, and those which are legal or administrative. Of the informal or voluntary controls, the more important are perhaps those by business itself, instituted in an attempt to regulate its own house. We should, however, also consider the controls by consumers, particularly since these have, during the late 1960's and early 1970's, exerted considerable pressure on advertising in almost every country of the world.

A. Control by Business

Business and marketing executives generally praise self-regulation as a responsible reaction to public demand for advertising to clean its own house. There are, however, some questions raised about it, such as the following [1, p. 11]: (1) Is it likely to conflict with the right of each firm to conduct its business freely as it sees fit? (2) Does it violate antitrust laws which are designed to encourage free and open competition? (3) Does it usurp the function of the government? (4) Is it a good idea to publish negative findings as a punitive technique? (5) Does vigorous promotion of complaint facilities elicit valid complaints or merely multiply frivolous ones? (6) Should self-regulation be conducted by practicing advertisers or by hired administrators?

Studies conducted in 1962 and 1971 [9] indicated that U.S. business executives were increasingly skeptical of management's abilities to enforce a code of advertising ethics, while they had increasing confidence in "a group of executives plus other members of the community" and in "a government agency" as regulators. More than half the respondents said that "if advertising cannot keep its house in order the government will have to."

Despite the pessimism, self-regulation has prospered in most countries during the 1970's [11]. This is a far cry from earlier times when, as Sandage, Fryburger and Rotzoll [10] point out:

> Prior to the 1970's it can be fairly asserted that the performance had not been meritorious.
> Simple disinterest, underfinancing, an absence of first-rate talent and an unwillingness to

submit judgment of potential competitors have all led to an overall lackluster performance. That the mechanisms were not always carefully conceived can be suggested by the fact that many emerged only during periods of outside agitation with the wolf close to the door if not inside the house.

Self-regulation has taken many forms with some organizations such as the National Advertising Review Board representing all segments of the industry; at the same time various associations and individual advertising agencies, advertisers, media have all set up their own regulatory mechanisms.

1. National Advertising Review Board   This Board is the focal point of a three-tiered system which involves local Better Business Bureaus, the National Advertising Division of the nationwide Council of Better Business Bureaus, and the National Advertising Review Board. Complaints are forwarded by the local Better Business Bureau to the National Advertising Division of the Council. A complaint does not go to the NARB until it has been completely evaluated by the NAD and the advertiser has had full opportunity to defend his advertising. Since its beginning in 1971, the NARB has received praise from the advertising industry but some skepticism from leaders of the consumer movement. There is, however, considerable evidence to indicate that it has been the most successful of the advertising industry's regulatory efforts in the United States and that it has been able to overcome some of the difficulties that have beset previous industry-wide efforts.

The NARB consists of 50 members, 30 representing national advertisers, 10 representing advertising agencies and 10 representing the public or the nonindustry sector. Complaints about advertising are referred to this Board which may receive them from the public, from other businessmen, or from other sources. The NAD evaluates the complaints, and if it seems justified confers with the advertiser or its agency in an attempt to seek changes in the advertising. If this attempt is not successful the complaint is appealed to the NARB which appoints five-member panels of three advertisers, one agency person, and one public representative to review complaints and the findings of the NAD staff up to that point. If the panel upholds the staff decision the advertiser is again asked to change or withdraw the advertising in question. If this is unsuccessful, either the NARB publicly identifies the advertisers, the nature of the complaint and the Board's findings, or the case is referred to the appropriate government agency (in most cases the Federal Trade Commission). Since the NARB and NAD were established in 1971 an average of 200 cases per year have been submitted to the NAD for review, most of these having come from complaints or monitoring by the local Better Business Bureau. The proportion of complaints from consumer groups have decreased as these groups have found a more receptive climate in the government agencies.

In a comprehensive study in which he attempted to evaluate the efforts of the NARB, Zanot [12] found that, in 1976, 36 percent of the cases were substantiated, 35 percent led to modifications, 28 percent were closed administratively, and only 1 percent reached the NARB panel level. He found that 52 percent were initiated as a result of monitoring by the National Advertising Division of the National Better Business Bureau, 26 percent by competitors and only 1 percent by consumer groups.

2. Better Business Bureaus The local bureaus are financed by business firms which want to stamp out unfair competition in a particular locality. Complaints to these bureaus come from individuals or businesses, in most instances; for example, an advertising message in a local newspaper or a local radio station may offer a late-model used car at a very low price. When someone checks with the dealer and finds out that this car has been sold and an attempt is made to sell a higher-priced model, this is a typical example of what the B B B calls "bait" advertising. If the bureau finds out that this is, indeed, a misleading advertisement, it tries to persuade the advertiser to change his ways. If he does not stop, publicity may be used as a weapon to stop him. If the publicity does not work, legal action, probably under the laws of the particular state, will be taken.

There were, in 1976, 150 separate BBB's under the general supervision of the Council of Better Business Bureaus in New York City. They were supported by more than 100,000 membership firms whose total membership dues were in excess of $6.5 million per year. Each bureau is organized as an independent nonprofit corporation usually supported by a diversity of business interests in the community. The board of directors of each local bureau appoints a manager and authorizes the addition of needed staff members.

3. Advertising Agencies Advertising agencies, both individually and cooperatively through the American Association of Advertising Agencies, attempt to exercise control over the advertising they plan and prepare for their clients. Individual agencies do much self-policing in an attempt to prevent either bad publicity or some sort of legal action. Such efforts by agencies are likely to increase since in recent years they have been held legally liable along with clients for misleading or fraudulent claims in their advertisements. Until recent years, liability had been judged to rest exclusively with the client which hired the agency and supposedly exercised careful surveillance over what was said in the advertising messages.

Most agencies have in-house legal counsel. Some will refuse to handle advertising for certain products, such as cigarettes, or proprietary medicines. Agencies are in a particularly good position to exercise even more control since most of the large ones have sophisticated researchers as well as lawyers on their staff and they are equipped to hire and work with outside research counsel.

What is needed in the agency field is the focusing of research efforts more on regulatory problems and perhaps less on problems of management of the advertising budget or on creative or media strategy per se.

4. Advertising Media   Almost all the major media carry on extensive regulation of the advertising they carry, both individually and through the associations of which they are members. For example, many newspapers have become famous for their refusal to accept questionable advertising. The *New York Times* has for more than fifty years had a strict set of standards administered by its own Advertising Acceptability Department. This department will not accept superlatives or claims which it feels might be misleading. It was decided in late 1977 to refuse advertising for movie theaters which promoted "X-rated" movies. Another comprehensive code is that of the Detroit News which bans advertisements for introductions to members of the opposite sex, those offering homework for pay, and those selling habit-forming drugs.

The fleeting nature of radio and television messages makes them especially difficult to police. In fact, many of them are never written at all but are merely ad-libbed by a studio announcer. However, many stations are quite selective about what they will or will not accept. Since they are government-licensed media, they must be particularly careful about what kind of advertising they carry since illegal advertising or even advertising in bad taste may constitute a black mark against them when their license comes up for renewal. Consequently, they rely more heavily than print media on advertising codes and are particularly concerned about techniques of presentation which may be misleading or offensive.

Some stations and networks have self-regulatory machinery for continuity acceptance departments which pass on all proposed advertising. Much of the regulation, however, is geared to the Television Review Board of the National Association of Broadcasters. This TV code, in effect since 1952, has gone through many revisions. However, it is quite specific in discouraging certain types of advertising as being not acceptable for television. Examples are: "bait" advertising, advertising for tip sheets, race track publications, fortune tellers, and astrologers. Advertising of liquor is banned with the exception of beer and wine. The TV code also limits the amount of broadcast time that may be devoted to commercials at different periods of the day. For example, in prime time the maximum allowed is nine and a half minutes and in nonprime time, sixteen minutes.

In the case of magazines, there is no industry-wide advertising code but many publishers have their own stringent rules. For example, management of *Good Housekeeping* claims it has a staff of 100 technicians and spends more than $1 million a year testing in the Good Housekeeping Institute products which advertise in its pages in order that advertising claims may be checked. It guarantees a refund for any product that does not live up to the advertised claim.

Almost all other media have an association which provide guidance in the policing of advertising carried by its members. For example, the Direct Marketing Association bans sending through the mail unsolicited merchandise, vulgar or immoral matter, and gambling devices. The Outdoor Advertising Association of

America adopts a code of acceptable practice which is concerned especially with tasteful design and construction of display and placement of billboards.

The advertising industry has within it, groups which focus on various regulatory problems in its field. The leading publication in the field, *Advertising Age,* wages a consistent battle for more truthful and tasteful advertising and has carried on campaigns against violations of good taste and truth by professionals.

At least three major advertising associations—the American Advertising Federation, American Association of Advertising Agencies, and the Association of National Advertisers—have helped in the regulation of advertising. For example, the AAF, which is a federation of advertising organizations, helped establish the FTC and the BBB grew out of its own early "vigilance committees." Because most local advertising clubs belong to the AAF it is in a particularly good position to influence local advertisers.

The AAAA exercises control over member agencies through its ability to deny membership to agencies which prepare false or misleading statements or testimonials which do not reflect the real choice of competent witnesses. Since almost all large national agencies belong to the AAAA it is in a position to exert considerable pressure.

The ANA is an organization representing most of the major manufacturers in the United States. It also has a code and attempts by working through its members and its member agencies to exert pressure for more truthful advertising.

B. Controls by Consumers

The rise of the consumer movement during the middle and latter part of the twentieth century has exerted strong pressure on advertising practices. In the 1950's and 1960's the advertising professionals were subjected to searching criticism. Laws were proposed to tax advertising, to increase the police powers of federal agencies, to restrict the placing of billboards along highways, and to prohibit subliminal advertising in the broadcast media. By the late 1960's the consumer movement was so well organized and had gained so much power that a new word (consumerism) was created to describe it.

Consumerism is much more complex than past consumer movements and it stems from a variety of causes. Among these have been the rise of technology, mass-produced and often unreliable products, soaring medical and dental costs, and pollution of air and water. Problems of the consumer have been dramatized by books such as Rachel Carson's *Silent Spring* and Ralph Nader's *Unsafe at Any Speed.* The educational and sophistication level of the American consumer has been higher than in past periods. There is evidence that advertisers were slow to realize the upgrading of mass tastes and that they underestimated consumer discontent, particularly among some of the better educated people who have served as leaders in the consumer movement.

Consumerism had both an indirect and a direct effect on the practice of advertising. Perhaps its most direct effect has been alerting advertisers to be more conscious of the claims they make, especially in advertisements directed to children or when the product advertised uses resources such as energy. An effect has been the growth of consumer organizations and government regulatory agencies. Consumerism is an effective control over advertising only where advertisers have adequate information on which to base their decision. Professor James Engel [13] has suggested that consumerism will result in more sophisticated consumer research in order that business can find out what consumers are really thinking and when they are likely to act. Many, but not all advertisers, cooperate with consumerist leaders in efforts to bring about more enlightened buying by consumers. Some advertisers look upon the rise of consumerism as an opportunity for growth and profit, rather than as a straitjacket. For example, studies by Greyser and Diamond [14] indicated that business people see consumerism as "an ally, a tool through which profits can be generated. . . . Eighty-six percent agree that company investment in consumer services and satisfaction will usually pay for itself."

Consumers have found several formal channels through which they can express loudly and clearly their opinions on advertising and marketing. Among the most important are the Consumer Federation of America and the National Consumer League. The CFA was formed in 1968 by representatives of 44 consumer organizations and 12 supporting groups. By 1976 it consisted of over 200 national, state and local groups, labor unions, and electric cooperatives, along with such organizations as The National Council of Senior Citizens and the National Board of the Y.M.C.A.

The National Consumer League was founded in 1899 to work for better labor conditions through public pressure. In recent years it has concentrated more on consumer issues.

A second type of channel for consumers is the private, nonprofit testing organization, such as Consumers Union and Consumers' Research. The latter which was founded as an outgrowth of the publication *Your Money's Worth* by Stewart Chase and F. J. Schlink, both early consumerists. Consumers' Research rates products and issues its findings monthly in *Consumer Bulletin*. Still another nonprofit organization, Underwriters Laboratory, tests products for safety and publishes lists of products it has found acceptable.

C. Controls Over Advertising By The Government

The most stringent and apparent controls over advertising are those based on laws passed by Congress, state legislatures, or local municipal authorities. Enforcement is up to government administrators who must decide what the laws really mean and take appropriate actions which are subject to challenge in the courts. The legislators, the judges and administrators are constantly changing, so it is not surprising that advertising people must consult lawyers. More and more they are also consulting researchers to find evidence of what consumers perceive in an advertisement or of its effect in the marketplace.

1. Federal Controls   Although controls are exercised at state and local levels, by far the most important is that at the Federal level. Federal control has evolved primarily through attempts to cope with such problems as unfair competition, deceptive practices, protection of brand names and literary rights. The Federal Trade Commission Act, which established the agency most active in control of advertising, was passed in 1914 to eliminate unfair competition and it originally contained no statement about advertising. Focus on advertising came later.

   a. Federal Trade Commission.   To most advertising professionals the FTC symbolizes regulation of national advertising. In 1916 the FTC decided that advertising of products falsely took unfair advantage of a competitor and therefore was illegal under the provisions of the Act which set up that body. The U.S. Supreme Court upheld this interpretation in 1922, confirming the FTC's right to regulate false labeling and advertising as unfair methods of competition. The Wheeler-Lea Amendments of 1938 significantly extended FTC powers and clarified its authority to regulate advertising.

   Although the FTC clearly has the power to cover all phases of "unfair competition" it had decided by the early 1970's according to one of its top officers, to give its highest priority to the enforcement of laws regarding advertising. One of the reasons given for this emphasis was the increasing amount of advertising and the decreasing tolerance of consumers for questionable advertising, as indicated by complaints of individual consumers and consumer groups as well as their Congressmen to the FTC. Because of the tremendous volume of advertising which had to be monitored by the late 1970s, the FTC set up a liaison with the Federal Communications Commission under which the FTC was provided with copies of complaints and orders involving broadcasters or broadcast advertising. The two agencies have extended the cooperation by making it possible for personnel of each to have access to confidential files of the other. The agencies also have agreed to inform each other when they obtain investigation leads of mutual interest.

   The FTC is also responsible for administering such laws as the Fur Products Labeling Act and the Robinson-Patman Act of 1936. The former protects advertising and labeling of fur products and the latter protects the small retailers against large outlets who because of their size gain a substantial price advantage.

   When a complaint is issued by the FTC the respondent has thirty days to reply. In cases where litigation is involved, hearings are held before a trial examiner employed by the FTC, but not under its discipline. His initial decision can be appealed to the FTC by either side. The FTC affirms or modifies the order, or the case may be dismissed. However, the decisions of the FTC, like any other government regulatory agency, are appealable to any Federal Court of Appeals.

   During the 1970s the FTC has extended its influence in areas which were once considered outside its province. For example, it has contended that agencies as well as clients are liable for false or misleading advertising which they place. It has required aut* automobile manufacturers to show documentation for specific claims made in their advertising. Among these are such claims as mileage, price and safety. It has insisted that pesticides should provide warnings.

The FTC has also mapped out new regulations such as the following: (1) unfairness doctrine (power to deal with what the FTC considers "unfair" practices), even these practices have no relation to monopolies or competition; (2) substantive rule-making power (making rules for procedure to be followed in questionable areas such as children's advertising on television); (3) ad substantiation (programs to educate the public on ways of substantiating claims); (4) unreasonable basis tests (emphasizing the point that advertisers must have substantiating data to back up any "unreasonable basis" for claims they make in advertising); (5) corrective advertising (ordered by FTC to advertisers who are deemed to have so deceived consumers that they msut devote a certain percentage of future ads to removal of "residual consumer deception").

The definition of "residual consumer deception" has been a troublesome one for both the regulators and the regulated. The FTC has attempted to determine how much deception might be lingering in the minds of prospective consumers, since this is the basis for requiring a certain percentage of future advertisements to remove this residue. There is a serious need for more research in this area.

In 1976, somewhat to the dismay of the U.S. Patent and Trademark Office, an FTC administrative judge decided that Borden should be required to license other companies to make Realemon (reconstituted lemon juice). This was the first attempt by a government agency or a court to require licensing of a trademark. The Department of Commerce disagreed with this decision of an administrative judge.

b. Food and Drug Administration. The Federal Food, Drug and Cosmetic Act of 1938 represented an attempt to eliminate some of the weaknesses and ambiguities of the original legislation setting up the Food and Drug Administration. The most important contributions were that it made failure to reveal material facts on a label an element of misbranding and thus a misdemeanor.

c. Federal Communications Commission. This Commission is empowered to operate our telecommunications system in "the public interest, convenience and necessity." These are the main criteria for awarding operating licenses for television and radio stations and for renewing them. Thus the FCC wields indirect control over the advertising because certain types of advertising and advertising practice are not considered to be in the public interest, convenience and necessity. In 1967 the FCC decided to apply the fairness doctrine to cigarette commercials with the rule that broadcasters must carry anticigarette announcements to counterbalance the cigarette commercials presently carried. The "counter ads" for cigarettes have been sighted by various social-action groups who want such ads as warning against drugs, autombiles and a host of other "controversial" products carried on TV stations. Also concerns of the FCC are length of commercials, number of commercials, piling up of commercials, middle commercials in a program, sponsor vs. sustaining programs, lotteries.

The FCC has no power of censorship and does not act on individual programs or commercials, per se, unless it has received complaints. Instead, each station is required to keep a complete log of all programs and commercials it transmits and these may be examined when the license renewal is due. In several cases false or misleading advertising has been cited as a reason for failure of the FCC to renew a license or to provide a present licensee with additional stations.

d. The United States Postal Service. The Postal Service controls advertising through the mails mainly in the areas of obscenity, lottery, and fraud. In order to exercise control over advertising that is not legally obscene but may shock the families who receive it, a law has been passed that is designed to curb "pandering" advertisements. Anyone receiving such an ad now has the authority to ask that no more mail be forwarded from that sender. An advertisement is "pandering" if in the opinion of the receiver it is "erotically arousing or sexually provocative." The Postmaster General has the authority to withhold mail which he deems to constitute a lottery.

The Postal Service also has indirect authority to regulate advertising through granting or withholding the Second Class Mailing privilege to periodicals. The Supreme Court has, however, limited its powers in this sphere by deciding that it cannot deny a Second Class permit on the grounds of taste or morals. Although revocation of a Second Class permit is a potentially powerful sanction, the revocation proposed by the judiciary and the reluctance on the part of the Post Office to impose this restriction have made a minimal effectiveness in advertising regulation.

e. Alcohol and Tobacco Tax Division. In 1935 the Federal Alcohol and Tobacco Tax Administration was created as a division of the Treasury Department, to control practices, including advertisements, in the brewing and liquor industry. This unit is now the Alcohol and Tobacco Tax Division of the Revenue Service of the Treasury Department. At present, not only can the agency take action against deceptive practices but can also require inclusion of certain types of information on labels and advertising as well as prohibiting other types of information. The unit has worked out an elaborate classification system regulating what can and cannot be said about alcoholic content, presence of neutral spirits and so on in both labels and ads. For example, ads may not contain curative or therapeutic claims, reference to the American flag, or such terms as "pure" and "double distilled."

f. Patent Office. Anyone who wants to protect a slogan or brand name from infringement by competitors must make his application to the U.S. Patent Office. These include any words, names, similar device, or combination thereof adopted and used by a manufacturer or merchant to identify his goods and distinguish them from those manufactured and sold by others. The mark identifying the product need not be physically affixed. The Lanham Act also protects service marks used to distinguish services rather than products, certification marks used by persons other than the owners to signify geographical origin, grade or quality and collective marks used to indicate membership in an organization. In 1976 there were 34,573 applications for trademark registration at the Patent Office. Registrations were issued to 33,931.

Since the modern marketer often has no direct contact with the ultimate consumer, he will look for some sign that indicates that the product came from a reliable firm. Often products are so similar in outward appearance that it is important that a distinctive mark be used to connote high quality. This is particularly important in the case of products which are sold on a self-service basis. Because of the increasing importance of identification marks, more and more court cases have been focused on the problem of whether a particular variation of existing brand name or identification is likely to confuse large numbers of people. This is obviously an important, though difficult, area for the courts, and lawyers and judges have consequently depended more and more on researchers to provide evidence of whether confusion is actually caused.

g. *Library of Congress.* The Library of Congress enforces the copyright laws which give authors and other creators a monopoly over their use for a certain period of time. Most advertising lawyers will suggest that advertisements be copyrighted and they qualify for the easiest kind of copyright notice in that all that is required is a © and the name of the advertiser. The copyrighting of the periodical in which an ad appears does not necessarily protect an ad from paraphrasing or from variations of that advertising message, only from direct quotation.

h. *Office of Consumer Protection.* In 1971 President Nixon created the Office of Consumer Protection. Among the publications issued by this office are a monthly newsletter, "Consumer Education Guidelines," and a column on consumer services that is distributed to 4,500 weekly newspapers.

2. *State Controls* Most advertising falls in the category of interstate commerce and thus is subject to Federal regulation. However, any activities that are primarily intrastate are regulated by the states themselves. Consequently, many states have passed variations of the *Printers Ink* "Model Statute," designed to make advertising more truthful. The statute, suggested by the advertising magazine, *Printers Ink,* said that any person who placed before the public an announcement that "contains any assertion, representation or statement of fact which is untrue, deceptive or misleading shall be guilty of a misdemeanor." This statute or some variation of it has been passed by all but three states; however, it is not stringently enforced because it is a criminal, not a civil, law and prosecutors know it is hard to get juries to convict under a criminal statute. Many states have also enacted laws that regulate lotteries, cosmetics, securities, bait and switch advertising, and advertising by special groups.

3. Municipal Control   Some municipal authorities have moved into the area of advertising control and into consumerism. For example, a former "Miss America," Bess Myerson, helped enforce New York City's Consumer Protection Act and helped in passing a regulation requiring New York City merchants to stamp the price per measure (unit measure) on supplies. She also backed strongly "open dating" on perishables which indicates the last day of acceptable use. Miss Myerson was succeeded by another well-known consumerist, Miss Betty Furness.

D. Control by the Courts

In practice, much advertising is controlled by court decision. When someone contests a law which is made by a regulatory agency, the court must render judgment. For example, in the Virginia State Board of Pharmacy *vs.* the Virginia Citizens Consumer Council, in 1976, the U.S. Supreme Court determined that advertising was, "contrary to previous decisions," protected by the First Amendment to the U.S. Constitution [1]. The law at issue was a Virginia statute, that a pharmacist would be "guilty of unprofessional conduct" and liable to discipline if he advertised or publicized or published the prices of discount terms for presecription drugs which he sold. The statute was attacked and suit was instituted by prescription drug users who argued that the First Amendment entitled users to receive such information from pharmacists. The courts decided the Statute was unconstitutional. This was a landmark decision because it held that advertising was protected under the First Amendment (as is nonadvertising material) as long as it is not misleading or does not promote an illegal product.

Many court battles have hinged on brand names and trademarks; for example, a Wisconsin court stopped Heileman from using "Light" for its beer on the basis that it infringed on Miller Brewing, which produces "lite" low-calorie beer. The judges decided that the critical question was the term "lite," which was descriptive or suggestive. If a word provides some direct information about a product it is descriptive; if the word stands for an idea that requires some imagination to associate it with the product it is suggestive. The judge decided that words like "lite" were suggestive and thus valid and protected as trademarks. Few beer drinkers, according to this judge, seriously believe that beer would actually cause them to weigh less. The other legal question was whether consumers would be confused. On this basis also the judge decided that Miller should be protected because "lite" and "light" are alike in sound and cannot easily be distinguished in conversation or oral communication or radio advertising.

III. FUTURE OF RESEARCH IN THE REGULATION OF ADVERTISING

The dilemma of the regulators came into sharp focus when the Federal Trade Commission in 1971 required the makers of Profile Bread to "correct" or remove "residual consumer deception" by running commercials that corrected false impressions implanted by earlier commercials. This was the first example of "corrective advertising." This commercial, narrated by Julia Mead, began in the following manner:

> I'd like to clear up any misunderstanding you may have about Profile Bread or even from its name. . . .

In early 1978 the Federal Trade Commission and the STP Corporation concluded an agreement that STP would purchase approximately $700,000 worth of advertising in national media to tell consumers that certain of its advertising claims may have been deceptive. FTC had little research on which to base this agreement but it stated that the settlement was designed to send businessmen a message that the agency henceforth seeks stronger enforcement measures against those accused of deceptive advertising. The corporation maintained that its claims that STP reduced automobile oil consumption were based on "defective oil consumption tests," but that these defective tests did not mean claims were untrue. The corrective advertisement pointed out that the company was carrying out an agreed-upon settlement with the Federal Trade Commission. As the *Wall Street Journal* pointed out at the time of the settlement, how many consumers would understand what such a statement was all about?

As we have seen, regulation lies in the hands of four primary groups: advertising professionals, government regulators, the courts, and the consumers themselves. These groups seem to agree only in very general terms. For example, most studies indicate that all favor better-informed consumers. However, when it comes to the specifics of how much information consumers need, how consumers perceive the claims they read or hear in advertisements, whether special provisions should be made for such special groups as children and many others, there seems to be wide disagreement. This disagreement seems to concentrate on three general areas: the value of research to policy makers, standards which can be used to interpret and compare findings, and the amount of interaction there should be between researchers and users.

A. Disagreement on Value of Research

During the 1970's most research publications in advertising and marketing have urged their readers to use research methodology to shed light on the various problems that so frequently trouble both the regulators and the regulated. They have been encouraged by increasing acceptance of research findings in court litigation—particularly in disputed trademark cases. There is, however, still far too little acceptance of research approaches by consumer advocates. For example, a study by Professor Steven Permut [15] in 1977 indicated only token acceptance of research by 89 executives in Federal and state regulatory agencies and in leading national consumer organizations. These conclusions emerged from his study:

1. Respondents in the public sector expressed little support for more research dealing with consumer information needs.
2. All respondents expressed skepticism regarding the contribution of research on information disclosure issues, primarily because such research is perceived as lacking recommendations as to specific actions to be taken.
3. Respondents in all groups view their own group (but not others) as being most capable of judging the real information needs of the consumer.

It is worth some examination as to why so many policy makers are so skeptical of research. Permut [12] has suggested that it is their background as lawyers and economists which leads them to believe that these approaches are more useful than the unfamiliar world of the behaviorist. There is undoubtedly some validity to this argument. Although the opinions of professional marketers was not included in this study, there is some reason to believe they would be more receptive than government regulators to research data. However, there is also reason to believe their superiors (the chief executive officers of corporations which are the largest advertisers) are less trustful of research. Most recent studies show that a financial or accounting executive is more likely to be the chief executive of a U.S. corporation than a marketing specialist.

Another reason for this skepticism may well be that the policymakers do not really like what they hear from the researchers. For example, six separate studies of consumers' use of nutrition information available to these consumers indicated that "the vast majority of consumers neither acquire such information when making a purchase decision nor comprehend most nutritional information once they do receive it [16]." This lack of use may be the result of poor methods of communication by the marketers. There is, however, some suspicion that large numbers of consumers are simply not anxious to be burdened with great amounts of information pro and con regarding a prospective purchase—and such a conclusion goes counter to the basic philosophy of most consumer advocates.

An additional reason for this skepticism is the complexity of the preception process. Even the most zealous researchers would certainly not claim that modern research methodolgy can provide definitive answers to such questions as how consumers perceive (or misperceive) advertising messages and how much information they can process when they can read these messages. Most people have the experience from time to time of reading a book and receiving an impression quite different from that of someone else who read that same book. One person exposed to a mass of stimuli from a message will select certain ones and reject others, while another reader may make an entirely different selection from these same stimuli.

Perception is a complex process in which people manipulate the incoming information and select certain stimuli, reject others. People are, for example, influenced by their own existing motives and predispositions. They will see or hear communications that are favorable to their own point of view and reject those that are unfavorable. They may even perceive a neutral message as conforming with what they happen to believe.

In spite of the complexity of the processes studied, however, research is still a much better guide for the regulators or for those trying to avoid undue regulation than the ''seat-of-the-pants'' opinion so often relied on by lawyers, economists and would-be communicators.

B. Need for Standards for Comparing Research Findings

A major problem in the use of research by government regulators, judges, business people and consumer advocates is the complexity of so many research reports. Most are not schooled in either statistics or research methodology and their most objective and sincere efforts to understand the research reports may be very frustrating. And it is true that many researchers have great difficulty—as do many lawyers and economists—in expressing what they mean in good clear English sentences. Others are overly afraid of not properly qualifying their findings and end up by giving the impression that they have not really found out anything at all.

What is to be done? One helpful step would be agreement between the researchers and the regulators on certain standards. For example, how much of a standard error would be acceptable in probability sampling? Such agreement might allay some of the widespread suspicion that samples are not really representative of the opinions or actions of consumers. Some agreement might also be possible on how far supervisors would be required to go in minimizing nonsampling errors.

Agreement might also be possible as to what topical areas should be included in each ''audit'' or ''research study'' of consumer perception. A parallel might be found in the broadcast audience field where there is wide agreement that program ratings, sets-in-use data, average audience, total audience and certain other types of data are useful guides as to audience reaction to the program fare offered by programmers. It is true that sophisticated researchers complain about the looseness of some of these concepts and the errors which often creep into implementing them. Yet few would throw them out and go back to the early days of radio when no one had much idea at all of audience reaction. In the case of the broadcasting industry these data have been generated by the nervousness of executives who know the riskiness of long-term television commitments and their obvious need for some guidance in minimizing this risk. There is riskiness also in the area of advertising regulation and both regulator and the regulated should be working on setting standards for data they need on a regular basis.

C. Need for Interaction Between Researchers and Users of Research

There is little doubt that greater interaction between the researchers and those who decide on policy would result in better policies. For example, there is a great deal more information on consumer behavior and perception already available than most policymakers seem to realize. There are several stumbling blocks which seem to inhibit this interaction.

One stumbling block is the complexity of the whole communication process and the lack of clearcut findings or guides for action that come out of much of our present day research. It is not surprising that many of the government and business executives in their search for clear-cut answers become disenchanted with research. This feeling comes at least in part from the fear of the unfamiliar in that most of these administrators do not have training in research.

Another problem is the orientation of many researchers to theory rather than to the solving of problems. More problem orientation on the part of researchers and better communication to nontechnical readers would improve their interaction between researchers and users. One need only to go through some of our marketing and advertising journals to see how many research articles are written to communicate to other researchers and not to the policymakers.

A third problem is the lack of background on the part of researchers in the legal framework in which regulators have to operate. A stronger effort should be made to school researchers in legalistic approaches and the problems faced by policy makers. This should continue on a regular basis with meetings or institutes set up to bring researchers and policymakers together on a regular basis.

There have been some encouraging steps in the direction of improving interaction between researchers and regulators. One was a series of hearings the first of which was held in 1973 at which leading researchers and advertising professionals attempted to explain to FTC commissioners and some of their staff what they have found out about how advertising works and how it influences consumers. The conferences helped the commissioners understand the extent to which large corporations, advertising agencies, independent research firms and advertising media are researching the communication process. They also found out how creative people translate these findings into television commercials and print advertisements. The conference resulted in heightened interest on the part of commissioners in behavioral research, in some effort to bring academic researchers to the FTC on a temporary basis, to add behavioral scientists to their staffs, in inviting marketing professors to spend a semester or two in Washington working with them and in greater acceptance in general of behavioral findings.

There is evidence also that policymakers are more interested in the wealth of research that has become available in the middle and later 1970's on "consumer information processing." Some of these studies have been summarized in an excellent monograph by Wilkie [17], published by the government.

IV. CONCLUSION

The mechanism for the regulation of advertising is a complicated, cumbersome, often slow-moving one. It is not surprising that both the regulators and the regulated at times become inpatient with its slowness and the often ambiguous resolution of so many regulatory problems. However, self-regulatory groups are certainly improving in efficiency and in stature in the eyes of fellow business people—especially the NARB. The consumer groups are militant but not particularly well organized, and certainly the most reluctant of all groups to use research in any meaningful way. All too often they are suspicious of it.

It is encouraging to see the Federal Trade Commission dip a tentative toe into the eddies of behavioral science, although it is clear that there is still much suspicion around the corridors of the Federal Trade Commission Building in Washington. It is encouraging also to find that courts are more and more open to research data and that consumer researchers are so much in demand as expert witnesses at court proceedings.

Complicated as it is to make real progress today in advertising regulation, certain approaches do hold out some promise for improvement. One is an organized effort to educate both the regulators and the regulated as to what we can expect from research and how it can if wisely used make regulation more efficient and more equitable for all. Another is the development of certain standards for comparing advertising and consumer behavior on a continuing basis. A third is the organization of a mechanism for continuing and fairly frequent interaction between the researchers and the regulators.

REFERENCES

1. Dunn, S. Watson, and Barban, Arnold M. *Advertising: Its Role in Modern Marketing,* 4th edition. Hinsdale, Ill: Dryden Press, 1978, p. 84.
2. Preston, Ivan L. *The Great American Blow-Up.* Madison, Wisc.: University of Wisconsin Press, 1975, p. 4.
3. Levitt, Theodore. "The Morality of Advertising." *Harvard Business Review,* July–August 1970.
4. Cunningham, Isabella C. M. and Cunningham, William H. "Standards for Advertising Regulation." *Journal of Marketing,* October 1977.
5. Gardner, David M. "Deception in Advertising: A Received-Channel Approach to Understanding." *Journal of Advertising,* Fall 1976, pp. 5–11.
6. Ward, Scott. "Effects of Television Advertising on Children." Boston: Marketing Science Institute, 1971, pp. 16–19; and "Children and Promotion," Boston, Mass.: Marketing Science Institute, 1972, pp. 9–13.
7. *FTC Staff Report on Television Advertising to Children.* Washington, D.C.: FTC, February 1978.

8. Griffin, Emilie. "What's Fair to Children? The Policy Need for New Research on Children's Perception of Advertising Content." *Journal of Advertising,* Spring 1976.
9. Greyser, Stephen A., and Reece, Bonnie B. "Businessmen Look Hard at Advertising." *Harvard Business Review,* May-June 1971, pp. 9-10; and S. Watson Dunn and David A. Yorke, "European Executives Look at Advertising," *Columbia Journal of World Business,* Winter 1974, pp. 54-60.
10. Stridsberg, Albert B. *Progress in Effective Advertising Self-Regulation.* New York: International Advertising Association, 1976.
11. Sandage, C. H., Fryburger, Vernon, and Rotzall, Kim. *Advertising Theory and Practice,* 10th edition. Homewood, Ill: Richard D. Irwin, 1979, pp. 656-657.
12. Zanot, Eric J. "The National Advertising Review Board: Precedents, Premises and Performance." Unpublished doctoral dissertation. University of Illinois, 1977, p. 202.
13. Engel, James F. "Advertising and the Consumer." *Journal of Advertising,* Summer 1974.
14. Greyser, Stephen A., and Diamond, Steven L. "Business is Adapting to Consumerism." *Harvard Business Review,* September-October 1974, p. 9.
15. Permut, Steven E. "Research on Consumer Information: Public Sector Perspectives." Paper delivered at International Symposium on Consumer Information, sponsored by the European Research Association for Consumer Affairs, and the Commission of the European Communities, Brussels, Belgium, November 23-25, 1977.
16. Jacoby, Jacob, Chestnut, Robert W., and Silverman, William. "Consumer Use and Comprehension of Nutrition Information." Purdue Papers in Consumer Psychology 163, 1976.
17. Wilkie, William L. *Assessment of Consumer Information Processing Research in Relation to Public Policy Needs.* Washington, D.C.: Government Printing Office, 1975.

THE ANALYSIS OF OPTIONS APPROACH TO NEW PRODUCT SCREENING

Theodore J. Mitchell and Thomas P. Hustad

The health of the modern firm lies in its ability to manage its product mix. This portfolio includes both new and existing products. In 1977, the addition of 1,218 new grocery and drug products to the U.S. market brought a 14-year total to 21,969 product introductions [1]. Even though many of these products were similar to others already on the market (some were simply new package sizes), this level of activity illustrates the importance of new products in many firms' product strategies.

New product decisions are often highly strategic. This is because new product programs can involve a long planning horizon, major commitments to new facilities and, perhaps, even to new distributors and markets [2, p. 32]. Thus it is not surprising that considerable attention has been focused on the problems of evaluating new product ideas.

This discussion will investigate methods for screening new products. First,

Research in Marketing, Volume 4, pages 143–179
Copyright © 1981 by JAI Press Inc.
All rights of reproduction in any form reserved.
ISBN: 0-89232-169-5

what is the nature of the product development process? Second, what problems are encountered while screening product ideas? Finally, a new approach to screening decisions will be described which addresses many of the limitations of present techniques.

I. PRODUCT DEVELOPMENT PROCESS

The contribution of new products to total sales varies across a variety of product types; however, sales of new products average 10 percent of total sales of U.S. manufactured products in 1960 and were projected to reach 17 percent of sales in 1970 [3]. This trend reflects the increasing importance of new products during the sixties. More recently, the pace of product development activity has been challenged by a variety of resource constraints [4]. This has contributed to a slowing of the rate of innovation [5], especially in high technology businesses [6,7]. The decline in innovation has not occurred uninformly in all industries or companies.

Since product mixes must change to reflect changes in the marketing and technological environments, resource constraints simply intensify the need for businesses to identify the most promising new product ideas at an early stage in the development process. Thus, it is not surprising that considerable attention has been focused on the problems of evaluating new product ideas.

Stages of the Development Process

Booz, Allen, and Hamilton [8] originally conceptualized the product development process as consisting of six discrete stages: idea generation, screening, business analysis, development, testing, and commercialization. Each evaluation stage (following the generation of ideas) requires incremental expenditures of time and money. A large number of ideas (estimated by Booz, Allen, and Hamilton to average 58) is required to obtain a single commercially successful product [8, p. 9]. The development program must, therefore, seek to eliminate the vast majority of inappropriate or low potential ideas quickly and efficiently. Even so, development of unsuccessful products accounted for 70 percent of new product expenditures [8, p. 11]. Waste was concentrated at the development stage.

A. S. Clausi [9] reported the experience of General Foods during an unspecified ten-year period. Over 600 ideas were examined. Table 1 shows the results of this program. Thirty successful products were added to the product mix at a total cost of $243 million. Over half of this expenditure was attributed to test marketing. It is possible that more effective screening procedures could have eliminated some of these latter expenses. While high technology industries experience markedly different patterns of expenditures (development costs can greatly exceed costs of field testing), more effective screening could still contribute to overall cost savings by reducing wasted development expense.

Table 1. Ten Years of New Product Development at General Foods Corporation

Stage of Development Process	Cost ($Millions)
Preliminary Screening of over 600 ideas	$ 76
Development of remaining 118 concepts	11
Test Marketing of 87 remaining products	156
Total Development Cost	$ 243

Development program resulted in 30 successful products and 10 failures of 40 products commercialized.

Based on data from A. S. Clausi, Vice President for Corporate Research, General Foods Corporation [9].

Role of Preliminary Screening Evaluation

In practice, the differences between screening and business analysis become blurred. In many cases a company will evaluate products using similar criteria at both stages of the development process. Screening relies on secondary data and qualitative judgments, while business analysis often requires collection of primary data on potential demand and a more exhaustive analysis of technical feasibility. Thus, it is possible to envision a single evaluation procedure for both stages of analysis that can be updated to reflect new information. Preliminary screening requires a broad, often qualitative, analysis while final screening examines key areas of uncertainty in more detail.

No matter what these stages are named, their goal is the reduction of expenditures on low potential projects. Funds may then be diverted to more promising programs. To achieve success a new product idea must be both technically and commercially feasible. References abound to projects where either or both dimensions were not properly controlled [10, 11].

Figure 1 [12, p. 3] details the procedures followed by an anonymous industrial products company. It depicts the complimentary nature of marketing and engineering inputs to the product development process.

II. IMPLEMENTATION OF PRODUCT SYSTEMS

The Conference Board [12] reported in 1973 that about half of 203 companies surveyed had a formal, written basis for evaluating new product or service ideas. A number (unreported) of these, in turn, used some form of weighted evaluation system. These systems typically operated by decomposing products into a series

Figure 1. Flow of Product Planning—An Industrial Products Company

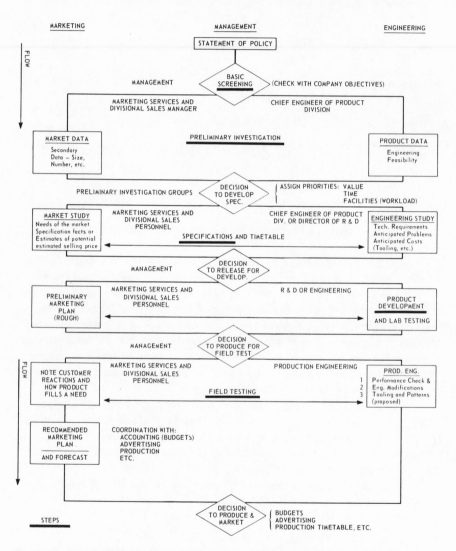

of analytical dimensions. Reservations in the use of such systems included the following:

1. Some proposals do not "fit" the established system;
2. What is the meaning of the overall score and can it mask critical deficiencies on individual evaluative criteria; and
3. Products which "fail" the evaluation might still be "desirable entries from the standpoint of competitive strategy [12, p. 32]."

The results, quite properly, are seen as useful input to the evaluation process, but not as a precise or final solution. These reservations indicate the need for a fundamental revision to new product screening procedures.

Types of Product Failure

There are two types of failures that can be associated with any screening process:

1. New product ideas that would have been successful in the market if they had passed the screening process (type 1 error).
2. New product ideas that passed through the screening process but subsequentially failed in the marketplace (type 2 error).

The type 1 errors (where the process causes good ideas to be rejected) are hidden errors. Type 1 errors are rarely documented within a company since rejected proposals are seldom accepted and subsequently marketed successfully by another firm. However, a relatively common objection raised by managers who eschew formal screening models is the claim that too many good ideas may be lost by forcing a rigorous structure on an ill-defined opportunity.

Causes of Product Failure

The type 2 errors (where the screening process has failed to reject an idea that failed in the marketplace) are more readily identified than type 1 errors. Many products fail after commercialization. Depending on definitions used, failure rates range between 20 percent and 30 percent [8, 13, 14, 15], but have been as high as 80 percent [16]. Of more concern than the level of failure are the reasons for failure. In many cases they are surprisingly basic. They include the following points cited by Cooper [17] and substantiated by other sources as shown:

1. Technical Problems [18, 19]:
   Technical difficulties/deficiencies with product; unable to produce product as desired.

Table 2.   Impact of Product Performance

Difference from Competitor	Of 50 Successes (%)	Of 50 Failures (%)
Significantly better performance, higher price	44	8
Marginally better performance, higher price	6	12
Better performance, same price	24	0
Same performance, lower price	8	0
Same performance, same price	16	30
Same performance, higher price	2	30
Worse performance, same or higher price	0	20
Total	100	100

Reprinted by permission of the *Harvard Business Review*. Exhibit I from "Why most new consumer brands fail" by J. Hugh Davidson (March-April 1976). Copyright © 1976 by the President and Fellows of Harvard College; all rights reserved.

2. Timing Too Late [19, 20]:
   Too late into the market; a me too product; competitors were firmly entrenched.

3. Lack of Understanding of Customers' Needs [14, 15, 18, 19, 21, 22]:
   Potential users overestimated; really no need for product; did not understand customer requirements.

4. Defensive Actions by Competitors [15, 19, 20]:
   Similar competing products introduced; competitors took defensive actions.

5. Lack of Understanding of Market Environment [15, 19]:
   Inadequate selling effort; misdirected selling effort; government action hurt sales.

6. Price Competition:
   Price too high; competitors lowered prices.

Perhaps the data cited by Davidson [23] are even more impressive. They are reproduced in Table 2. Many product failures simply do not offer the buyer any appreciable improvement. The case for meaningful product differentiation is also made by Lemont [24]. In allowing such products to reach the market, present screening procedures are not performing adequately.

Breakdown in Traditional Screening Systems

Why do screening systems fail to anticipate such basic reasons for failure? Lazo [13] maintains that "all the assorted causes for failure are in control of the company itself." Undoubtedly this overstates the problem. Certainly, prior to commercialization, research data have some very important limitations. In particular, Tull [25] has maintained that forecasting market size is one of the most difficult tasks facing management.

Other reasons for product failure include inflexible methods, bureaucratic red tape, and arbitrary management vetos [26]. Crawford [27] focuses on the imperfect interface between marketing researchers and decision makers. In fact, some product failures may be more attributable to the nature of the sponsoring organizations than to the nature of the screening procedure itself. Because of the strategic importance of product decisions, organizational behavior can become very political. Janis [28] suggested that groups can make faulty decisions because of this political behavior. Specifically, he discussed how groups discount unfavorable information, assume they are of invulnerable, limit disagreement, and assume unanimity of opinion. Bennett [29] bluntly asks, "how many products are being lost by interdepartment warfare?"

The Assumption of Rational Action. All checklists assume implicitly a consistent "application of principles in order to select the optimal alternative. . . . The basic concepts of these models of rational action are: 1) Goals and Objectives . . . ; 2) Alternatives . . . ; 3) Consequences . . . ; 4) Choice. Rational choice consists simply of selecting that alternative whose consequences rank highest in the decision maker's payoff function [30]."

In reality rationality is limited. First, it is impossible to conceive of a complete set of alternatives [2, 30]. Second, not all consequences may be foreseen. Third, the payoff function must link all consequences to all goals. These functions, broadly construed, can contain a variety of noneconomic, even political, dimensions. Certainly, risk becomes an integral component of the function as well. Thus, at best, rational action implies a bounded form of rationality based on available information. More than this implies "powers of prescience and capacities for computation resembling those we usually attribute to God [31]."

Organizational Contributions to New Product Failure. Organizations, in their planning processes, further contribute to the problem of limited rationality. Typically, the quality of business performance is judged by the degree of coincidence of the plan and the actual results. This contributes to a tendency to be conservative, developing plans from a simple extrapolation of the past. The focus of these plans can be limited to modest, tactical changes, excluding reevaluations of basic strategy. Indeed, critical estimates and assumptions may go unchallenged simply because they serve the purposes of the decision makers.

Unfortunately, the ideal way to evaluate the quality of an organization's performance requires complete knowledge of all strategic and tactical alternatives. Actual performance would thus be compared to this ideal. This is a delightful but, of course, impossible prospect. More generally, Simon has commented on the simplifying assumptions commonly made by human problem solvers [31]:

1. Problems, being complex, must be factored into parts. These parts, in turn, are handled individually.
2. Search continues until a satisfactory alternative is found. Thus, the order in which alternatives are located becomes critical.

3. Uncertainty is avoided and organizations develop "repertories" which constitute the set of actions in response to recurring situations.

In addition to the problem of limited rationality, present screening systems fail to recognize that evaluations are made by employees drawn from a conglomerate of semi-independent departments. Screening decisions, then, reflect these independent outputs, partially coordinated by the participating executives. Nevertheless, responses are strongly influenced by the operating procedures of each department. Allison [30, p. 146] noted that leaders have "competitive, not homogeneous interests; priorities and perceptions are shaped by positions;... management of piecemeal streams of decisions is more important than steady-state choices...."

In short, present evaluation systems do not appear to obtain satisfactory answers to basic questions governing new product success. Efforts to improve systems have focused on obtaining more information and not in examining how organizations use information. Tightening procedures has often created more bureaucratic, less flexible systems without improving efficiency. As a final irony, these bureaucratic organizations can have "a tendency to stifle innovation [32, p. 265]."

The Philosophy of Present Evaluation Systems

Although modern marketers are quick to disavow a production orientation in favor of a customer orientation, they appear to be relatively content to treat new product screening as a type of operations problem. This approach makes several implicit assumptions. First, a vast reservoir of new product ideas exists. Second, these ideas can be easily sorted into categories of acceptable or unacceptable potential. Third, the probability that any given idea is successful is low. Thus, the evaluation problem has been traditionally viewed as one of checking a large number of ideas to identify those few which will be successful.

Viewed as an operations problem, a logical solution appears to lie with the application of traditional testing techniques associated with quality control. Although each new product idea is unique, it is decomposed into basic attributes such as profit, payback, technical feasibility, market acceptability, operational compatibility, and congruence with organizational goals. Once the product has been standardized into a set of homogeneous attributes, the evaluation problem is reduced to finding the appropriate level of each attribute to guarantee success. The concept of new product screening is derived directly from this mechanical approach. Efficient techniques are deemed to be those that allow for large numbers of ideas to be evaluated with as few tests as possible, and greater efficiency results from increased standardization.

Problems Caused by the Traditional Approach

The fundamental problems in new product screening can be traced to this production orientation. A strategic decision is transformed into an exercise in operational mechanics. To design a production line of new product ideas demands that the partisan and political environment associated with all new product adoptions be assumed away. Once this happens, the most crucial attribute of strategic stability can be lost.

A new product idea can be viewed as a strategic alternative which is presented to relevant decision makers for their support. The product will be a success if all the decision makers (e.g., customers, suppliers, distributors, bankers, top management, key departments) accept it. A new product program that can secure the support of all relevant decision makers for its duration has strategic stability. Alternatively, if a relevant decision maker can improve his position by withdrawing support, the new product program is strategically unstable. His departure will cause it to fail.

New Product Development as an Entrepreneurial Process

The strategic nature of new product evaluations requires a shift from the current production orientation to a political orientation. A political orientation begins with the most primitive process of new product adoption, the case of an entrepreneur who seeks to build a company around a new product idea. The entrepreneur sequentially approaches each of the decision makers whose support is critical for the success of his venture. He sells, bargains, and compromises his vision of the ideal product and delivery system as he deals with bankers, investment houses, shareholders, channel partners, suppliers, customers and key employees to gain their support. Each of the relevant decision makers must support the new product idea and be prepared to play a specific role in the future program.

Entrepreneurial Decisions in the Large Corporation. When the scene is changed from the open market of new ideas and venture capital to the inside of a large corporation, the role of the entrepreneur is assumed by the new product's champion. Many of the relevent decision makers are the managers drawn from the controller's office, production, research and development, and marketing. The entrepreneurial process of selling, bargaining, and compromising will not cease simply because the activities become embedded in an institutional framework; however, current evaluation techniques often give the illusion that this partisian activity does not exist in the modern, optimizing organization.

The new product screening process is a strategic problem because it is an attempt to identify and evaluate the future relationship that would exist among the decision makers if the introduction of the new product were attempted. In the extreme, a new product innovation can cause major shifts in the behavior of the decision makers involved, and these shifts will stabilize into totally new markets and institutions.

Checklists in a Partisan Environment.   Current screening techniques are inadequate because they fail to reflect the reality of interactive decision making in a partisan environment. New product proposals may pass through all the hurdles imposed by formal committees and checklists, but any proposal which is not strategically stable will fail in the marketplace. It is left to the people who make the screening decisions to evaluate the strategic aspects of a new product proposal informally. The results of a formal screening analysis may have very little impact on the informal strategic evaluation. Current evaluation procedures could be cited as a classic example of the problems inherent in operationalizing strategic decisions. Grayson has stated the following:

> It is standard operating procedure for most management science people to strip away so much of a real problem with simplifying assumptions that the remaining carcass of the problem and its attendant solution bear little resemblance to the reality with which the manager must deal [33, p. 44].

Use of the Delphi Method.   Most management scientists have preferred to simplify by overlooking the political aspects of new product screening. However, some have identified the problem and attempted to model around it. For example, Chambers et al. [34] identified a negative aspect of group discussion making which they called the "bandwagon effect." They suggest organizational politics could be circumvented by using a derivative of the Delphi Method. "For the Delphi Method, the human environment is not a concern, since openness, interaction and trust are neither sought nor necessary [p. 112]." However, modeling around political problems is only an expediency. It maintains the fiction that new product evaluation occurs in a depoliticized environment where managers attempt to make objective decisions.

Current screening techniques represent the result of simplifying the process by assuming away its strategic structure. If screening techniques are to be made more relevent to those who attempt to use them, it is necessary for each new product proposal to be judged within a formal, coherent framework that deals with the strategic structure of the proposal and recognizes the political nature of the evaluation process.

III. A STRATEGIC VIEW OF THE NEW PRODUCT PROPOSAL

At any point in time, a person could attempt to write a history of a firm's operations, including a description of its relationships with other decision makers in the environment. The history would revolve around the successes and failures of various products and marketing strategies employed by both firm and its competitors. Similarly, a person could attempt to describe a firm's future. Unlike history, a large number of possible futures could be described. Each future scenario would be developed in terms of anticipated product and marketing strategies.

The New Product Proposal as a Scenario of the Future

A new product proposal is the champion's perception of anticipated relationships among the company and its suppliers, competitors, channel members, and customers if the new product were introduced. The complete scenario (not just the physical new product) is evaluated by managers who control new product introductions.

The champion of the new product attempts to sell this entire scenario, emphasizing its impact on the future role of his company. If it is accepted, the new product will be introduced. If the external decision makers follow the roles predicted for them, the new product launch will be successful.

Strategic Evaluation of a New Product Scenario

The new product proposal may be adopted after a series of evaluations and modifications. Current screening techniques tend to focus attention on both technical aspects and *pro forma* financial statements, leaving the strategic feasibility of the scenario less developed; however, the managerial evaluation of the strategic feasibility of the proposal is the crucial part of the evaluation process.

Since new product proposals must move through a series of formal screening stages, implicit approval is required at each stage to make the proposal strategically viable. Yet, because of the emphasis on formal technical and cost evaluations, the strategic evaluations are often deferred until considerable time and money have been spent on the operational evaluation of the proposal. They are very easy to postpone since they represent difficult, judgmental issues complicated by political and partisan overtones. Unfortunately, proper strategic evaluation becomes more difficult the longer the delay, due to the assumed acceptance of the proposal's strategic validity at each prior stage of the evaluation process.

Cases where a new product fails to gain a market position can easily be blamed on the inadequacies of market measurement, but many failures reflect a failure to evaluate and identify a new product scenario that was strategically unstable. New product proposals that are inherently unstable are scenarios that combine future events that cannot occur simultaneously. Such proposals should be rejected. It is not necessary to analyze their economic potential. The rejection of a new product proposal does not necessarily imply rejection of the new product, but it does demand that the idea be recast in a different scenario prior to evaluation of its economic worth.

The new product proposal is evaluated strategically by various members of the screening committee who test the proposed scenario with a series of counter and "what-if" scenarios. Whenever a new product scenario is being actively evaluated, its champion demonstrates the stability of his scenario by showing the infeasibility of these counter-scenarios. When a counter-scenario is encountered that cannot be rejected, the new product proposal must be modified to reflect this aspect of the strategic structure. If the modified proposal does not meet the organization's technical or cost requirements, the new product idea is rejected. Of course, a determined champion of a rejected new product proposal may start again by completely rewriting his description of the future. Since many scenarios exist, new product ideas may be shelved, only to be proposed again at a future date.

The essence of efficient new product evaluations lies in the ability of people on a screening committee to develop arguments systematically. It can be argued that the more rigorous this procedure is, the more likely it is that the proper scenario will be evaluated.

The Strategic Formulation of a New Product Scenario

Evaluation of the strategic structure of a new product proposal first requires identifying the decision making centers having a role in the particular scenario. The list of actors affected by the introduction of the new product would depend on the characteristics of the product being evaluated, but the list would typically include:

1. suppliers
2. production department
3. marketing department
4. channel members
5. customers in target market
6. competitors
7. regulatory or government agencies

The new product proposal is a scenario of the future relationship among these decision makers and notes the anticipations of each center. The amount of detail provided for each role description depends on the proposal's stage of development. As with current evaluation techniques, the new product proposal is expected to become progressively more detailed as the new product advances through the screening process; however, at the preliminary screening stages, the role descriptions will be rather general in nature. For example, the following initial role description may be anticipated:

1. Supplier: will provide quantities on a flexible shipment schedule;
2. Production Department: will modify production scheduling to accommodate peak level demands;

Table 3.   Description of a What—If Scenario

DECISION MAKERS	OPTIONS	WHAT–IF SCENARIO	PROPOSED NEW PRODUCT SCENARIO
Raw Material Supplier	– uses flexible shipment schedule	1	1
Production Department	– peak level demand scheduling	1	1
Marketing Department	– incentives for salesman	1	1
Channel Members	– carry 4 week inventory supply	1	1
Customers	– 40% awareness levels	1	1
	– usage rate of 2 units/month	1	1
Competitor	– does not change list prices	0	1
Regulatory Agencies	– will grant patent	1	1
Company Executive	– introduces new product at $x retail	1	1

3. Marketing Department: will provide sufficient incentives for salesmen to promote product;
4. Channel Members: will maintain a four week supply of inventory at projected demand levels;
5. Customers in Target Market: will achieve an awareness level of 40 percent in first year and exhibit an average usage rate of two units/month;
6. Competitor: will not change his list prices; and
7. Regulatory Agencies: will accept patent proposals

The list of decision makers and their expected behavior describes the new product scenario found in a new product proposal. The strategic evaluation of the new product scenario can begin once management accepts that the proposal is internally consistent and provides reasonable estimates.

The strategic evaluation attempts to define a what-if scenario that demonstrates the instability of the proposed scenario. If this is possible, the original scenario is discredited since it could not possibly be an actual description of the future. The what-if scenarios are based on decision options. For example, the competitor might decide to change his price. The proposed and what-if scenarios can be illustrated by listing the decision makers and their options as in Table 3. Options followed are indicated by the number 1, while options not followed are noted by the number 0. The number 0 beside the competitor's option can be interpreted to mean lower prices will be implemented.

The introduction of the new product is a decision of the firm's executive, and many of the options are meaningful if and only if the new product is introduced. Therefore, the executive option of actually introducing the new product is also included in the table for a total of nine options. Thus, 512 (2^9) scenarios could be represented by this list of decision makers and options.

Stability of a Scenario.   Screening committee members generally select a particular what-if scenario for one of two reasons:

1. Finding the worst possible scenario from the company's point of view;
2. finding options that a decision maker (e.g., the competitor) prefers to the role specified by the proposed scenario.

This selection process is used to test the validity of the proposed new product scenario.

The objective in finding the worst possible scenario is to evaluate the project's risk. If the worst possible scenario with the new product is found to be preferred to the status quo, the company may have a guaranteed improvement by introducing the new product. Of course very few new product introductions are this attractive.

A more reasonable set of arguments against the proposed scenario evolves from a search for reasons why particular decision makers prefer to follow different roles from those specified in the new product proposal. However, finding that a decision maker prefers a different role is not a sufficient reason for abandoning the proposal as unstable. The only situation where a new product proposal is clearly unstable is when some decision maker can be shown to have a guaranteed improvement from the proposed scenario.

The existence of a guaranteed improvement implies that there are no sanctions or threat of sanctions that the firm or other decision makers could bring to bear on the defecting decision maker. For example, the competitor may prefer to lower his prices. He may be confident that if the executives of the firm lower the proposed retail price of the new product, their distributors would not carry sufficient inventory. Thus, the competitor experiences a guaranteed improvement if there is no change in roles of other decision makers that would make him regret his defection. This would indicate an unstable proposal. Strategic stability is not a sufficient condition for new product success but it is certainly a necessary condition. Thus, the presence of a guaranteed improvement leads to the rejection of a proposed scenario.

A Formal Classification of Scenario Stability.   The Analysis of Options technique is a formal method for testing the strategic stability of future scenarios. Used in this manner, it can ensure that only strategically stable new product scenarios will be evaluated. In addition, the technique can provide a means to identify the conditions that permit the potential stability of a proposal. For example, a new product scenario where channel members support the new product with cooperative advertising may be stable only if the firm maintains its current level of national advertising for the complete line. The cost of meeting this condition could cause a new product proposal to be rejected even though it was feasible in all other respects. Thus, another important aspect of the overall evaluation of a proposal is noting the conditions of strategic stability.

The Analysis of Options technique is a managerial algorithm developed by Howard, based on his development of metagame theory [35]. The theory of metagames rigorously defines a set of conditions that allows a decision maker's scenario to be stable. A scenario can be stable for a decision maker if the following conditions are met:

1. If the decision maker has no unilateral improvement away from the scenario;
2. if the decision maker believes a sanction will be applied if he moves away from the scenario; or
3. if the decision maker has no guaranteed improvement by moving away from the scenario.

A scenario is certainly unstable if the decision maker has a guaranteed improvement by moving away from that scenario. To be stable a scenario must be stable for every decision maker, operating singly or in coalitions.

Figure 2 shows the three possible conditions of potential scenario stability and an unstable scenario. The row decision maker represented in Figure 2 has two different decision problems. Each of the problems includes four possible scenarios. He must evaluate each scenario for strategic stability from his point of view. Only his rank order preferences for the scenarios are shown. Although he must evaluate the strategic stability of the scenarios, he cannot choose a scenario per se. He is limited to choosing an option in each problem. His options are represented by rows R and S in Problem 1, and rows T and U in Problem 2. The column decision maker's choice of options are represented by the columns C, D and E, F, respectively. His preferences are not shown since they are not required to determine the strategic structure of a scenario from the row decision maker's point of view.

Figure 2.   Stability of Scenarios

column decision maker

	option C	option D
option R	scenario (RC) 3	scenario (RD) 2
option S	scenario (SC) 4	scenario (SD) 1

row decision maker

Problem #1

The numbers in each scenario represent row players rank order preferences.

4=best   1=worst

column decision maker

	option E	option F
option T	scenario (TE) 2	scenario (TF) 3
option U	scenario (UE) 4	scenario (UF) 1

row decision maker

Problem #2

The eight scenarios represented in Figure 2 would have their strategic stability evaluated from a row player's point of view as follows:

1. Scenarios (SC) (RD) (UE) (TF) are potentially stable because there is no unilateral improvement for the row decision maker in changing his choice of options.

2. Scenario (RC) is potentially stable because there is a sanction to deter the unilateral move from (RC) to (SC). The sanction is contained in the column decision maker's threat to choose option D which would result in either (RD) or (SD), both of which are less preferred than (RC).

3. Scenario (TE) is potentially stable because there is no guaranteed improvement in the shift from option T to U for the decision maker. Although scenario (UE) is preferred to (TE), scenario (UF) is not preferred to (TE).
4. Scenarios (SD) and (UF) are not stable because the row decision maker has a guaranteed improvement in changing his role if he finds himself in either scenario. From scenario (SD), the shift to option R would result in scenarios (RC) or (RD), both of which are preferred to (SD).

A complete evaluation of the strategic structure of any scenario in Figure 2 also requires the column decision maker's preferences. The impact of a coalition would also be studied. However, even from the point of view of the row decision maker alone, scenarios (SD) and (UF) are unstable. If either of these scenarios were contained in a new product proposal, the proposal should be rejected.

Analysis of Options Technique

The Analysis of Options technique is very general and can be applied whenever managers face complex decision problems and would find a benefit in identifying the strategic structure of a problem. It does not provide solutions in the sense of classical decision models such as linear programming or game theory. For many managers, the value of models is in the insights gained by structuring the problem rather than accepting the solution. The Analysis of Options technique provides the benefit of structure without burdening managers with the generation of many quantitative estimates necessary for models which generate optimal solutions.

The Analysis of Options technique only requires that a manager have the ability to make preference judgments between two scenarios. This does not preclude a manager from developing financial or other quantitative indices to help him judge his preferences. The advantage of the Analysis of Options technique is that it does not force the manager to give quantitative estimates for every evaluation. This is particularly important for new product screening. At the early stages of the screening process, there is very little quantitative data available; consequently, decisions must be made on the basis of qualitative judgment.

The Analysis of Options technique is built on the philosophy that good decisions frequently depend upon having a clear understanding of the strategic structure of the problem. This differs from the more conventional assumption that decisions based on quantitative data are superior to those based on qualitative judgments. Furthermore, the qualitative evaluations within the strategic structure more clearly indicate where the effort to develop quantitative estimates should be concentrated.

The Analysis of Options approach is very flexible. Traditional (solution-orientated) models are constructed around a set of stated objectives and constraints. If this set is changed, a new model must be developed. The Analysis of Options technique allows new decision makers and new options for current decision makers to be added (or deleted) as they are identified. This open-ended aspect of the technique is particularly important in the strategic evaluation of new product scenarios since the list of decision makers and options is likely to be changed as the screening process proceeds.

A formal procedure for evaluating the potential stability of a future scenario is shown in Figure 3. The process starts with the premise that all the pertinent decision makers and their alternative courses of action can be identified during the course of the analysis. The exercise of listing decision makers and their options is in itself a difficult task. The choice and wording of the options must be selected with some care to keep the number of potential scenarios limited to those of strategic importance.

The selection of a particular scenario is an important step in the analysis since the evaluation of its relationship with other scenarios often identifies other interesting scenarios for analysis. The selection of a particular decision maker or coalition is not as crucial. The theoretically complete evaluation of a particular scenario requires that it be considered from the point of view of each decision maker and coalition.

Evaluation of a particular scenario begins by locating all the unilateral improvements for the decision maker whose viewpoint is being considered. All other decision makers are assumed to have their options frozen, and only the decision maker under consideration can change his options in an attempt to create unilaterally preferred scenarios. If no unilateral improvements for the decision maker can be found, the scenario is deemed potentially stable for that particular decision maker. In game theoretic terms, the absence of a unilateral improvement is equivalent to finding a rational outcome for that player. If no unilateral improvements are found for any individual decision maker from a particular scenario, then the stability of that scenario corresponds to a Nash equilibrium found in a mixed motive game [36].

Even when a unilateral improvement has been identified, the scenario under consideration may still be stable for that decision maker if a sanction is found to exist. A sanction exists if the other decision makers follow an option (or combination of options) which prevents the decision maker under analysis from finding a scenario he prefers to the particular scenario. The existence of a sanction implies that the particular scenario can be potentially stable from the decision maker's point of view. If sanctions exist for every decision maker, that particular scenario is potentially stable and corresponds to a symmetric equilibrium in metagame theory [35]. The actual stability of a particular scenario will depend on the credibility of the sanction.

Even if no sanctions are identified, the scenario could be potentially stable for a decision maker if the unilateral improvement he is considering does not provide a guaranteed improvement. The last step in the formal Analysis of Options is to

Figure 3.   Procedure for Analysis of Options

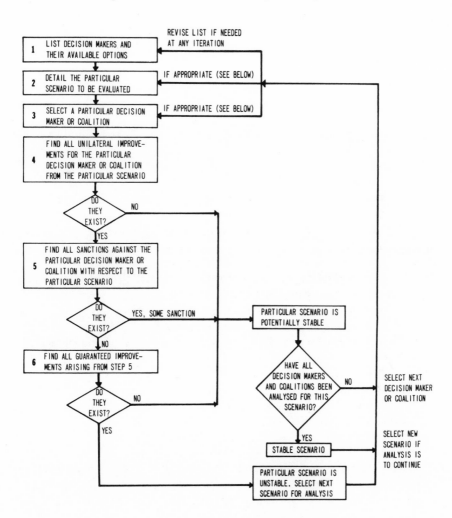

identify the existence of a guaranteed improvement for the decision maker. This requires that all possible reactions of the other decision makers be considered. If they cannot create a scenario that is less preferred to the scenario under analysis for the defector, then a guaranteed improvement exists.

Radford [37] has provided detailed examples of formal procedures for the Analysis of Options technique. However, the formal technique is somewhat cumbersome for new product scenario analysis. A modified form of the analysis is more appropriate for use by a new product screening committee.

Analysis of New Product Scenarios.   The procedure for the analysis of new product scenarios begins when a new product proposal has been presented to a screening committee. The new product proposal identifies every strategic decision maker and his proposed role in the scenario. Each committee member assumes the role and partisan point of view of one of the decision makers specified in the proposal. Ideally, there would be one committee member for each role in the scenario.

The process consists of two major phases. The first phase tests the new product proposal for strategic stability while the second compares the general acceptability of the new product scenario to the status quo. Both phases are quite separate problems of analysis, and the search for strategic stability clearly differentiates this form of analysis from the conventional checklists used to evaluate new product proposals.

The flow diagram in Figure 3 illustrates the basic steps in the analysis of a new product scenario. The routine is followed for each decision maker individually or operating in coalitions of decision makers. There are four possible results at the end of a single analysis:

1. The new product proposal S is stable and is preferred to the status quo Q for that particular decision maker M_i $(S \epsilon \tilde{M}_i Q)$.
2. The new product proposal S is stable and is not preferred to the status quo Q for that particular decision maker M_i $(S \epsilon M_i Q)$.
3. The new product proposal S is not stable and the scenario that represents a guaranteed improvement S' is not preferred to the status quo Q for that particular decision maker M_i $(S' \epsilon M_i Q)$.
4. The new product proposal S is not stable and the scenario that represents a guaranteed improvement S' is preferred to the status quo Q for that particular decision maker $(S' \epsilon \tilde{M}_i Q)$.

If the new product proposal is found to be stable and preferred to the status quo (Result #1), the new product proposal is classified as potentially acceptable to that decision maker. It is unlikely that every decision maker will find the new product proposal preferred to the status quo. For example, competitors and channel members may find the proposal stable but not preferred to the status quo (Result #2). This result indicates that the proposal most be modified. The modifications must indicate both how the scenario is to be achieved and the cost of implementing the conditions necessary for stability. Of course, further analysis is necessary once a decision maker finds the proposal strategically unstable.

If a decision maker has a guaranteed improvement away from the new product scenario, the proposal is rejected; however, rejection of a proposal does not imply complete rejection of the new product. For example, the marketing or production department may find a guaranteed improvement by using different

Figure 4.   Analysis of Proposal Stability

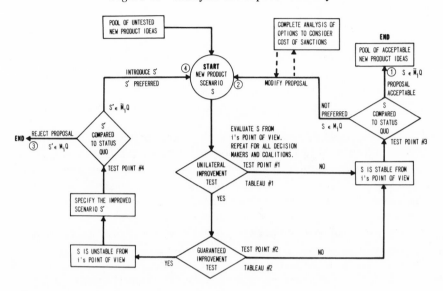

options than those specified in the proposal. It may also prefer the new scenario to the status quo (Result #4). This new scenario replaces the current proposal, and the analysis is repeated with the scenario now being championed by the decision maker who discovered it. The decision maker who finds a guaranteed improvement but still prefers the status quo (Result #3) will simply reject the new product proposal.

Figure 4 presents a flow diagram of the analysis of the new product options process. Test points #1 and #2 in the flow diagram comprise the checks for strategic stability. Test points #3 and #4 evaluate scenarios against the status quo. The existence of strategic stability determines whether test point #3 or test point #4 is reached.

Test point #1 occurs where each committee member searches for a unilateral improvement from the point of view of the decision maker he represents. The committee member may add options he feels are available to the decision maker, but which have been neglected in the proposal.

Test point #2 is reached if a unilateral improvement is found for a decision maker. That unilateral improvement is evaluated for the possibility that it is a guaranteed improvement.

Test point #3 is reached if a new product proposal has the property of being strategically stable for that particular decision maker. The objective is to compare the description of the future with and without the proposed product.

Test point #4 is reached if a new product proposal is strategically unstable from a decision maker's point of view. The objective is to compare the guaranteed improvement scenario found by the decision maker with the status quo.

The Search for Strategic Stability.   The format permits independent, simultaneous analysis of each decision maker by a different committee member. Obviously, the quality of the analysis depends upon the level of knowledge a committee member has of the goals, values, and capabilities of the assigned role.

After each member of the new product screening committee has been assigned a role, his first objective is to find a change of options or roles that would lead to a unilateral improvement for the decision maker he represents. For example, a committee member assigned the role of a channel member any identify an improved scenario. This could involve returning all old products in stock made obsolete by the introduction of the new product rather than attempting to sell them as specified in the new product proposal. The production department's representative may find it preferable to buy different tooling than that specified in the scenario. The marketing department representative may find that a different allocation of salesmen is preferable to that specified.

If none of the committee members can find strategic alternatives that are preferred to those in the new product proposal, then the new product is potentially stable. When the new product proposal is found to be strategically stable, further effort should be invested to identify whether or not the new product scenario is preferred to the status quo.

Each committee member who finds a unilateral improvement must immediately test that scenario to see if it represents a guaranteed improvement. If it is a guaranteed improvement, the new product scenario is strategically unstable and should be rejected. The rejection of the new product scenario requires that the new product proposal be rewritten and resubmitted to the committee.

The first two steps of a potential analysis are summarized in the form of Tableau #1 shown in Table 4. The example builds on the new product scenario developed in Table 3. The first tableau represents the unilateral improvement from the proposed new product scenario found by the committee member while representing the channel member's point of view.

Having found a unilateral improvement in the first tableau, the committee member uses Tableau #2, shown in Table 5, to determine if the preferred scenario is a guaranteed improvement for the channel member. Rather than hold all the other decision makers' options constant as was done in the first tableau, the options are marked with a dash and changed. The objective is to find a combination of options that will create a new scenario which is not preferred to the proposed scenario. If any scenario can be found which makes the unilateral improvement less attractive than the particular scenario, then a guaranteed improvement does not exist. Thus, the proposed scenario would have some basis (as yet not identified) for being strategically stable from the channel member's point of view.

Table 4.   A Tableau Illustrating a Channel Member's Point of View

Decision Makers	Options	Scenario Preferred	Proposed Scenario	Scenario Not Preferred
raw material supplier	—uses flexible shipment schedule	1	1	
production dept.	—peak level demand scheduling	1	1	
marketing dept.	—incentives for salesmen	1	1	these options remain fixed
channel members	—carry 4 week inventory supply	0	1	
customers	—40% awareness levels	1	1	
	—usage rate of 2 units/month	1	1	
competitor	—does not change list prices	1	1	
regulatory agencies	—will grant patent	1	1	
company executives	—introduces new product at $x retail	1	1	

A unilateral imiprovement is found.

Tableau #1:   Unilateral Improvements
Point of View: Channel Members
Note: The channel members would prefer to hold two weeks inventory rather than four weeks as suggested in the new product proposal.

The example in Table 5 provides a tableau where no combination of options could be found that would make the scenario build on the channel member's unilateral improvement of holding just two weeks inventory. The worst possible options (from the channel member's point of view) taken by the other decision makers are shown in the brackets beside each dash. Since the worst possible options taken by the other decision makers still leave the scenario in the preferred column, any other combination of options will also leave it in the preferred column. Thus, this is a guaranteed improvement. The supporting analysis of the channel member's guaranteed improvement can be detailed in a note attached to the tableau.

The committee member who represents the channel does not attempt to judge the desirability or credibility of the worst case options from any other decision maker's point of view. The objective of this analysis is to ensure that the partisan aspects of new product adoption are clearly identified. After preparing both tableaux, the committee member knows whether or not the new product proposal is potentially stable from the assigned decision maker's point of view. If the new product proposal is found to be stable from all possible points of view, it has the potential to be strategically viable. However, it only takes the discovery of one decision maker having a guaranteed improvement away from the proposed scenario to effectively veto the new product proposal. Although the initial em-

Table 5.   Guaranteed Improvement Tableau Illustrating
Channel Member's Point of View

Decision Makers	Options	Scenario Preferred	Proposed Scenario	Scenario Not Preferred
raw material supplier	—uses flexible shipment schedule	−(−)	1	
production dept.	—peak level demand scheduling	−(−)	1	
marketing dept.	—incentives for salesmen	−(−)	1	
channel members	—carry 4 week inventory supply	0	1 $\Big\}$ ———	this option fixed
customer	—40% awareness levels	−(0)	1	
	—usage rate of 2 units/month	−(0)	1	
competitor	—does not change list prices	−(0)	1	
regulatory agencies	—will grant patent	−(0)	1	
company executive	—introduces new product at $x retail	−(1) ↑ a guaranteed improvement has been identified	1	

Tableau #2:   Guaranteed Improvements
Point of View: Channel Members

Note: The channel member is indifferent to changes in supplier, production and marketing options. He is, however, sensitive to the possibilities that the consumer's awareness levels and usage rate may be lower, the competitor may lower list prices, and that our firm fails to get the patent and refuses to reduce our introductory price. These effects do alter his preference for the new scenario. He continues to prefer the two-week inventory option to the proposed new product scenario. This constitutes a guaranteed improvement.

Recommendation: Reject new product scenario. Suggest adding marketing option of increased dealer margins since the channel member feels that present margins are inadequate to support a four-week inventory.

phasis of the analysis is to test the new product proposal for strategic viability, the comparison of scenarios to the status quo provides a first cut at the potential acceptability of the proposal.

The Evaluation of Scenarios

The analysis of the new product scenario relies on a manager's ability to make a simple qualitative judgment between two scenarios. It does not require that he rank a number of scenarios or assign weights to his preferences. This simplicity is possible because the mathematics of metagame theory only requires that a manager's preference function M_i be reflexive. The stability of a scenario can be established even if a manager has some intransitive preferences. Although the technique demands only that managers do not claim a scenario to be strictly preferred to itself, it does not preclude managers from using quantitative estimates of profit, market share, sales volume and/or costs to help them make a preference judgment. The objective is to provide a technique where important judgments, such as strategic stability, are not postponed until sufficient numerical estimates become available.

A committee member is not even required to provide ranked reasons why a decision maker may prefer one scenario to another. It is only important that committee members think about the overall impact of a particular scenario in terms of the decision maker's goals and values.

These goals and values are often difficult to operationalize since they involve things such as leadership, risk, growth, and loss of face. Although it is difficult for managers to specify exactly why one scenario is preferred to another, this technique relies on the fact that managers can make these judgements without detailed specifications.

There are two types of judgments being made in the analysis. The first type concerns the evaluation of scenarios within Analysis of Options tableaux. These judgments are well constrained. The decision is based on a comparison of scenarios within a well specified set of options. Alternative scenarios are determined to be strictly preferred (or not) compared to the new product scenario.

The second type of judgment is when the new product scenario (or modified scenario) is compared to the status quo. The status quo scenario may be defined outside the options provided in the tableau; however, each committee member must have a formal description of the status quo for the decision maker he represents. Comparing the new product scenario to the status quo can help identify new options and new decision makers that may be of strategic importance. For example, a channel member may have a special arrangement with a trucking firm or a bank that is constraining his options in the new product scenario. These may represent decision makers and options that are of strategic importance even though they are only indirectly involved in the new product decision. Naturally, these indirect decision makers may only be of strategic importance in some of the new product scenarios.

The creation of modified new product proposals is an important aspect of a successful analysis. For example, if three or four committee members each submit tableaux, these can be combined into a single new tableau of players and options. Such a tableau may provide players and options that had been missed by other members of the committee and their inclusion may change their strategic evaluations of the proposal. Therefore, it is reasonable for committee members to expect a new product proposal to move through the analysis several times as options of strategic importance are identified.

Even if a decision maker finds a stable new product proposal not preferred to the status quo, the proposal may not be rejected. Some decision makers, such as competitors, channel members, or suppliers, may not prefer a particularly new product. This should sensitize the company to problems of implementing a product proposal in an environment of conflict. For example, a channel member may not prefer a product or marketing innovation to the status quo; however, he would prefer to distribute the new product rather than switch to a different supplier. The analysis of these conflict situations and the cost of appropriate implementation policies is an important aspect of a new product program.

The presence of conflict within a new product proposal may demand an in-depth use of the Analysis of Options technique in order to identify the strategic basis for stability of the new product scenario. The Analysis of Options technique will determine whether a scenario is stable because a sanction exists or because no guaranteed improvement can be found. After the reasons for a scenario's stability have been identified, the operational costs (if any) of establishing the credibility of a sanction can be added to the costs of the new product launch. For example, it may be necessary to engage in costly high-profile negotiations with a potential alternative channel member or suppliers to keep current channel members or suppliers aware of the options available.

IV. THE ROLE OF CONVENTIONAL EVALUATION METHODS

The use of the options framework shifts the evaluation orientation from being perceived as a series of quality control checks to a strategic analysis of possible futures for the firm and the decision makers with which it interacts. However, stable new product proposals must still be evaluated and conventional methods are useful.

The conventional techniques can be broadly classified as follows:

1. ad hoc procedures
2. checklists; or
3. weighted checklists

Each will be discussed in turn. Other forms of quantitative models will not be examined since they typically require data not available at the time of initial screening. A review of some of these models is contained in Montgomery and Urban [38]. A recent paper by Silk and Urban [39] described a system for assessing market potential at the final screening stage; however, market potential is only a portion of the information needed for a screening evaluation.

Ad Hoc Procedures

For a variety of reasons, some firms may adopt an unstructured or ad hoc system for analyzing new product opportunities. These reasons may include a reluctance to impose structure on an ill-defined set of opportunities or a belief that the business's product alternatives are so diverse as to preclude the use of a common analytical framework. In many cases the lack of a systematic review system is likely accompanied by the absence of a statement of product policy.

Table 6. Types of Strategic New Product Options

Degree of Market Newness	Degree of Technological Newness		
	No Change	Improved Technology	New Technology
No Change		Reformulation	Replacement
Strengthen Market	Remerchandising	Improved Product	Line Extension
New Market	New Use	Market Extension	Diversification

Source: Adapted from Johnson and Jones (41) and Pessemier (50, pg 9)

Such a statement can be very powerful in directing the business's product development process. Principally, it can provide a framework for guiding product development and selection [11, 16, 40]. Thus it can apply the firm's resources to desired areas of growth. One of the most fundamental approaches to forming a product policy is shown in Table 6 [41]. Strategic choices can be based on the interrelationship of both market and technological factors [42].

The essence of a product policy statement attempts to summarize the business characteristics products must possess to have a reasonable chance of success. The literature contains guidelines for developing policy statements [40, 43]. Statements can be limiting in controlling product development; however, this is quite desirable for many of the ideas routinely evaluated. Yet, the organization must remain committed to altering its policy in response to company, market, and technological changes [44], the absence of flexibility, can contribute to the classic problems of marketing myopia [45].

The Analysis of Options framework suggests the product policy statement must be supplemented with a statement about the goals and objectives of the other decision makers in the new product process. This assumption is more realistic than assuming that a company has a unified and operationally valid statement of goals and objectives which was necessary to maintain the fiction that evaluating new product proposals could be treated as a quality control problem. Different departments often interpret corporate objectives in different ways. In fact, a company is a rather loose coalition, bound together because of past product ideas which were successful. The future relationship within the coalition will be determined by the success of future new products. For example, the champion of a major new product success is invariably rewarded by being promoted up the corporate ranks.

Checklists

In the conventional approach, it is assumed that it is possible to construct a set of objectives for new products added to the product mix. These objectives can lead in turn to a set of evaluative criteria that serves as a "hurdle" for each proposed project. Frequently, these criteria are organized in the form of a checklist. This is often particularly appropriate for the task of qualitative preliminary screening; however, checklists remain suitable for use as a summary of all known data and judgements throughout the product development process. For instance, early subjective sales estimates can be revised during the final screening process. New information will be used to update the earlier evaluation forms.

Lists of evaluative criteria for use in checklist systems can be found in several sources [12, 46, 47, 48, 49, 50]. Such a list can contain very general statements relating to the product, its market, and financial projections. Alternately, it may consist of factors that are highly company and industry specific. In either case, such a system forces a systematic review which can be more complete and efficient than a totally ad hoc approach. It serves to organize the analysis along specific attributes expected from a new product.

Just as in the case of product policy statements, objectives and evaluative criteria must be subject to change. The desirability of a particular project may change as the market changes or even as the mix of other projects being developed changes. Williams has noted the following [51, p. 369]:

> If the resources required for a project are already committed, then the project might be rejected (or postponed) even though it might have greater potential worth than another company-funded project, already in progress. . . . Since the projects arise at different points in time, the phasing in of new worthwhile projects requiring scarce resources must be equated with the problem of maintaining stability in the projects in progress, so that new projects do not cause frequent curtailment of satisfactory projects still in progress. . . . Thus while projects in progress might have been selected according to their financial worth, further proposals initiated later might be accepted or rejected according to their utilization of resources, so that this objective assumes greater importance relative to the financial objectives than before.

Clearly, this creates pressures to suboptimize project decisions [2]. In so doing, it can likely lead to heated discussion within the firm. In part, this problem can be lessened if projects are grouped with others which share similar resources prior to their evaluation [52]; however, ideas do not often arrive in such neatly organized packages.

Weighted Checklists

The most commonly reported screening device in the product development literature is the weighted checklist. This type of rating scheme is presented as a compromise between the comparatively unstructured approach of a checklist and the impossibility of *directly* estimating a product's attractiveness on a single, summary scale. In practice, relevant evaluative criteria are assigned numeric weights based on their relative importance. Also, a numeric scale is established for each evaluative criterion. The resulting weighted sum score of evaluations on all criteria yields a single score of product attractiveness [53].

This procedure presumably gained favor because of its believed similarity to a decision maker's reasoning process. As well, it is more detailed than either an ad hoc or single criterion system and more structured than a checklist. Clearly, the sum score need not necessarily be a linear combination of the evaluative criteria. Various transformations could be employed to reflect diminishing returns on certain dimensions once critical levels have been surpassed. Noncompensatory scoring systems could also be introduced. For instance, Hart [48] reports a logarithmic transformation of criteria prior to establishing the final product index. Like other weighted checklist systems reported, no attempt was described to establish the validity of the system. This is critical since no justification is presented for violating parsimony.

The project indices may be combined with financial data to form measures that correlate with projected return on development costs or "probability weighted" measures of estimated profitability [54]. In practice, however, this approach is fraught with difficulty [55, 56]. Can a reliable set of weights be obtained? Are evaluative criteria truly independent? Are the weights independent of the product scores? Do weights remain constant over time and across products?

The question of independence of criteria becomes very important in a weighted checklist system. The literature contains several references to proposed solutions. Williams [51] reports an attempt to create a model based on a weighted sum of factor scores. The attempt was not successful because there was no agreement among decision makers about the way particular evaluative criteria related to overall objectives.

An earlier attempt to resolve the lack of independence problem applied linear discriminant analysis [47] to the screening system in O'Meara [49]. A likelihood ratio of success to failure for a hypothetical product was calculated. In this approach, the entire set of 17 scores on all evaluative criteria is thus used to describe the state of nature. This system requires two 17-dimensional vectors for comparison, one each of scores from successful and unsuccessful products.

In further work using a similar approach, Freimer and Simon [57] suggested a very disturbing finding. The final score in a weighted screening system is extremely insensitive to changes in either individual ratings or criterion weights. Most decisions would be resolved in favor of continuing development. The authors conclude "it appears possible that many screening models are much more insensitive devices for screening new product opportunities than had heretofore been believed [p. 124]."

The theoretical and empirical shortcomings of checklists are primarily due to the operational objectives demanded of them in a screening role. If the checklists are simply used in the role of a guide to help ensure a more complete and thorough evaluation of scenarios, objections to their use must be reduced.

At times, the manager attempting to evaluate two scenarios may find his experience too limited and the scenarios too similar to make a confident judgment, even if aided with a checklist. This manager could then direct his operations research or support staff to assist him with the construction of a simulation model that will compare the two specific scenarios in terms of quantitative analysis. A model building task that is specifically directed by the Analysis of Options and scenarios is far simpler than attempting the construction of a general model that will compare all scenarios to each other.

The Analysis of Options approach ensures that each manager is evaluating scenarios from a specific point of view, employing a specific scenario as a reference point. He is only asked to determine if a scenario is strictly preferred or not to some other scenario. The manager making this evaluation should use checklists and simulations whenever it assists him in making a better judgment.

V. A COMPARISON OF METHODS

Larréché and Montgomery [58] have described a framework for comparing a variety of marketing models. Many of their evaluative criteria are also relevant for comparing the alternative screening procedures described here.

Checklists

It would appear that the benefits of outlining a systematic system incorporating a simple checklist far outweight the initial costs. Such a system is easy to use and understand, being somewhat similar to the manager's thought process. Especially when used for new products using familiar technology and restricted to familiar markets this approach is quite adequate. Its ability to deal with politics, new situations, and the general strategic realities of the decision process is, however, extremely limited.

Weighted Checklists

Adding weights increases both initial costs and complexity while doing nothing to lessen the limitations of simple checklists. Furthermore, new problems of attribute independence, importance and meaning of overall scores are added. It would appear that weights would only lead to an overall improvement when decisions are highly similar to past experience. Even then, one could question the need for such a formal procedure unless a very large number of ideas were being evaluated.

Other Current Procedures

Procedures (such as Delphi) which model around organizational politics begin to address the limitations of the foregoing techniques. They do require higher initial costs for implementation, simply because managers must be trained in their use. They are somewhat more complex, thus tending to limit their use. Likely, such an approach would be reserved for decisions thought to be of major strategic importance and/or quite unlike past evaluations made by the organization.

Advantages of the Analysis of Options

The Analysis of Options approach to new product screening does not provide any indication that the new product proposal is the best available. It is a methodology for systematically exploring the strategic stability of a proposal and seeks to ensure that the reality of the partisan environment surrounding new product development is handled in an explicit and rigorous manner. It is far too easy for the proponents of a new product idea to start believing their own rhetoric created as a necessary part of new product adoption. Formal checklists and weighted ranking schemes have been used to keep the evaluations as objective as possible. The idea behind the Analysis of Options approach is to make the political proceedings as objective as possible.

Because the analysis has a clear mathematical structure, the tableaux used in the analysis can be stored in a computer. In fact, some of the advantages become even more apparent when members of the screening committee each have access to a conversational computer link. With the computer, each member can do his share of the analysis in his own time outside the committee room. The computer handles the bookkeeping and draws the individual analysis into a comprehensive mapping of the problem. The computer will also cue the representative doing the analysis to scenarios that need consideration and assist in the evaluation of sanctions and their credibility.

The tableaux form the basis for an audit of the strategic policies developed for a new product launch. With or without the computer, the procedure based on the Analysis of Options technique has some important advantages.

- Efficiency: Because the process is a systematic application of logic, the committee loses less time through rehashing old scenarios and circularity of arguments.
- Learning: Because the process forces the person to evaluate a package of options that define a scenario rather than individual

                                          options, there is less risk of people championing a single option and having the screening degenerate into a win-lose contest.

- Qualitative: Because the structure of the analysis can be developed without making explicit quantitative estimates, the process gives full allowance to a manager's qualitative judgment.

- Simplicity: Because the process only requires a preference judgment between two scenarios at any one time, there is no need for any ranking procedures.

- Quantification: To the extent that a manager wishes to use quantitative analysis to assist him in judging preferences between scenarios, it is much simpler to quantify two separate scenarios rather than to work out comprehensive algorithms for the total problem.

- Open Analysis: To the extent that new players and new options can be added to the game as their impact becomes appreciated by the screening committee, the analysis grows and matures without a need to rebuild the model each time.

- Clarity: Because all the assumptions and preferences are made explicitly, any contradictions or misunderstanding can be detected and set right immediately.

- Variety: Because the problem is examined from many points of view, the chances of making decisions on erroneous extrapolations of the status quo are avoided.

- Recording: The process provides a permanent record of the structure and rational of the policies that are required to achieve scenarios. In this sense, the analysis can be built upon by successive managers as the product moves through various stages of development and on into the complete life cycle of the product. The process can be used as a product policy accounting system when the product comes under periodic review.

Members of the screening committee are not required to have an intimate knowledge of mathematical model building to use the process, even though they are in fact building a decision model. If a computer is used, only the knowledge of how to record preferences is required of the member. "The air of mystery associated with the use of mathematical model-building techniques disappears and all involved see the Analysis of Options as a common-sense (although curiously logical) discussion of practical matters, with which they are comfortingly familiar [37, p. 168]."

Comparing Current Methods to Analysis of Options

None of the current screening procedures compensate automatically for organizational politics. It is far from clear that they can ever do so in the absence of mutually held goals held in an environment of trust and cooperation. Thus, the Analysis of New Product Options technique is the only procedure which attempts to address the realistic constraints imposed on the evaluation and decision process. As an unfamiliar technique, it unquestionably suffers from high initial costs and what initially seems an imposing structure. Nevertheless, the technique can offer high value when applied to major strategic decisions. Its use becomes repetitive and thus learning effects are high. It has been validated in a number of decision situations [35, 37].

From this analysis, a pattern seems to emerge. Simple checklists seem to dominate weighted ones for more routine types of analysis. For more strategic evaluations the Analysis of New Product Options is theoretically preferable to Delphi approaches. Both techniques are more costly than checklists but a more thorough analysis can result. Given a comparable amount of organizational experience, the cost of the Options Analysis need not exceed a Delphi approach. Checklists can provide a useful system to aid in the evaluation of stable scenarios.

VI. SUMMARY

New product decisions are of fundamental importance to any business. They have great influence on the options open to the firm in the future. It is generally accepted that new product decisions must be guided by a clear statement of corporate strategy and objectives. This, it is hoped, will provide a set of uniform criteria to ensure that program evaluations and product decisions are consistent across departmental boundaries over time.

In reality, corporations often fall short of this ideal. Benefits to the total corporation become subordinated to those which accrue to individual departments or divisions. "The important consideration becomes protecting departmental interests rather than furthering interdepartmental cooperation [32, p. 364]." Any tendency to optimize the contribution of each department can have the effect of suboptimizing the total program [2]. As organizations grow more complex, this can become a perpetual problem. Organizational complexity is worsened by the fact that corporations have multiple, sometimes conflicting, objectives. Since departmental goals are derived from corporate objectives, the organization's environment becomes very political whenever departmental goals conflict. Politics and suboptimization are particularly evident in the new product screening process because of the visibility and strategic importance of the decisions.

The fundamental weakness in current screening methods is their operational orientation. The current orientation treats the stream of new ideas as a production process, each proposal being inspected and tested for quality with checklists of criteria. To establish a consistent set of operational criteria requires the assumption that there is a consistent set of unified goals applicable to all new products the company considers. This assumption of using a single point of view (the firm) and a single point of reference (the customer) assumes away the strategic nature of the new product adoption process.

Formal operational methodologies, such as statements of corporate goals and checklists, can be useful if they are employed within a formal framework, such as the Analysis of Options, that will reflect the strategic reality of the new product decisions.

The strategic reality is that the new product adoptions are very political in nature. New product ideas must be sold to the relevant decision makers, and interaction between decision makers involved negotiation and compromise. It is clear that the future success of a firm is closely associated with the ability of a firm to establish a larger pool of potentially successful new ideas and this means that a larger number of ideas must be evaluated. To evaluate larger numbers of ideas demands that the process be routinized in some way; however, if the process is to be successful, it must take into account the political and partisan nature of new product adoptions. Current screening techniques reflect an attempt to routinize the evaluation process by assuming away the partisan environment.

The natural behavior of product champions is to sell their ideas to the relevant decision makers regardless of the formal checklists and evaluation schemes imposed on the process. The existence of many formal checks may ensure that only those product ideas that are enthusiastically supported will be proposed and pushed through the system. To the extent that there may be a correlation between the enthusiasm of the idea's proponents and the probability of eventual market success, then even the worst screening bureaucracy may succeed in allowing very good ideas to be tried; however, a bandwagon effect can push bad ideas through. When the analysis loses objectivity, these failures occur for the basic reasons discussed in Section II, concerning the role of preliminary screening evaluation.

The Analysis of Options approach does not attempt to model the negotiation process per se. Rather, it makes the assumption that the proponents of the new product idea can be extremely successful at the selling job, and that all the relevant decision makers are on the "bandwagon." The objective of the analysis is to find out who has an incentive for getting off, once the direction of the bandwagon becomes known.

The new venture can only be successful if all the relevant decision makers stay on the bandwagon. If a decision maker has a guaranteed improvement for himself by changing his role, the strategic viability of the venture is destroyed. The Analysis of Options technique addresses the problem of identifying who has incentive to adopt a different role and those who might regret participating but have no incentive to deviate from the new product scenario.

There is little reason for managers to spend large amounts of effort attempting to quantify the attributes of any particular new product idea until the strategic stability of the idea is established. The Analysis of Options provides a formal framework that reflects the partisan environment of the new product adoption process and gives current, formal evaluation techniques a greater relevance to the strategic nature of the process.

REFERENCES

1. "New Product News," quoted in *Business Week* 92 (March 6, 1978).
2. O'Dell, William F., Ruppel, Andrew C., Trent, Robert H. *Marketing Decision Making: Analytic Framework and Cases.* Cincinnati: South-Western Publishing Co., 1976.
3. McGraw-Hill Department of Economics, *Business Week* 34 (April 29, 1961) and 73 (May 13, 1967), quoted in Edgar A. Pessemier, *Product Management: Strategy and Organization.* Santa Barbara, Calif.: Wiley/Hamilton, 1977.
4. "The Two-Way Squeeze on New Products," *Business Week* 130–132 (August 10, 1974).
5. "Innovation: Has America Lost Its Edge." *Newsweek* 56–68 (July 4, 1979).
6. "The Breakdown of U.S. Innovation." *Business Week* 56–68 (February 16, 1976).
7. "Vanishing Innovation." *Business Week* 46–54 (July 3, 1978).
8. *Management of New Products.* Chicago: Booz, Allen and Hamilton, Management Consultants, 1968.
9. "The Rebuilding Job at General Foods." *Business Week* 50 (August 25, 1973), cited in Ben M. Enis, *Marketing Principles,* 2nd edition. Santa Monica. Calif.: Goodyear Publishing Co., 1977.
10. "How Fusion Systems Blundered to Success with Exotic Product." *Wall Street Journal* (November 17, 1977).
11. Zarecor, William D. "High-Technology Product Planning." *Harvard Business Review* 53: 108–115 (January–February 1975).
12. McGuire, E. Patrick. *Evaluating New-Product Proposals.* New York: The Conference Board, 1973.
13. Lazo, Hector. "Finding a Key to Success in New Product Failures." *Industrial Marketing:* 74–77 (November 1964).
14. "20% of New Products Fail, Study Reveals." *Advertising Age* 4 (June 21, 1971).
15. "Why New Products Fail." *The Conference Board Record,* 1964.
16. Bogarty, Herman. "Development of New Consumer Products—Ways to Improve Your Chances of Success." *Research Management* 17: 26–30, July 1974.
17. Cooper, Robert G. *Winning the New Product Game.* Montreal: McGill University, 1976.
18. Hlavacek, James D. "Toward More Successful Venture Management." *Journal of Marketing* 38: 56–60, October 1974.
19. *Market Testing Consumer Products.* New York: The Conference Board, 1967.
20. Napier, J. P. "How to Reduce the Cost of 'Point-of-View' Errors." *The Nielsen Researcher* 2–6, November 1957, quoted in Thomas L. Berg, *Mismarketing.* New York: Anchor Books, 1971.
21. Angelus, Theodore L. "Why Most New Products Fail." *Advertising Age* 85–86, March 24, 1969.
22. Konopa, L. J. "New Products: Assessing Commerical Potential," *Management Bulletin* 88. New York: American Management Association, 1966. Cited in Cooper [17].
23. Davidson, J. Hugh. "Why Most New Consumer Brands Fail." *Harvard Business Review* 54: 119, March–April 1976.

24. Lemont, Fred L. "New Products: How They Differ; Why They Fail; How to Help Them Do Better." *Advertising Age:* 43–45, April 5, 1971.
25. Tull, Donald S. "Relationships of Actual and Predicted Sales and Profits in New-Product Introductions." *Journal of Business* 40: 233–50 July 1967.
26. Weiss, E. B. "Slash New Product Costs With Conceptual Testing." *Advertising Age* 76+ February 3, 1969.
27. Crawford, C. Merle. "Marketing Research and the New Product Failure Rate." *Journal of Marketing* 41: 51–61, April 1977.
28. Janis, Irvin L. "Groupthink." *Psychology Today* 43–46+ November 1971.
29. Bennett, K. W. "Reducing New Product Mortalities." *Iron Age* 202: 48–49 December 19, 1968.
30. Allison, Graham T. *Essence of Decision.* Boston: Little, Brown, 1971.
31. Simon, Herbert. *Models of Man,* New York: John Wiley, 1957.
32. Hlavacek, James D., and Thompson, Victor A. "Bureaucracy and New Product Innovation." *Academy of Management Journal* 16: 361–372, September 1973.
33. Grayson, C. J. Jr. "Management Science and Business Practice." *Harvard Business Review* 51: 41–48 July–August 1973.
34. Chambers, John C., Mullick, Satinder, K., and Goodman, David A. "Catalytic Agent for Effective Planning." *Harvard Business Review* 49: 110–119 January–February 1971.
35. Howard, Nigel. *Paradoxes of Rationality.* Cambridge, Mass.: M.I.T. Press, 1971.
36. Nash, J. F. "Two-Person Cooperative Games." *Econometrica* 21: 128–142, 1953.
37. Radford, K. J. *Managerial Decision Making.* Reston, Va.: Reston Publishing Co., 1975.
38. Montgomery, David B., and Urban, Glen L. *Management Science in Marketing.* Englewood Cliffs, N.J.: Prentice-Hall, 1969.
39. Silk, Alvin J., and Urban, Glen L. "Pre-Test Market Evaluation of New Packaged Goods: A Model and Management Methodology." *Journal of Marketing Research* 15: 171–191 May 1978.
40. Kline, Charles H. "The Strategy of Product Policy." *Harvard Business Review* 33: 91–100 July–August 1955.
41. Johnson, Samuel C., and Jones, Conrad. "How to Organize For New Products." *Harvard Business Review* 35: 49–62 May–June 1957.
42. Corey, E. Raymond. "Key Options in Market Selection and Product Planning." *Harvard Business Review* 53: 119–28 September–October 1975.
43. Crawford, C. Merle. "Strategies For New Product Development." *Business Horizons* 15: 49–58 December 1972.
44. Wrapp, H. Edward. "Good Managers Don't Make Policy Decisions." *Harvard Business Review* 45: 91–99 September–October 1967.
45. Levitt, Theodore. "Marketing Myopia." *Harvard Business Review:* 45–56, July–August 1960.
46. Christian, Richard S. "A Check List for New Industrial Products." *Journal of Marketing* 24: 70–73 July 1959.
47. Freimer, Marshall, and Simon, Leonard S. "The Evaluation of Potential New Product Alternatives." *Management Science* 13: 279–292 February 1967.
48. Hart, A. "A Chart for Evaluating Product Research and Development Projects." *Operational Research Quarterly* 17: 347–358 December 1966.
49. O'Meara, John T., Jr. "Selecting Profitable Products." *Harvard Business Review* 39: 83–59 January–February 1961.
50. Pessemier, Edgar A. *Product Management: Strategy and Organization.* Santa Barbara, Calif.: Wiley/Hamilton, 1977.
51. Williams, D. J. "A Study of a Decision Model for R & D Project Selection." *Operational Research Quarterly* 20: 361–373 September 1969.
52. Locander, William B., and Scamell, Richard W. "Screening New Product Ideas—A Two-Phase Approach." *Research Management* 19: 14–18, March 1976.

53. Richman, Barry M. "A Rating Scale for Product Innovations." *Business Horizons* 5: 37–44 Summer 1962.
54. "Modern Packaging Machinery Corporation." Boston: Intercollegiate Case Clearing House, 1962.
55. Alderson, Wroe, and Green, Paul E. *Planning and Problem Solving in in Marketing.* Homewood, Ill.: Richard D. Irwin, 1964.
56. Shocker, Allan D., Gensch, Dennis, and Simon, Leonard S. "Toward the Improvement of New Product Search and Screening." *Proceedings,* pp. 168–175. Fall Conference, American Marketing Association, 1969.
57. Freimer, Marshall, and Simon, Leonard S. "Screening New Product Ideas." *Proceedings,* pp. 99–104. Fall Conference, American Marketing Association, 1968.
58. Larréché, Jean-Claude, and Montgomery, David B. "A Framework for the Comparison of Marketing Models: A Delphi Study." *Journal of Marketing Research* 14: 487–498 November 1977.

A THEORY OF SHORT-RUN RESPONSE TO ADVERTISING

Otto Ottesen

I. INTRODUCTION

This article deals with advertising effect and decision making. In Section II we[1] (1) propose a *theory of the individual purchase response function,* i.e., the relationship between an individual's purchase of a brand in a planning period and the number of times he is exposed to a given ad in the period,[2] dealing in particular with the *shape* of the function (see Figure 1). (2) On the basis of this theory, *a statement is made regarding in particular the shape of the short-run relationship between advertising effort[3] and sales volume or value[4] on a media and market level.* Our conclusion is that as advertising effort is being increased, *returns in sales* must generally be expected to diminish: the advertising sales function is degressive!

In Section III we discuss *some extensions and practical implications of the theory.* During the time that has lapsed since the theory was originally stated in 1973, it has, in fact, had some impact upon practical thinking and decision

Research in Marketing, Volume 4, pages 181–222
Copyright © 1981 by JAI Press Inc.
All rights of reproduction in any form reserved.
ISBN: 0–89232–169–5

Figure 1.   The Individual Purchase Response Function: Some Examples.

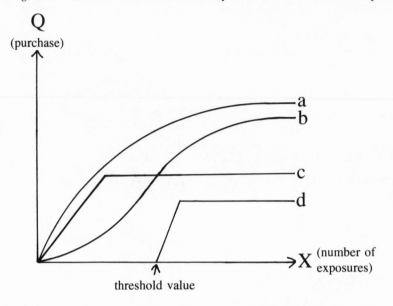

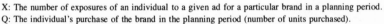

X: The number of exposures of an individual to a given ad for a particular brand in a planning period.
Q: The individual's purchase of the brand in the planning period (number of units purchased).

making.[5] In particular we deal with the question of *how the theory may be used as a basis for defining meaningful communication segments (target groups) and for adapting advertising decisions to the various stages of development of a brand in a market.* In addition, we touch upon subjects such as *repetition and concentration in media planning* and upon the problem of timing, i.e., of allocating the advertising effort over time in a planning period.

The managerial and societal relevance of the main characteristics of the individual purchase response function and advertising sales function is evident. For example, the shape has implications for decisions regarding how much to spend on advertising, and for media selection, repetition and timing. Nevertheless, at the time when our theory was first proposed in 1973 practically no *theoretical* research had been done on the shape and other main characteristics of these functions. In advertising and marketing literature, as well as among advertising practitioners, it had for years been a fairly deep-rooted *supposition* that the advertising sales function is S-shaped—an assumption implying an individual response function with an S-shape or with a threshold value of some kind. (See Figure 2 and the curves b and d in Figure 1.) For example, Rao [30] typically had assumed the S-curve to describe the typical advertising-sales relationship (p. 17, Figure 3.1.) as had Boyd and Massy [6], writing with reference to their Figure 2,

Figure 2.   An S-shaped Advertising Sales Function.

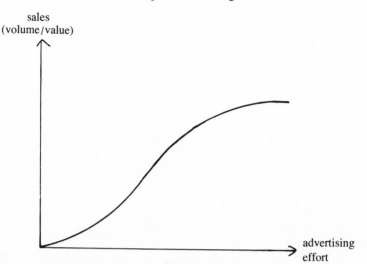

Sales: Sales value or volume, i.e., number of units of a brand sold in a planning period.
Advertising effort, e.g., number of insertions of an ad in a medium/group of media or size of advertising budget.

"A hypothetical relationship between advertising and sales": "The graph implies that increases in the advertising budget will increase sales only a little so long as the budget is small but that further increases will produce much better returns until some ultimate saturation level is reached" (p. 17). However, theoretical arguments for the S-shape hypothesis had either been lacking in the literature or had taken the form of references to micro-economic literature or to opinions of practitioners. Dealing with the shape of "the advertising demand function," Kotler [16] had cited from Dean's *Managerial Economics* [9]. As to the practitioner's belief in the S-shape, this could be seen as embedded in a slogan like "Keeping everlastingly at it leads to success," once championed by one of the major American agencies, or in advertising planning "proverbs" like the following, popular among Scandinavian practitioners during the 1950's and 1960's: "Concentrate, dominate—and repeat!"

To be true, the S-shape assumption had not been completely dominant. First, it had been challenged directly by Simon [36, 37] on the basis of results from empirical studies bearing on the subject, pointing, in his view, in the direction of a degressive type of relationship. Furthermore, the question of the shape had been touched upon in a series of articles appearing in the British journal *AdMap* during 1967-1969, e.g., Carpenter [8], Marc [24], Adams and Twymann [2], Fischer et al. [13] and Lawrence [19]. These articles had, in part, been initiated by a paper on response functions in media planning by Broadbent and Segnit [7].

Working on the basis of available empirical data, these writers had dealt with
several conceivable shapes, and had stated that "We are free to conclude from
the examination of the data . . . that thresholds, a low effectiveness at a small
number of insertions and the rest of it are rarely if ever supported by evidence.
S-shaped functions may well exist, but if so let the data be produced" (p. 51) and
that ". . . we consider a convex (i.e., degressive) response function is indicated
by such data as are available" (p. 55). In the United States, Kotler [16], among
other writers, had considered two distinct shapes—the S- and the concave (i.e.,
degressive) shape (p. 31). However, the existing discussions and challenges had
all been based on references to results of empirical studies, including a large
amount of mail order data (see, e.g., Ornstien [25].

In short, the main characteristics of the situation in 1973 were (1) that the
S-shape assumption prevailed in literature and practice; (2) that no serious attempts had been made in order to develop theories regarding the shape and other
main characteristics of the individual response function and/or advertising sales
function; and (3) that the available empirical evidence did *not* seem to support
the S-shape hypothesis.

The present situation does not differ much. In the last five or six years more
empirical studies bearing on the subject have been made. Simon and Arndt [38]
have reviewed the available data, concluding that, taken together, the studies
using physical (i.e., exposure, number of insertions of an ad or the like) and
momentary variables add up to the very strong conclusion that there are no
increasing returns to advertising, that is, no S-shaped response function. However, serious attempts at theory building are still lacking and the S-shape assumption does not seem to have lost (much) ground. Rao [31], for example, assumes
that the advertising response function is S-shaped (Figure 1, p. 9). Aaker and
Myers [1] seemingly regard the S-shape as typical of the advertising sales function (pp. 52–54, Figure 3–1), although the question of the shape is, upon reference to among others, Simon [36, 37] in principle left more or less open. The
authors conclude: "Of course, there is no definite word that would hold for all
products in all situations. The truth must include a qualified 'it depends'" (p.
54).

When it comes to theoretical justifications, references are still typically made,
e.g., to micro-economic literature or opinions of practitioners. Dealing with the
S-shape hypothesis, Kotler [16, p. 352] cites Dean [9]. Aaker and Myers [1],
referring to Longman [22, p. 232], writes:

> Some justification, however, can be presented for the S-shaped curve. . . . Longman, an
> agency executive, states that advertising professionals generally believe that 1) there is always
> some sales return for additional advertising investment, but that the rate of return will decline
> as more money is spent; 2) no amount of advertising investment could push sales above some
> limit imposed by the culture and competitive environment; 3) there are threshold levels of
> advertising such that expenditures below the threshold have no effect on sales; and 4) some
> sales will be made even with no advertising investment (p. 53).

Given this state of affairs, the following discussion may be of interest. It should be considered as an attempt to take a step on the road toward the development of a body of theory regarding a subject of practical importance.[6] Our ideas on the following are definitely incompatible with the S-shape assumption.

Before continuing, we would like to point out that for simplicity we will assume that a brand is being marketed in one single variant, e.g., concerning quality and packing. Also we will frequently exemplify by consumer advertising in print media, such as newspapers and magazines.

II. THE ADVERTISING SALES FUNCTION

A. Individual Response Function. Buyer Behavior

First, the content of the concept "response function" and the underlying assumptions of this function should be discussed more fully. As stated earlier, the dependent variable, Q, represents an individual's purchase and the independent variable, X, the number of exposures of the individual in a given planning period (see Figure 1). Especially, X should be defined more exactly.

"Exposures" should be interpreted as exposures independent of each other. For example, an individual who *looks for* an ad he has seen before, may be exposed, say, twice. However, as the second exposure is a function of the preceding one, only the first one "counts." X, then, stands for exposures of an individual produced by other factors than reading in or looking through a newspaper or a magazine with the purpose of finding an ad seen previously.

Also, there is a problem with the time dimension. One possible solution would be to say that everything happens simultaneously in the planning period. We find, however, that an assumption of this kind would be just too unrealistic. Instead, we will assume that the exposures are "evenly distributed from the beginning in the planning period," i.e., the first few exposures take place at the beginning of the period, the next few exposures in the middle of the period, and those that follow at the end of the period, etc.

Secondly, the model of consumer behavior underlying our theory should be outlined. The model is illustrated in Figure 3. The content of its concept may be indicated as follows:

Stimuli (S) are external influences that can "excite" one or more of the sense organs of the individual. The individual is exposed to a stimulus when at least one sense organ is being "excited" by the stimulus. Normally, only a part of a stimulus or a set of stimuli to which an individual is exposed "gets through" the sense organ(s), i.e., the individual will become aware of only some of the stimuli that he can perceive.

The organism variables (O) include all types of inner characteristics of the individual, characteristics which can be indicated by words such as "motives," "attitudes," "images," "expectations," "plans," and "intelligence." (R) stands for *behavior* (reaction).

Figure 3.   The Variables of the Reference Model in Greater Detail.

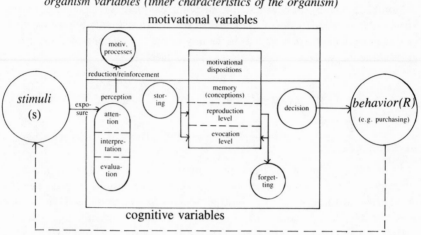

(O)
organism variables (inner characteristics of the organism)

1. *Stimuli* (S): External influences that can excite an individual's sense organs (sight, hearing, taste, smell or touch). For instance, products and communication messages.
2. *Behavior* (R): For instance: The purchase of a brand and information seeking.
3. *Exposure:* The fact that a stimulus excites a sensory organ.
4. *Inner characteristics* (0): Characteristics of the individual's organism. There are two main groups: 1) Motivational, and 2) cognitive variables.

The *main hypothesis* of this model is that behavior (R) is a function of stimuli (S) and inner characteristics (O)[7]:

$$R = R (S, O)$$

Also, a given inner variable, Ō, is assumed to be a function of both O- and S-variables:

$$\bar{O} = \bar{O} (S, O)$$

For example, a change in an individual's conceptions of his social and physical environment (Ō) is assumed to depend on for example what he reads (S) as well as his initial ideas about "the world" (O).

Organism variables may be changed by sensory processes. The arrow outside "the box" in Figure 3 indicates an important, dynamic aspect: That a behavior produced by one set of stimuli generally leads to exposure to new sets of stimuli possibly influencing behavior, and so on.

The motivational processes can be characterized as states of tension or imbalance which the individual will seek to neutralize through, among other things, exposing himself to stimuli expected to be relevant for this purpose. The processes are assumed to be functions of both inner physiological variables and stimuli. Stimuli, then, can neutralize as well as create tensions, which may be described by words such as "need," "fear," "dislike," and "hunger." Neutralization, when it occurs, is accompanied by positive feelings such as satiety, pleasure, a feeling of safety and contentment. A stimulus can either be directly (non)satisfying (e.g., a brand) or serve as a means to obtain (avoid) a directly (non)satisfying stimulus *(e.g., an ad containing information about a brand).*

The cognitive variables describe the intellectual apparatus, a main function of which is to "regulate" the behavior of the individual toward satisfaction of motives. We will be working with three main categories of cognitive variables, i.e., perception, memory and decision:

a. Perception This includes attention to, interpretation and evaluation of stimuli: i.e.:

Attention (awareness): The concentration of one or more senses on a stimulus or set of stimuli, e.g., on one or more elements in an ad.

Interpretation: A process by which it is "decided" what one or more stimuli, which the individual is attentive to, represent (e.g., the meaning of a sentence in an ad). It is assumed that interpretation normally is connected with uncertainty as to 1) what a stimulus may alternatively be conceived to represent or be, and 2) the probability of either of these alternatives being the truth.

Evaluation: The interpretation of a stimulus is followed by an evaluation concerning its believability and relevance. This variable is assumed to run from negative to positive values. Negative evaluation of an ad, then, is tantamount to the fact that the individual does not consider its content, as interpreted by him, a) instrumental in relation to the solution of a problem, i.e., satisfaction of one or more motives, and/or b) sufficiently believable.

b. Memory In memory the individual stores conceptions or impressions of his social and physical environments, events, etc. What a memory contains is partly a function of attention to and interpretations and evaluations of, stimuli. Also, memory is influenced by oblivion: Impressions fade and slide "down" on a level where they can no longer be recalled spontaneously, i.e., from the "reproduction level" to the "evocation level," or are forgotten completely.

c. Decision A decision is a process by which the individual chooses between two or more alternatives, e.g., between different brands or between purchasing and further information seeking. In short, the consumer acts as a *problem-solving individual.* Basically, he is striving toward maximization of motive satisfaction within given limits as to the amount of money, time and energy available. His

main problem is normally under conditions of great uncertainty to choose between alternative behaviors, possibly leading to motive satisfaction. According
to our model all necessary behavioral energy stems from motivation in the sense
that neutralization of tensions is the *fundamental* problem of the individual:
Without motivation, no behavior. A basic function of the cognitive apparatus is
to "regulate" or direct behavior through attention to, interpretation and evaluation of, stimuli, storage of impressions, etc. In addition, motivational processes
are to a large extent initiated and stimulated by stimuli "mediated through" the
cognitive apparatus.

We do not assume that the individual, *ex ante,* behaves rationally. Choices are
more often than not made on the basis of incomplete or/and unrealistic conceptions of the environment, a lack of ability to deal with a complex and dynamic
reality, and to a large extent on sheer routines. What is supposed is a tendency in
a specific situation to choose the alternative which seems or has earlier been
learned to be considered as the most favorable to the solution of the relevant
problem(s), i.e., the satisfaction of the relevant motive(s). The model also assumes that all processes in the individual can take place on different levels of
consciousness.

Our reference model is—as regards theoretical perspective—by no means
incompatible with frameworks suggested by Howard and Sheth [14] and Engel et
al. [11]. However, there are differences, stemming among other things from the
fact that frameworks such as the above-mentioned have been made for other and
more far-reaching purposes than ours, for example in order "to provide a theoretical structure that, in addition to serving the usual functions of a theory, focuses
the findings in behavioral science on issues of public and private practice, thus
building 'pathways' along which the buyer behavior specialist can 'find his way'
to the body of knowledge of basic science and the basic scientist can approach the
problems of buyer behavior" [Howard and Sheth [14, p. vii]. One might say that
the reference model above—exposing certain concepts and relations—has been
"tailor-made" for our specific purpose.

Through the above discussion we have given a rough outline of the reference
model and some basic concepts constituting our platform for formulating the
more specific hypotheses on which our theory will be based. However, before we
start on the theory-building, several important *assumptions underlying the response function should be stated more explicitly.*

a. One given ad for one given brand is considered.
b. The "stimulus situation" is given and the same for all media.
   The "stimulus situation" is defined as all stimuli in a medium (e.g.,
   editorial elements and ads) and in the environment (e.g., other people
   talking, an open TV set or radio) exposing the individual simultaneously
   with the considered ad.

c. The values of all decision variables such as the quality and price of the considered brand as well as other kinds of communication than the ad are given and remain fixed in the planning period. The same goes for decision variables of competitors, "nature" variables and the like.

d. The brand is accessible in most retail shops in the market.

e. An individual enters the planning period with a given set of inner characteristics. Relevant changes in these characteristics can, *in the course of the period, takes place only as a result of exposure to the ad currently being considered.* The physical and social environment that surrounds the individual is also given. Note that the concept *"individual characteristics"* covers 1) inner characteristics of the individual as well as 2) his physical and social environment, e.g., messages communicated by competitors, stimuli from nature, other people etc.

B. The Response Function for a Nondurable Brand

We will *attack the problem regarding the individual response function in two steps:*

(1) Frist we will discuss whether the response function can be assumed to start from the X-axis after

    a. a few exposures (low X-values),

    b. many exposures (high X-values) or whether

    c. all X-values are just as probable as the "starting point", i.e., the X-value where the purchase variable (Q) becomes positive.

Roughly: From where on the X-axis is the function likely to start?

(2) Thereafter the *"rest of the function,"* i.e., its further course, will be investigated.

Considering first the response function for a new, *nondurable* brand[8] we assume that a consumer's purchases of a nondurable product is evenly distributed from the beginning in the planning period, and that the purchased quantity is a constant. "Evenly distributed purchases" should be matched with "evenly distributed exposures."

The first step in our analysis concerns the problem of *how the response function "starts" from the X-axis.* Let us, for the present, focus on the first time an individual purchases a unit of a new brand, e.g., on the trial purchase. Certain conditions must be met for an exposure to an ad to cause a trial purchase:

1. The individual must have become aware of the ad. As a result of this, interpretation and evaluation processes must have taken place together with a decision to make a trial purchase.

2. The result of the perceptual processes and/or the decision to try the brand

must have been stored in memory sufficiently long for the trial purchase to be released, i.e., the individual must not forget the impression made by the ad or the resulting decision.

Accordingly, hypotheses concerning perception and memory msut be of relevance to our problem.

Figure 4 illustrates (and structures) the relevant *hypotheses concerning perception*. The model concerns the result of one exposure to an ad. An important characteristic of the model is that it distinguishes between initial and continued awareness. The concept ''initial awareness'' covers the initial change from exposure to concentration of the sense of sight on a stimulus in the ad, while ''continued awareness'' covers a possible concentration on further stimuli, i.e., continued reading of the ad. Perception, then, is a dynamic process; it starts with some specific stimulus and may stop after attention to, interpretation and evaluation of any number of stimuli. That is, the individual can read the whole ad or any part of the ad.

The hypotheses are:

1. Initial awareness is a function of (a) the concrete formulation of the ad (i.e., ''the stimulus structure'') and (b) of earlier experiences with the ad, i.e., impressions of the ad. Among other things, the familiarity of a stimulus influences the probability of initial awareness in a positive direction.

2. Continued awareness is determined by the individual's evaluation of the stimulus he has initially become aware of: Positive relevance evaluation produces continued awareness, while negative relevance evaluation ''breaks off'' attention. Furthermore: Relevance evaluation is a function of interpretation and thereby the conceptions the individual has about the meaning of words, figures, etc., i.e. the individual's ''alphabet.''

Relevance evaluation also depends on the individual's motivation, choice criteria (i.e., characteristics concerning product, price, service, etc., found salient by the individual), conceptions of other brands, possible impressions of the ad and a possible previous decision not to make a trial purchase (stored in memory). Positive relevance evaluation implies that the individual perceives a relation between brand and motives (solution of a problem), that he does not know of other brands which he evaluates as better, *that* the ad has not previously been rejected as irrelevant or *that* the individual has not previously made up his mind not to make a trial purchase.

Underlying these hypotheses is the basic assumption that awareness is selective and concentrates on stimuli relevant to the individual. Given these hypotheses, imagine an individual being exposed to the given ad one, two, three, four, etc., times. The ''alphabet,'' motivation, choice criteria, and conceptions of other brands are, according to our assumptions, given individual characteristics (see section IIA, last paragraphs). Conceptions of the ad and a decision of (not) making a trial purchase are part of the model both as individual characteris-

Figure 4. Hypotheses Concerning Perception.

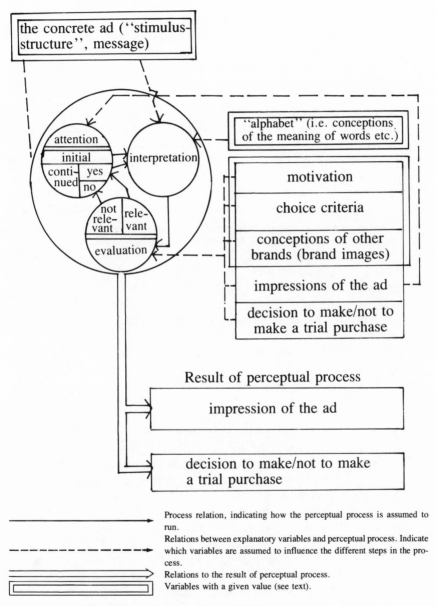

the concrete ad ("stimulus-structure", message)

attention
initial
conti-
nued
yes
no
interpretation
not rele-vant
rele-vant
evaluation

"alphabet" (i.e. conceptions of the meaning of words etc.)

motivation

choice criteria

conceptions of other brands (brand images)

impressions of the ad

decision to make/not to make a trial purchase

Result of perceptual process

impression of the ad

decision to make/not to make a trial purchase

Process relation, indicating how the perceptual process is assumed to run.

Relations between explanatory variables and perceptual process. Indicate which variables are assumed to influence the different steps in the process.

Relations to the result of perceptual process.

Variables with a given value (see text).

The model concerns one exposure to a given ad.

191

tics and as a possible result of an exposure. Obviously, impressions of the ad and of a decision of (not) making a trial purchase cannot exist previously to the first exposure.

As far as reaction to exposure is concerned, the alternatives are as follows:

1. The individual has characteristics implying that he does not become aware of the ad. Now, the characteristics are given, i.e., nothing happens to them in the planning period that can cause awareness as a result of a second, third, etc., exposure. Consequently, the individual has a response function which coincides with the X-axis, i.e., a *zero function*. He does not purchase the brand no matter how many times he is exposed to the ad. (See A in Figure 5.)

2. The individual has characteristics producing awareness as a consequence of the first exposure. (See B in Figure 5.) In this case the possibilities are:

a. The individual reacts to exposure with initial and possibly also continued awareness, but on account of negative evaluation of the ad or other causes the process does not result in a decision to make a trial purchase. According to our hypotheses, further exposures will result in initial, but not in continued awareness, due to the impressions the individual has of the ad stemming from the first exposure, together with the previous decision not to make a trial purchase. The individual's experience with the ad will, if anything, produce a "faster" rejection by a second, third, etc., exposure.

Consequently such an individual must have a *zero function* (see C_1 and C_2 in Figure 5).

b. The individual has characteristics causing initial and continued awareness. He evaluates the ad positively and makes a decision to make a trial purchase. (See D in Figure 5.) Further exposures also cause awareness, but these perceptions are only necessary for the trial purchase to take place in case the individual forgets the trial purchase decision and repeated perception of the ad is assumed to influence retention, i.e., the time the result of a perceptual process is stored in memory. This means that the answer to the question of how the response function "starts" from the X-axis also depends on memory. Relevant hypotheses concerning *memory* are:

1. Retention of an impression depends on its relevance: The more relevant it is considered by the individual, the longer the impression is retained.

2. Also, retention of an impression is a function of the number of perceptions of the actual stimulus/set of stimuli (i.e., repetition): The larger the number of repetitions, the longer the impression is stored. Furthermore, the effect of repetition is positively related to the degree of relevance.

3. Memory is also affected by the degree of difficulty, i.e., the degree to which the individual, when "dealing" with a stimulus or a set of stimuli, is in a position to make use of previous experience, i.e., the extent to which a communication message implies new kinds of actions, new combinations of and/or new relationships between "elements" in reality, contains new concepts, etc.

Figure 5. Possible Types of Response Functions for a Nondurable Brand. Outline of the Main Line of Reasoning.

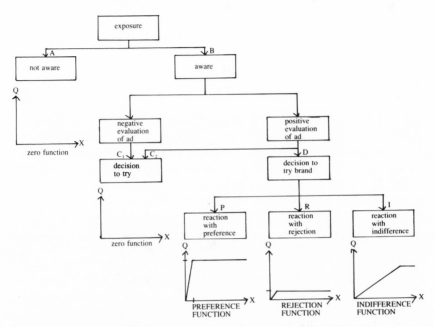

The figure illustrates the possible reactions of one individual. The reader should keep in mind the assumptions concerning individual characteristics, a given product quality and price, a given ad.

All response functions have been drawn under the assumption that the individual reacts with a trial purchase to the first exposure ($X = 1$). *One exposure* is considered a reasonable approximation to *one or few exposures.*

X: Number of exposures.
Q: Number of units of brand purchased.

For example, the degree of difficulty may have to do with the ''size'' of a stimulus or set of stimuli, e.g., the number of ''elements'' in an ad (for example how many facts it contains), as well as its ''structure'' (a highly structured ad may be perceived as less difficult).

4. There is a relationship between the degree of difficulty and the degree of relevance. That is, if an ad becomes ''too difficult,'' i.e., the individual does not understand (much of) it, the probability of continued awareness is assumed to be very small, regardless of the fact that the content might potentially be of relevance to the individual. Nò interpretation and evaluation cannot result in positive relevance evaluation. Consequently, the value of the variables, ''degree of relevance'' and ''degree of difficulty,'' is critical for the answer to our problem. Concerning the degree of difficulty, the following may be said on a pure common-sense basis:

As far as ads are concerned, the degree of difficulty will normally be low. In most cases, an individual will be in a position to make use of previous experience to a rather large extent: ads deal with "elements of reality" with which he is more or less familiar. For example: Most often does an ad "demand" behavior with which he is familiar, e.g., making a purchase of a specific product in a particular type of shops, or behavior of a kind more or less similar to one the individual knows, such as baking with cake mix instead of flour, butter, etc. Besides, in connection with the problem of exposure producing a trial purchase, it is clearly sufficient that the individual recalls the decision to try the brand and the brand name. There are, then, various ways in which the individual can simplify and concentrate on the most important features: It is not necessary for him to remember the whole of a communication message. Consequently the quantitative dimension of the degree of difficulty may be assumed to have a low value.

The degree of relevance must be high, the reason for this being that the individual in question, as a consequence of the perceptual processes following the first exposure to the ad, must have evaluated it positively and have decided to make a trial purchase, implying perception of a high degree of relevance. It follows, then, that:

1. The degree of relevance is high; the individual considers the ad relatively important, implying that the perceptual result of an exposure will be stored for a relatively long time in memory. Also, repetition will be relatively effective.

2. The degree of difficulty is low. The relationship between degree of difficulty and retention is negative.

All these hypotheses in combination point to the following conclusion: An individual who makes a trial purchase reacts after one or few exposures to an ad. Later, we shall elaborate on the concept "few exposures." The main point is that an individual with the characteristics producing reaction with a trial purchase, given that the message "gets through," logically also must have the characteristics necessary to get the message through, i.e., the characteristics that produce awareness, positive evaluation and sufficient retention without many repetitions. It follows from this that we reject the possibility of the response function "starting after" a large number of exposures, i.e., "from" a high X-value. Because this would, in fact, be tantamount to an incompatible combination of a low degree of retention, a low degree of difficulty and a high degree of relevance. Consequently, the answer to the question "from where on the X-axis may the response function be assumed to start" must be: *It starts after one or few exposures.*

Note that this conclusion does not contradict the rather well-known hypothesis that an individual, as a consequence of an increasing number of exposures to and perceptions of a set of stimuli (e.g., an ad text), will learn to reproduce an increasing part of it. Numerous laboratory experiments indicate that repetition has this effect. Learning, though, implies some kind of "motivation." In a typical experimental situation the researcher and the research design motivate the individual to expose himself to the stimulus set, perceive it and try to recall it. In a real exposure situation the effect of the ad itself is the important variable, since a negative evaluation at the first exposure will eliminate the "motivation" to learn from additional exposures.

If, on the other hand, the ad is evaluated positively, motivation is "supplied" and the effect of an exposure increased. Also, it does not follow from our conclusion that nondurable products and information about nondurable products generally are relevant or important to the individual. What we have hypothesized is that relevance is a necessary condition for reaction to exposure. A postulate saying that a high degree of relevance will normally hold good for only a relatively small proportion of the buyers implies that "target groups" are small and that the effect of advertising is "marginal."

Let us move on to the second problem: *The "rest" of the response function, i.e., its further course after a trial purchase has taken place.*

A trial purchase may have one of three different outcomes:

1. The individual reacts with *preference* for the brand, i.e., considers it better than other brands known to him.

2. The individual *rejects* the brand, i.e., considers its quality as poorer than that of other known brands.

3. The individual reacts with *indifference*, i.e., considers the brands quality equal to that of the best of other known brands. "Known brands" should be interpreted as brands on the reproduction level and brands which experiences in connection with the trial purchase may possibly "bring up" from the evocation level. (See "Memory" in Section II A.)

Preference for the brand implies that the individual has experienced something relevant, i.e., an improvement of motive satisfaction. The degree of difficulty can normally be assumed to be low in connection with the direct experience of a nondurable brand.[9] According to our hypotheses concerning retention, the "good" experience will therefore be stored and "kept" on the reproduction level, i.e., it is rather unlikely that the individual will forget that he has found a better brand. Consequently, additional exposures to the ad are not necessary for further purchases of the brand to take place, although at the same time the probability of initial awareness will be high or even growing on account of the increasing familiarity with the stimulus.[10] In fact, the "good" experience will induce the individual to choose the considered brand instead of others every time he purchases the product in the planning period. Consequently the response function "runs" from a small value on the X-axis directly "up" and "levels out" at a Q-value corresponding to the total quantity of the product that the individual buys and consumes during the planning period. In the following we shall call this quantity "the total quantity consumed." (See P in Figure 5.)

If the brand is *rejected*, this also is an event of relevance to the individual. He has, so to speak, experienced the poor quality of the brand "on his own body." Under these circumstances further exposures to the same ad which triggered the trial purchase will obviously not produce additional purchases. At any rate, it is sufficient that the negative "conclusion" is stored in memory on the evocation level: New perceptions of the brand will evoke the negative experience. Consequently, the response function of a rejecter "runs" from a small value on the X-axis directly up and "levels out" on a Q-level corresponding to the trial purchase quantity. (See R in Figure 5.)

The consequences of *indifference* for the effect of additional exposures to the ad is more problematic to trace. According to our hypotheses one can assume that the brand, i.e., the name and conceptions of it, will be quickly forgotten soon after the trial purchase: What the individual has experienced is neither something that can increase motive satisfaction nor something to be avoided. Now, in order to remain on the highest possible "known" level of satisfaction it is not necessary for the individual to store a whole range of equally favorable alternatives on the reproduction level: One brand is sufficient. The ad is, on the other hand, a familiar set of stimuli, i.e., the probability is high that further exposures will produce initial awareness. This awareness may, despite the low degree of relevance, be sufficient for "keeping" the brand name on the reproduction level in memory, provided that the ad is formulated so that the name of the brand becomes the object of the initial awareness. This means that additional exposures in case of indifference may have a *reminder effect,* in that continuous exposures to the ad will "keep" more brands that the individual considers to be of equal quality on the reproduction level. Together, these brands form a category of product units from which the individual chooses, so to say, at random, in the same way that he chooses among units of one specific brand.

An indifference-response function, then, must in part depend on the number of brands on the reproduction level. If, for example, the number of brands is two, i.e., if the individual chooses at random among product units of two brands A and B, then 50 percent of the total quantity consumed during the planning period will consist of units of brand A and 50 percent of units of brand B. Consequently, the "leveling out" value of Q in the response function for A will be 50 percent of the total quantity consumed. If four brands are stored on the reproduction level, the total quantity will be divided among these four. Thus, "the levling-out" value of Q falls with an increasing number of brands on the reproduction level. But then again, the number of brands on the reproduction level is, among other things, a function of the competitors' communication effort, an increase in which implies more brands on the reproduction level and therefore a smaller "leveling-out" value of Q.

The course of the response function up to the "leveling-out" value of Q must depend on the *purchase frequency.* The higher the individuals purchase frequency in the planning period, the more opportunities exist where exposure to the ad may produce a reminder effect. Also, the retention effect on an exposure is important. The greater this effect, the fewer exposures are necessary to maintain the brand on the reproduction level.[11] Consequently, the response function "runs" from the X-axis up to the "leveling-out" value of Q in a stepwise manner. Each reminder produces an effect, the size of which depends on the quantity bought per purchase, i.e., the total quantity consumed divided by the purchase frequency, the number of brands on the reproduction level and the retention effect of an exposure. The relevance of this last variable stems from the fact that in-between exposures may occur that are not necessary for the brand to "exist" on the reproduction level when a given purchase is made. If, however, the retention effect of an exposure is not substantial or/and if the purchase frequency is not very low, a linear function will be a reasonable approximation: The steps will be numerous and small. Accordingly, as far as a typical nondurable brand is concerned, we may conclude that the indifference response function "runs" linearly from a small value on the X-axis and "up to" a leveling-out" value of Q.[12] (See Figure 6 where two examples are explained. See also I in Figure 5.) This value depends, among other things, on the total quantity consumed of the considered product, and of the number of brands on the reproduction level.

We conclude, then, that the response function for a nondurable brand is a kind of step function, which after one or few exposures "runs" directly from the X-axis "up to" a "leveling out value" of Q. What "few exposures" should stand for depends on the weight one puts on the hypotheses concerning the importance of the degree of relevance for retention and for the effect of repetition combined with the fact that an individual having the characteristics producing a trial purchase, given that the message "comes through," logically also must ascribe a high degree of relevance to the ad. Our assumption will be that "one exposure" is a reasonable approximation to "one or few exposures." Accordingly, *with respect to a new nondurable brand there are four main types of response functions:*

1. Preference functions,
2. rejection functions, and
3. indifference functions, all of which "start" in origo—and
4. zero functions.

So far, we have dealt with a new brand. However, given that the quality of an established brand, its price and other relevant variables have had the same values in all planning periods during which the brand has existed, the market will be composed of the following categories of individuals:

1. Individuals that have earlier tried the brand and a) reacted with preference, b) rejection, or c) indifference. The individuals in the categories a and b must have zero functions in the considered period. Additional exposures to the ad will have no effect: Those who have earlier tried and rejected the brand will not buy as a consequence of new exposures. Those who prefer the brand will buy it anyway. Individuals in category c must have indifference functions.[13]

2. Individuals a) having earlier evaluated the ad negatively and having decided

OTTO OTTESEN

Figure 6.   The Indifference Response Function.

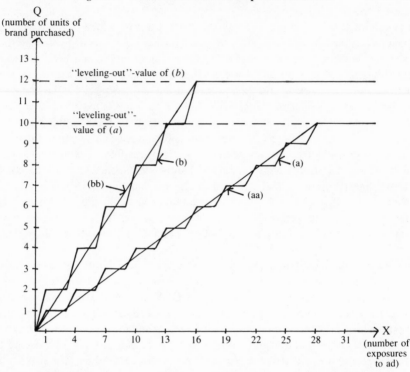

The two functions are called (a) and (b); (aa) = approximation to (a). (bb) = approximation to (b).
For both functions we assume that every third exposure is necessary for keeping the brand on the reproduction level.
Each step represents a quantity corresponding to the number of product units bought in three purchases divided by the number of brands on the reproduction level,

$$\frac{\dfrac{\text{total quantity consumed} \times 3}{\text{purchase frequency}}}{\text{Number of brands on repro-}\atop\text{duction level}}$$

i.e.

One step in function (a) represents one product unit, one step in function (b) two units. A two-unit step corresponds e.g. to a total quantity consumed of 24, a purchase frequency of 18 and two brands on the reproduction level. (a) has a somewhat lower "leveling-out" value than (b) and also reflects a higher purchase frequency.
X: Number of exposures.
Q: Number of units purchased.

not to make a trial purchase, and b) individuals having been exposed to the ad without becoming aware of it must have a zero function.

3. Individuals who have not been exposed to the ad before. For individuals of this category the brand is new. Consequently, all four kinds of response functions may occur. Hence, as far as our theory is concerned, it does not matter whether the brand is established or not, the only difference being that if the brand is not

Figure 7. Possible Types of Response Functions for a Durable Brand.

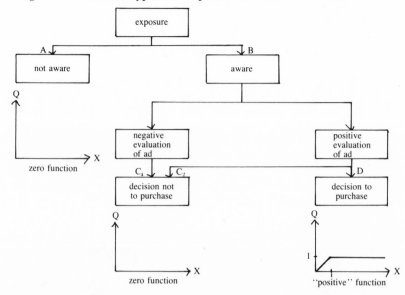

The reasoning behind this figure is analogous to that behind Figure 5. The difference stems from 1) the fact that the concept "trial purchase" has no meaning in connection with a durable brand, and 2) the fact that "the leveling-out" value of Q in a "positive" response function is equal to 1.

X: Number of exposures.   Q: Number of units purchased.

new, some individuals will have a zero function because they have tried the brand and reacted with rejection or preference.[14]

C. The Response Function for a Durable Brand

The reason why it is necessary to distinguish between durable and nondurable brands is an important difference between the two: A consumer will normally buy only one unit of a specific durable brand during a planning period, e.g., not two or three identical TV sets or refrigerators. Thus, when speaking of a durable brand,

1. the concept "trial purchase" is irrelevant, and

2. the "leveling-out-value" of Q in a response function can at maximum be 1.

Given these differences, a reasoning analogous to the one carried through in section B leads to the conclusion that there are *two possible kinds of response functions* (see Figure 7):

1. A function "running" from origo directly "up to" a leveling-out value" of Q equal to 1 for $X = 1$, i.e. a positive function.

2. A zero function.

Figure 8.   The Individual Purchase Response Function. Illustration of Two
Functions, A and B, with Different Speeds of Growth.

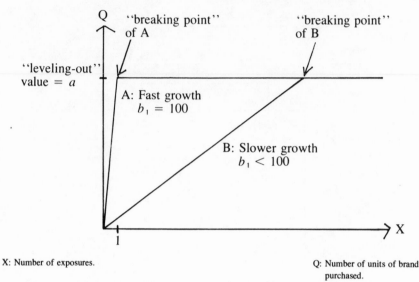

X: Number of exposures.

Q: Number of units of brand
purchased.

D. Conclusion

The Shape of the Advertising Sales Function

We may conclude as follows:

1. The individual purchase response function is a kind of "degressive-looking" step function, starting in origo in the form of a straight line, "breaking" and "leveling out" at a certain value of the purchase variable. The function is characterized by (see Figure 8):

a) A "leveling-out"-value. We will label it a.
b) A speed of (linear) growth "up to" the "leveling-out" value, which we choose to symbolize by a parameter b so that $0 \leq b \leq 100$, and $b = 100$ means that the function "breaks" at one exposure ($X = 1$).

2. For a nondurable brand and a durable brand, respectively, the following main types of response functions exist (see Figure 9):

A nondurable brand:
1. Preference functions,
2. rejection functions,

Figure 9. The Main Characteristics of the Different Types of Individual Response Functions

Functions	(A) "Breaking Point" O	(B) "Leveling-Out Value" (a) is	(C) Speed of Growth (b) is
A nondurable brand			
Preference functions	one exposure	equal to the total quantity consumed of product	large ($b = 100$) (See also [A].)
Rejection functions	one exposure	equal to trial purchase quantity	large ($b = 100$). (See also [A].)
Indifference functions	several exposures	a function of the total quantity consumed, the number of brands on the reproduction level, and, consequently, of competitors' communication effort	smaller, i.e., b is smaller and a function of a.o.t. the purchase frequency and the retention effect of an exposure
Zero functions			
A durable brand			
"Positive" functions	one exposure	equal to one ($=1$).	large ($b = 100$). (See also [A].)
Zero functions			

3. indifference functions, and
4. zero functions.
A durable brand:
1. "Positive functions", and
2. zero functions.

3. The main characteristics of the different categories of response functions are outlined in Figures 9 and 10.

Let:

a = "leveling-out" value,

X^* = the number of exposures (X-value) at which the function "breaks" and becomes horizontal, i.e., reaches a,

and

b = the growth rate.

A response function may then generally be written as

$$Q = \frac{a \times b}{100} X \text{ when X is smaller than or equal to } X^*$$

and

$Q = a$, when X is larger than X^*,

given that

$$b = \frac{100}{X} \text{ and } 0 \leq b \leq 100.$$

The value of a may in principle vary between 0 and infinite; b is defined so that its value indicates what percentage of a the individual buys as a consequence of the first exposure. For instance, if b is equal to 10, the effect of the first exposure will be a number of units purchased equal to

$\frac{a \times 10}{100} = \frac{a}{10}$. A b-value of 100, then, means that the function "runs up to" the "leveling-out" value, a, at the first exposure.

1. Hence, *for a durable brand*
   $X^* = 1$, $b = 100$, and $a = 1$ in a "positive" response function,

2. and *for a nondurable brand*
   $X^* = 1$ and $b = 100$ *in preference and rejection functions.*

In indifference functions X will be considerably larger than 1 and $0 < b < 100$.

Figure 10.   Review of the Possible Types of Response Functions and Their
Characteristics Regarding the Value of *a* and *b*.

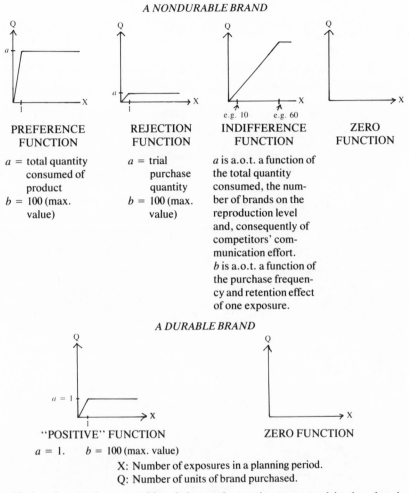

A NONDURABLE BRAND

PREFERENCE FUNCTION	REJECTION FUNCTION	INDIFFERENCE FUNCTION	ZERO FUNCTION
a = total quantity consumed of product b = 100 (max. value)	a = trial purchase quantity b = 100 (max. value)	a is a.o.t. a function of the total quantity consumed, the number of brands on the reproduction level and, consequently of competitors' communication effort. b is a.o.t. a function of the purchase frequency and retention effect of one exposure.	

A DURABLE BRAND

"POSITIVE" FUNCTION   ZERO FUNCTION

a = 1. b = 100 (max. value)

X: Number of exposures in a planning period.
Q: Number of units of brand purchased.

Notice that we have considered the total quantity consumed in the planning period as a constant. This assumption may be quite realistic in situations where *the product* to which the brand "belongs" is well established in the market, i.e., most individuals know about, have experience with it and know how to use it. This will normally be the case in practice. However, if the product is relatively new in the market, the total quantity consumed may be a function of the communication effort of the seller. In such a situation this effect must be considered when the "leveling-out"-value (*a*) of a response function is estimated.

The theory clearly implies that *the relationship between advertising effort and the number of units sold of a brand* is degressive, as there is no way in which an

S-shape can be generated from a degressive type of individual response. If advertising has any effect at all in a market, *sales volume increases with the advertising effort, but at a decreasing rate. Returns are diminishing.* As, in principle, sales value is equal to the product of the two factors "quantity sold" and "unit price," of which the latter must be regarded as a constant, this conclusion holds also for the advertising-dollar/kroner sales function. According to the theory, on a media level, for example, the relationship between advertising and sales volume has *two main characteristics,* as illustrated in Figure 11:

1) A "leveling-out"-value (see (B) in Figure 11).
2) A speed of growth (see (A) in Figure 11).

With respect to a nondurable brand, the "leveling-out" value is determined by the maximum number of individuals that can possibly be reached through the

Figure 11.   The Main Characteristics of the Advertising Sales Function.

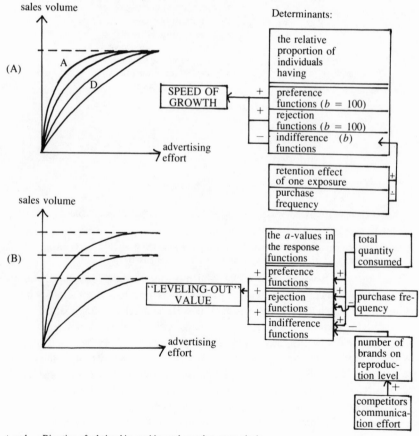

+ and −: Direction of relationship, positive and negative, respectively.

medium;[15] the a-values in the response functions; and the relative distribution of buyers with regard to the different values of a.

The speed of growth depends on the b-values in the indifference functions and the relative proportion of the buyers having preference, rejection and indifference functions, respectively.[16]

Hence, if the relative proportion of consumers with preference and/or rejection functions is large, the relationship will be extremely degressive, like the curve A in Figure 11 (A). On the other hand, if most of the relevant buyers have indifference functions and the b-values in these functions in addition are small, the first part of the relationship will be almost linear, like for instance the curve D in Figure 11 (A). The relationship for a durable brand will generally be extremely degressive, due to the fact that in all "positive" response functions the speed of growth is at maximum ($b = 100$).

Not only does the theory have implications regarding the shape of the advertising sales function "clashing" heavily with the popular notions of threshold values and S-shape, but for a nondurable brand it also provides some clues as to variables determining the main characteristics of the function, some of which, e.g., the total quantity consumed, the purchase frequency and the number of brands on the reproduction level, are easy to estimate. This may be of use in connection with interpretation of advertising-sales relationships in theoretical and empirical as well as practical advertising research. The clues are summarized in Figure 11.

III. EXTENSIONS AND IMPLICATIONS OF THE THEORY

A. Decision Rules of Thumb Connected with the S-shape Hypothesis

As will be apparent to anyone with insight into practical life, rules of thumb are important determinants of decisions. Considering the complexity of societies, markets and organizations, this is as it must be. However, the "soundness" of a rule of thumb may certainly vary. The origin of some rules are very difficult, if not impossible, to discover, while the basis of others is relatively easily traced, frequently in the form of a specific view of "a piece of the world," i.e., of how certain things are, interrelationships and functions. In fact, one basic assumption in such a "world view" may generate a whole cluster of rules of thumb, thus constituting a very important guideline for practical decision making. In our view the S-shape hypothesis is such a basic assumption, being widespread and deeply rooted in the world of advertising. Consider, for example, the following extremely influential rules, connected with the S-shape hypothesis and the notion of threshold values:

1. Advertising budgets should be large. A small budget is tantamount to waste.
2. In media planning one should aim at concentration and repetition, e.g., buy

a large number of insertions in a few media, those with the largest target group reach/cost ratio.

3. In spite of the considerable amount of discussion about segmentation, advertising people are still arguing about *the* message and defining *the* target group. The same pattern of thought is found in practical working manuals of advertising agencies and advertisers, describing the decision process. Here again, we clearly see the influence of the S-shape idea: In order to get the most out of one's effort, one should concentrate on a single target group and a single message.

Substitution of the S-shape hypothesis with a diminishing-returns hypothesis implies the *replacement of these well-established rules of thumb by new ones,* which are, in fact, pure reversals of the old ones:

1. Advertising budgets should not be too large. The first 1,000 kroner/dollars spent yields the highest per-krone/dollar returns in sales. Generally it is economically perfectly sound to operate with small and middle-sized budgets.

2. In media planning, one should usually go for dispersion, not concentration, and repetition should be moderate. The media plan should contain a wide range of media, e.g., also the second, third, etc., largest magazine or newspaper in an area. According to our theory, concentration and repetition will, within limits, be relevant only in situations where most of the consumers have indifference functions (possibly also with small b-values).

3. It should become a habit to talk about target groups (or segments) and messages: "What are our target group*s*? What are our message*s*?" Individuals differ. As each conceivable segment and message will show up diminishing returns, a decision maker will, more often than not, be better off to start thinking in plural.

Thus, the presented theory of the purchase response function has *some* clear-cut implications for the practical decision maker, whether he operates on a market, media or individual level. In fact, the theory explicitly points to *a way of segmenting the relevant buyers into meaningful subgroups.* This is illustrated in Figure 12. As regards a durable brand, the figure speaks for itself. As far as a nondurable brand is concerned, it shows a two-step process. First, the potential buyers in the market are structured into four main categories according to type of response function. Second, the individuals in each main category are divided into segments corresponding to expected "leveling-out" values (a-values) and speed of growth (b-values). The answer to the question of how many segments one should work with depends largely on the important criterion: How inaccurate can one be and still make a good decision? In our experience, more often than not, one need not to be too precise.[17]

A meaningful segmentation of a market is always difficult to carry through. We would, however, underline the fact that there are several ways in which the described segmentation process may be supported by practical advertising research. For a nondurable brand, knowledge of relatively easily measured var-

Figure 12. Outline of the Segmentation Process.

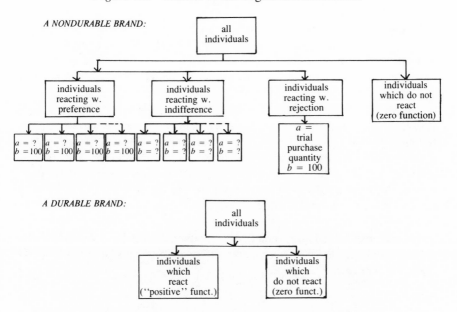

Step 1: Structure the consumers into four main categories according to type of response.
Step 2: Divide the individuals in each main category into segments according to a- and b-values.

iables like total quantity consumed in the planning period, purchase frequency and number of brands on the reproduction level may form a basis for making practically sufficient estimates of the parameters a and b. Also, a product test like research, or even controlled experiments (test marketing), may yield clues as to the distribution of consumers on main response categories. With regard to the frequently discussed question of "getting away from the usual economic-demographic" criteria in advertising planning, the described approach represents a practical possibility.

B. Dynamic Advertising Planning for a Nondurable Brand

The theory may also be used as a basis for "dynamic decision making," i.e., as a tool for making necessary adaptions of advertising strategy to the different stages of development of a nondurable brand in a market.[18] That such adaptions should be made is due to the fact that the market for a *new* brand differs in several important respects from that of an *established* one. Although this normative linkage between development stage and advertising decisions is obvious, it is often being ignored in practical advertising planning. An important reason is the widespread use of segmentation variables (i.e., consumer characteristics) which do not reflect changes in the "market situation" of a brand. This is true of the well-known and very heavily used economic-demographic variables such as income, age, education, and family life cycle. However, it also holds good with a number of variables of more recent origin, such as "life style" and "opinion leadership." A supplementation of the more traditionally used segmentation variables with some of the ideas embedded in our theory represents a practical possibility of a more dynamic, and thereby more realistic advertising planning.

Consider the "life" of a brand from the point in time when it is *new* to the point in time *well established* in the market. Let us assume that in the period of time considered, no salient exogeneously produced changes occur in the values of variables having to do with the quality, the price or the availability of the brand, competition, and characteristics of the consumers. The development of the "market situation" of a brand may then on the basis of the theory be modeled as visualized in Figure 13.

When a brand is new, the number of consumers knowing it is zero. Also, the market may be made up of any number of buyers belonging to any of the four main response categories: Reaction with

1. preference,
2. rejection,
3. indifference, or
4. no reaction.

For the sake of simplicity, let us label consumers belonging to the four categories P's, R's, I's and N's. As the brand penetrates the market, the number of individuals who know about it and have tried it increases. P's and R's reacting to communication will "move" into the N category, although P's will continue to buy. I's being exposed and reacting will, provided the brand is not being "overlearned," continue to have indifference functions. What goes on, then, is a process by which the market is being "drained" of P's and R's. When the brand has become well established, the market will consist exclusively of I's and N's. It goes almost without saying that the larger the advertising effort is for the brand, the sooner this stage will be reached.[19]

The main implications of this for decision making are rather obvious. In a new-brand situation, the purpose of advertising should be to produce brand awareness and trials. Any size and mix of response categories are conceivable, as are any budget size and different kinds of messages and media usage.

However, when the brand has become well established, the advertising problem is one of *reminding*. The message should concentrate on brand name and packing. As far as the budget is concerned, the critical variables to consider are the number and "quality"[20] of the I's in the market, and also the degree of overlearning the brand. Because the aggregate response of this consumer cate-

Figure 13.

(A): *Kind of response functions initially:*	*Developmental stage:* Brand is
	new · · · · · · · · · · · well established

indifference
functions

preference or
rejection
functions

zero functions

Buyers trying brand and reacting with indifference

Buyers with preference
or rejected
functions   (drainage)
                                    (drainage)
            (drainage)

Buyers with zero resp. function

(B):   TIME

	BRAND NEW	BRAND WELL ESTABLISHED
Main characteristics of market:		
Response functions:	Any number of buyers in any of the four response categories conceivable.	Buyers have either indifference or zero functions.
Brand awareness (proportion of buyers knowing of brand):	Zero or low	High
Brand trial proportion of buyers having tried brand,	Zero or small	Large
Advertising strategy:		
Purpose:	Produce brand awareness and trials.	Remind
Budget:	Any size conceivable.	Zero or of some size
Message(s):	Several different messages conceivable.	Concentrate on brand name and packing
Media usage:	Several different kinds conceivable.	In store media extremely relevant.

gory, will, up to a point, be fairly proportional, the problem will usually be one of deciding between a budget of *some* size and no effort at all. As regards media usage, in-store media will be of obvious relevance.

Several factors may, of course, interfere with the described process. Changes in the quality and/or the price of the brand may start the process anew. Exogenous forces may cause the number of buyers in the market to increase or decrease, or may produce changes in consumer characteristics or/and competition. Salient shifts in the values of this latter kind of variables are most likely to take place in early stages in the life cycle of a *product*. If it is well established, this being the normal situation for most products in a market, the pattern of a brand's development may be pretty much as described. Otherwise the process will have to be interpreted in light of current changes in the mentioned variables.

At this point it may be of interest to take a quick look at a practical tool, i.e., a combined planning and control device developed by the author a few years ago for the purpose of showing how some of the above reasoning may be put into practical use.[21] As can be seen from Figure 14, the Market Map, as it has come to be called, structures the market of a nondurable brand at a specific point in time into the following main buyer categories:

Buyers who:
1. do not know of the brand,
2. know of the brand, but have not tried it,

Figure 14.   The Market Map.

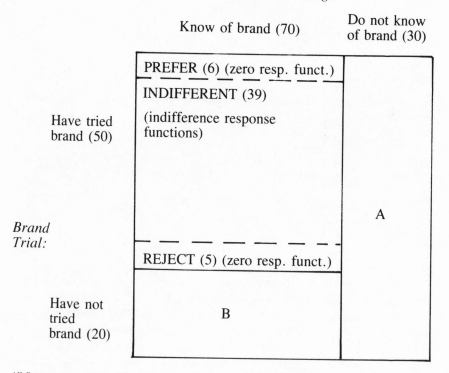

Brand Knowledge:

All figures are percentages of the total number of buyers of the product in question.

3. know of the brand, have tried it and
   a. prefer it,
   b. have rejected it, or
   c. are indifferent to it.

All figures are percentages of the total number of individuals actually buying the product in question.

The crude market "picture" provided by the map contains several "clues" of relevance to the decisionmaker. Firstly, the development stage of the brand is being indicated by the variables "brand knowledge (or awareness)" and "brand trial," i.e. by the relative size of the boxes A and B: The larger/smaller these are, the earlier/later the stage. This is further visualized in Figure 15, showing a "prototype" map for new and well-established brands. Secondly, on the basis of a given map one can calculate the following figures:

$$\text{A preference proportion figure} = \frac{\text{prop. preferring} \times 100}{\text{prop. having tried brand}}$$

$$\text{An indifference proportion figure} = \frac{\text{prop. having reacted with indiff.} \times 100}{\text{prop. having tried brand}}$$

$$\text{A rejection proportion figure} = \frac{\text{prop. having rejected brand} \times 100}{\text{prop. having tried brand}}$$

Figure 15. "Prototype" Market Maps, Typical for Three Different Developmental Stages of Brand

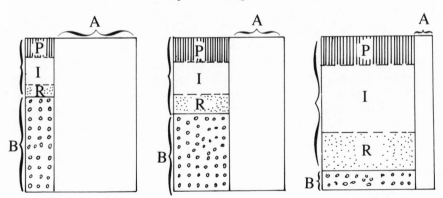

A: Do not know of brand.
B: Know of but have not tried brand.
C: Know of and have tried brand.
P: Prefers brand.
I: Indifferent toward brand.
R: Have rejected brand.

Using the data in Figure 14:

$$\text{Preference proportion figure} = \frac{6 \times 100}{50} = 12$$

$$\text{Indifference proportion figure} = \frac{39 \times 100}{50} = 78$$

$$\text{Rejection proportion figure} = \frac{5 \times 100}{50} = 10$$

Under the realistic assumption that a (nationally launched) brand enters and penetrates a market from "the easy end," these figures may give a decision maker some idea as to how consumers who do not yet know of and/or have not yet tried the brand are distributed with regard to main response categories. Referring to the proportion figures above, not more than 12 percent and 78 percent of the buyers who have not yet tried the brand may be expected to have preference functions and indifference functions. Most likely these proportions will even be considerably reduced among consumers who do not yet know the brand, especially at a late stage of development. On the other hand, the larger these figures are, the larger the expected return on advertising effort.

Thirdly, the Map reflects the proportion of buyers having zero and indifference functions as a result of trial purchases and reaction with preference/rejection (P and R in Figure 15) and indifference (I in Figure 15), respectively. By providing maps more or less continuously, e.g., every three, six or twelve months, a decision maker will be able to keep track of the development and potential of a brand and to adopt his decisions accordingly.

Superficially the Market Map may remind one of response hierarchy models like DAGMAR, DAGMAR MOD II, or CAPP (see Aaker and Myers [1, pp. 106–133]. Brand knowledge and trial are familiar variables and undoubtedly the Map contains a hierarchy notion, i.e., brand knowledge-trial-evaluation/ reaction. However, the Map's distinctiveness stems from the fact that it has been constructed and should be interpreted on the basis of a specific theory of the individual response function. At its core is the structuring of one's thinking around the theory's four main response categories of buyers, the consequent possibility of making estimates regarding past as well as future levels and types of response *and* the ensuing interpretations and implications as to decision making concerning budget size, messages and media usage. (See also Figure 13.)

Consider, for example, the following two statements, whose meaning rests solely on the underlying theory:

If a map indicates:
1. Brand new—brand awareness low—brand trial low—preference and indifference proportion figures low: Consider not to advertise.
2. Brand well established—brand awareness high—brand trial high—number of buyers having indifference response functions low: It may be better not to advertise.

Figure 16. The Market Map: Different Developmental Stages of a Brand, Exemplified by Maps for Six Different Brands.

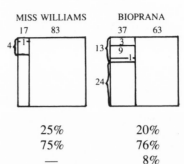

	MISS WILLIAMS	BIOPRANA
Preference proportion figure:	25%	20%
Indifference proportion figure:	75%	76%
Rejection proportion figure:	—	8%

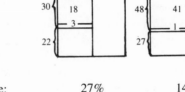

	PRANA	CORAL
Preference proportion figure:	27%	14%
Indifference proportion figure	63%	85%
Rejection proportion figure:	10%	2%

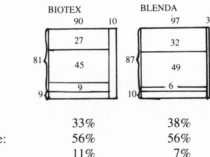

	BIOTEX	BLENDA
Preference proportion figure:	33%	38%
Indifference proportion figure:	56%	56%
Rejection proportion figure:	11%	7%

Empirically, the Market Map can be "filled in" easily on the basis of answers to a few simple questions which can be incorporated into an omnibus type of representative market analysis. Actually, practitioners in Denmark and Norway early became interested in the basic idea embedded in the Map. Some—and especially Kvaerk [17]—have been working on and continuously been doing experiments regarding the measurement of its variables. As a result of this work, several market research firms now offer Market Map data as part of their standard assortment. So, during the last few years the Map has been used to some extent by Danish as well as Norwegian advertisers and agencies.[22]

Figure 16 shows examples of factual Market Maps and proportion figures for six brands in different development stages. Further, Figure 17 shows how Market Map data, in connection with the definition of target groups, may advantageously be combined with traditional economic-demographic data. As appears from Figure 17, Map and proportion figures may vary considerably from one age group or type of population area to another. The same has been shown to hold good for audiences of different media.[23]

The experiences gained with the Market Map so far have resulted in the detection of problems as well as improvements concerning the question of how to measure the different buyer categories. Also, a number of refinements have been suggested.[24] Reports from decision makers indicate that the advantages connected with the Market Map way of looking at a market tend to grow with continued use. First, the angle generally seems to give one a good grasp of the basic market structure of a brand. Secondly, it is felt that one's thinking about budget size as well as messages and media usage tends to become more dynamic as one learns to interpret the Map. For instance, in a situation where a brand is well established with an unsatisfactory market share, one's line of thought "logically" will run toward a reduction of the advertising budget and/or a change in the quality and/or the price of the brand and *not* in to the more traditional and "static" solution: A larger effort in order to "crack" the market.

C. Two Important Assumptions and the Problem of Timing

Our reasoning regarding the individual purchase response function in Section II was based upon two important assumptions:

1. The individual characteristics[25] of the buyers do not change exogenously during the considered planning period as a consequence of developments in the social or/and physical environment.
2. Exposures of an individual are evenly distributed from the beginning in a planning period,[26] implying an analogous timing of advertising effort.

Certainly, only in some instances will these assumptions be sufficiently realistic. The purpose of this last section is to discuss what may be done in situations where they are considered unrealistic and to touch upon the question as to which market conditions offer sufficient realism. The discussion puts us in the position of making some rather crude statements regarding the problem of timing of an advertising effort within a planning period for a nondurable and a durable brand respectively.

In instances where the assumption about stable individual characteristics must be considered unrealistic, one possible way to tackle this problem is to divide the planning period into a number of shorter *subperiods,* so that sufficiently stable

Figure 17. The Market Map: Some Examples.

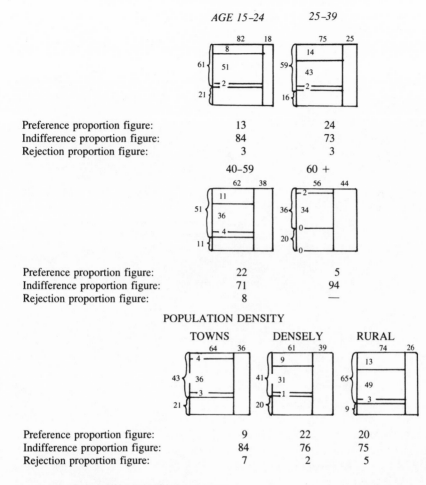

AGE 15–24   25–39

	15–24	25–39
Preference proportion figure:	13	24
Indifference proportion figure:	84	73
Rejection proportion figure:	3	3

40–59   60 +

	40–59	60 +
Preference proportion figure:	22	5
Indifference proportion figure:	71	94
Rejection proportion figure:	8	—

POPULATION DENSITY

TOWNS   DENSELY   RURAL

	TOWNS	DENSELY	RURAL
Preference proportion figure:	9	22	20
Indifference proportion figure:	84	76	75
Rejection proportion figure:	7	2	5

Brand: EVA LONGS (pantyhose)

individual characteristics may be expected within any of the subperiods. Accordingly, if the expected changes are large or/and frequent, the subperiods should be short, and vice versa. As shown in Figure 18 with a planning period divided into two subperiods, this procedure allows one to make adjustments regarding size and kind of buyer segments "between" subperiods and decisions regarding size of budgets, etc., with respect to each subperiod. The result of working with such a *multiperiod model* will be an advertising plan in which the timing of the effort is based not on an assumption, but on estimated changes in salient exogenous variables in the planning period.

Consider the *question of timing for a nondurable brand.* For the sake of

Figure 18.   The Principal Structure of a Multiperiod Model.

A planning period divided into
two sub-periods:

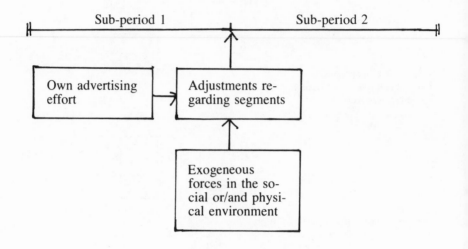

simplicity, let the problem be one of allocating a given budget. One important factor to take into account is, as emphasized above, changes in the number and characteristics of consumers produced by exogenous forces. A second relevant factor is the main response characteristics of the consumers. Other things being equal, it makes no difference *when* in a planning period a buyer with an indifference function or a rejection function is being exposed. On the other hand, the earlier a preference is created, the more a consumer will (be able to) buy of the brand. A large proportion of consumers with preference functions and/or high *a*-values in these functions implies that a relatively large part of the budget should be spent in early subperiods. Thus, there *are two main factors to consider:*

1) *The (possible) advantage connected with an early exposure of consumers with preference functions.*
2) *Exogenously produced changes in number and "quality" of buyers.*

As mentioned in Section III B, exogenously produced changes in the individual characteristics of the buyers are most likely to occur at early stages in the life of a product. According to one *product life-cycle model,* [27] three stages may be distinguished: The pioneer, the competitive, and the saturation stage. As indicated in Figure 19, the pioneer and competitive stages are both characterized by a high probability of large and frequent changes. At the pioneer stage, following intro-

Figure 19. Hypothesized Relationship Between Product Life Cycle Stage and Exogenous Changes in Characteristics of Buyers.

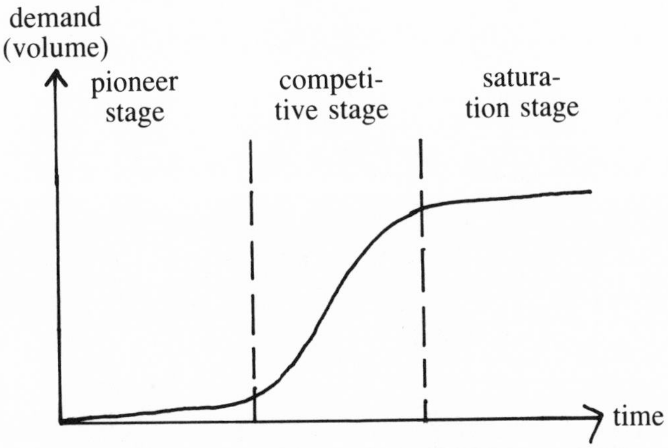

demand
(volume)

	pioneer stage	competitive stage	saturation stage
Exogeneous changes in number and characteristics of buyers probable?	YES: Increase in number of buyers and marketers. Normally increase in demand will outweight the effect of growing competition.	YES: Considerable growth in the number of buyers and competitors.	NO: No or small changes.
Is assumption about stable buyer characteristics sufficiently realistic?	NO: As a rule, consider working with a MULTIPERIOD model	NO: As a rule consider working with a MULTI-PERIOD model	YES

duction of the product, the number of marketers is at first small. Also, only a few pioneer consumers buy the product. However, the number of buyers is growing, due to an increasing social acceptance of the product, as is the number of sellers. At the competitive stage the number of buyers as well as demand increases rapidly and competition is hard, with frequent changes in marketing decision variables. On the other hand, the saturation stage is characterized by more

Figure 20. Timing the Advertising Effort for a Nondurable Brand in a Planning Period: An Example of How to Think about Timing.

Brand	Product on	
	PIONEER STAGE	SATURATION STAGE
NEW	A large number of buyers will have preference functions. Number and "quality" of buyers will be increasing. I.e.: The two main factors produce opposing forces. *Decision rule:* DISTRIBUTE ADVERTISING, EFFORT EVENLY (FROM BEGINNING OF PLANNING PERIOD) adv. effort / time / planning period	The number of buyers having preference functions is large. Number and quality of buyers will be stable. I.e.: The first factor dominates. *Decision rule:* A LARGER SHARE OF BUDGET SHOULD BE USED IN FIRST PART OF PLANNING PERIOD. adv. effort / time / planning period
WELL ESTAB-LISHED	The number of buyers having preference functions will be small. Number and "quality" of buyers will be increasing. I.e.: The second main factor dominates. *Decision rule:* A LARGER SHARE OF BUDGET SHOULD BE USED IN LATER PART OF PLANNING PERIOD. adv. effort / time / planning period	The number of buyers with preference functions is small. Most buyers with "positive" response functions have indifference functions. No or small changes in number and characteristics of buyers. I.e.: None of the two main factors of importance. *Decision rule:* DISTRIBUTE ADV. EFFORT EVENLY (FROM BEGINNING OF PLANNING PERIOD.) adv. effort / time / planning period

x) Relatively in relation to the total number of buyers of the product of any given point in time.
The two main factors referred to above are:
1. Advantage connected with producing a possible preference early in the planning period.
2. Exogenously produced changes in individual characteristics.
The figure should not be interpreted too literally, but is rather a demonstration of "how to think about timing" on the basis of the variables and relationships discussed.

stability regarding demand as well as competition. Consequently, if the product with which a decision maker is working is considered to be on the pioneer or competitive stage, our assumption about stable individual characteristics should probably not be accepted as realistic, i.e., decision making should be based on a multiperiod model. If, however, the product is regarded as being in the saturation stage, the assumption may most likely be accepted as sufficiently realistic. Due to the fact that most of the products existing at a given point in time will be at this stage, this will be the case more often than not. (See Figure 19.]

Returning to the question of timing: As shown in Section III B, the second important factor to consider, i.e., the main response characteristics of the buyers, is correlated with the degree to which a brand is established in the market. Consequently, some "prototype" situations may be constructed and some very crude statements made about timing by "cross-tabulating" the life cycle stages of a product with the development stages of a brand, as shown in Figure 20.

The figure speaks for itself. The only thing we would like to emphasize is that, in the kind of situation occurring rather frequently in practice, *product on saturation level and brand well established,* a distribution of the advertising effort in the planning period in accordance with our initial assumption: an *even distribution from the beginning of the planning period is recommended.* In this kind of situation, the market conditions are relatively stable and most relevant buyers have indifference response functions. Subsequently, there are no arguments for an *uneven* distribution. Indifference functions imply dispersion of exposures and, consequently, of reminder advertising.

Regarding the question of *timing for a durable brand,* the only really important fact to be emphasized here is that, typically, changes in individual characteristics will be large and frequent during a planning period of, for example, six or twelve months. Consumers motivated to buy a unit of the product continuously "pour" into the market, make a purchase and then "disappear" from the market for some period of time (years), the rate of this process changing and being dependent upon the time elapsed since the product was being introduced, the speed of introduction, the market "life time" of the product and seasonal forces. As a consequence:

1. The *assumption about stable individual characteristics during a planning period will never be realistic: A decision maker should always work with a multiperiod model!*
2. An even distribution of an advertising effort within a planning period will normally not be optimal. On the contrary, *some kind of uneven distribution*—following for instance a seasonal pattern—*is recommended.*

NOTES

1. That is, has the opportunity to see or/and hear.
2. As far as the definition of "short run" is concerned, we are considering a planning period of

say, one year, the "planning period" being the time period for which one makes advertising plans in a firm.

3. Advertising effort may be defined in different ways, e.g., "the number of insertions of an ad in a medium/group of media" or "the size of the advertising budget" (in advertising kroner (Danish currency)/dollars).

4. "Sales value" = "sales volume" times "unit price."

5. Section II of this article is a slightly adapted version of "The response function: A theory of the short-run effect of repetition of a marketing communication message, exemplified by advertising," in M. Berg et al. (eds.): *Current Theories in Scandinavian Mass Communication Research, Grenaa, Denmark, 1977. This paper is, in turn, a shortened version of chapter 6 in O. Ottesen, "Studier i virksomhedens mediabeslutninger,"* Copenhagen [27]. Section III is in part based on *chapters 9, 10, and 11 in O. Ottesen* [27] and chapters 5, 16, and 17 in O. Ottesen: *Innfoering i markedskommunikasjon,* Copenhagen and Oslo [28].

6. A growing interest in the subject is indicated by the so-called "Stanford Repetition Project" [34]. On the other hand, recent advertising research revies by Arndt [3] and Banks and Hart [4] do not deal with the subject at all.

7. Concerning the reference model and the specific behavioral hypotheses we are greatly indebted to, among others, authors like Madsen [23], Berelson and Steiner [5] and Wärneryd [40].

8. A nondurable brand is a brand that "belongs to" a nondurable product. A nondurable product has a "life time" in the market shorter than the planning period (e.g., beer). On the other hand, the "life time" of a durable product is longer than the planning period (e.g., cars).

9. Here the concept "degree of difficulty" relates to retention of the experiences with the brand.

10. In fact, we have here a possible explanation of a well-known phenomenon indicated, e.g., by Starch data, that actual users of a brand are the dominant group among readers of magazine ads.

11. We would like to remind the reader of two important assumptions implicitly underlying these deductions:

a) that the exposures are evenly distributed from the beginning in the planning period;
b) that the purchases a consumer makes of a nondurable product is evenly distributed from the outset of the planning period, and that the quantity purchased each time is the same.

12. After many exposures to the ad and/or purchases, a brand may be *overlearned,* i.e., become so well stored in an indifferent individual's memory that further exposures are *not* necessary in order to "keep" the brand name on the reproduction level. Our reasoning, though, concerns a new brand and a planning period of one year. Accordingly, we find it realistic to disregard the overlearning possibility. The consequence of overlearning may, however, easily be deduced: An individual who in one planning period has an indifference function may in the next have a zero function. Further exposures are not necessary for the brand to "stay" on the reproduction level in memory.

13. Provided the brand has not been overlearned.

14. Remember the assumption that the quality of the brand, its price, the ad, etc., are given and the same in all the planning periods considered. If the values of these variables change from one period to the next, the picture will be different. Individuals who have formerly rejected the brand may then, depending on the circumstances, react with preference or indifference, e.g., as a consequence of a price reduction. A new ad may get "new" individuals to try the brand. In short, the possibilities are not equally as "locked" as a consequence of the individual's former experiences with the brand. This follows from the fact that something new is offered, the message is new, etc. Notice, though, that variations in the values of such variables are unimportant to the conclusion regarding the possible types of response functions for a nondurable brand. (For further discussion, see Section III C.)

15. In the literature usually labeled "accumulated coverage" or "maximum reach" of a medium.

16. The speed of growth is also a function of, among other things, "loyalty" toward media (e.g., readership frequency in connection with newspapers and magazines).

17. Results of a sensitivity analysis by the author in testing the loss of profit due to incorrect

estimation of segments and the parameters a and b in response functions suggest that estimates precise enough for practical purposes can be made. (See Ottesen [27].)

18. The problems regarding "dynamic decision making" and timing have been addressed e.g. by Kennedy and Corkindale [15], Aaker and Myers [1], Kotler [16], Little [20], Sasieni [35], Ehrenberg [12], Strong [39], and Lodish [21].

19. Regarding overlearning, see footnote 12. Note that our reasoning may be relevant in connection with construction and/or interpretation of so-called carry-over effect models. Referring to the terminology of Kotler [16, Chapter 5], what we have said has to do with customer holdover effects. Thus, considering the effect in one period of an effort made in the preceding one, we 'ssume a retention rate of zero for R's, of 100 for P's and of zero or more for I's, depending u, arning. And, while a further effort made in the second period may neutralize a decay in s ω I's, i.e., reminder advertising, this is not the case as regards R's.

20. That is, the a - and b - values in the response functions.

21. See Kvaerk and O. Ottesen [18] and Kvaerk [17]. At present, Kvaerk's is the only existing paper dealing with the Market Map and its problems in English.

22. A Market Map for a brand may be bought at a very reasonable cost (1979), for less than Danish Kroner 15.000. Regarding measurement of the variables, see Kvaerk [17].

23. Figures 16 and 17 are adapted from Figures 14 and 17 in Kvaerk [17]. The data were collected in Norway in the mid-seventies.

24. The Market Map may be refined in many ways. For instance, buyers who react with preference or indifference may be grouped according to how many and which brands they know or have tried. Individuals who know the brand but have not yet tried may be described with regard to impression of brand, brand image or attitude. Regarding refinements, see Kvaerk [17].

25. See Section II A, third last paragraph.

26. See Section II A, third paragraph.

27. See Rasmussen [32].

REFERENCES

1. Aaker, D. A., and Myers, J. G. *Advertising management.* Englewood Cliffs, N.J., 1975.
2. Adams, J. R. and Twymann, W. A. "How Many Advertising Response Curves Are There?" *AdMap,* June 1968.
3. Arndt, J. "Research in Advertising. A State-of-the-Art Review." *European Journal of Marketing* 4, 1976.
4. Banks, S., and Hart, E. W. "Advertising and promotional methods." In R. Ferber (ed.): *Selected Aspects of Consumer Behavior.* Washington D.C., 1977.
5. Berelson, B., and Steiner, G. A. *Human Behavior.* New York, 1964.
6. Boyd, H. W., and Massy, W. F. *Marketing Management.* New York, 1972.
7. Broadbent, S. R., and Segnit, S. "Response Functions in Media Planning." In The Thomson Medals and Awards, London, 1967.
8. Carpenter, R. C. "Response functions. Problems and Limitations." *AdMap,* June 1967 and March 1968.
9. Dean, J. *Managerial Economics.* Englewood Cliffs, N.J., 1951.
10. Doyle, P., and Fenwick, I. "Advertising Tactics and Marketing Strategy." Market Research Society Conference, March 1975.
11. Engel, J. F. et al. *Consumer behavior.* New York, 1968.
12. Ehrenberg, A. S. C. "Repetitive Advertising and the Consumer." *Journal of Advertising Research,* April 1974.
13. Fischer, T. et al. "People Are Different." *AdMap,* January and February 1968.
14. Howard, J. A. and Sheth, J. A. *The Theory of Buyer Behavior.* New York, 1969.

15. Kennedy, S. H., and Corkindale, D. R. *Managing the Advertising Process*. Westmead (England), 1975.
16. Kotler, P. *Marketing Decisionmaking: A Model Building Approach*. New York, 1971.
17. Kvaerk, A. "The Market Map." The Association of Norwegian Magazine Publishers. Mimeograph, Oslo 1978.
18. Kvaerk, A., and Ottesen, O. "Segmentering og mediavalg for dagligvarer på basis av merkekjennskap, merkeerfaring og merkeinntrykk." *Markedsfoering* 1, 1973.
19. Lawrence, R. J. "Media Scheduling: The Case for a Return to Square One." *AdMap*, January 1969.
20. Little, J. D. C. "A Model for Adaptive Control of Promotional Spending." *Operations Research*, November 1966.
21. Lodish, L. M. "Empirical Studies of Individual Response Exposure Patterns." In H. L. Davis and J. J. Silk, *Behavioral and Management Science in Marketing*. New York, 1978.
22. Longman, K. A. *Advertising*. New York, 1971.
23. Madsen, K. B. *Moderne psykologiske teorier*. Copenhagen, 1960.
24. Marc, M. "Response Functions. Beware the Pitfalls." *AdMap*, March 1968.
25. Ornstien, E. J. *Mail Order Marketing*. London, 1970.
26. Otterlihy, C. "*Making Advertising Profitable for the Advertiser.*" AdMap, August 1976.
27. Ottesen, O. *Studier i virksomhedens mediabeslutninger*. Copenhagen, 1973.
28. _____. *Innfoering i markedskommunikasjon*. Copenhagen and Oslo, 1977.
29. Parsons, L. J. "The Product Life Cycle and Time-Varying Advertising Elasticities." *Journal of Marketing Research*, November 1975.
30. Rao, A. G. *Quantitative Theories in Advertising*. New York, 1970.
31. Rao, A. G., and Miller, P. B. "Advertising/Sales Response Functions." *Journal of Advertising Research*, April 1975.
32. Rasmussen, A. *Pristeori eller parameterteori*. Copenhagen, 1972.
33. Ray, M. L. "Frequency Effects Revisited". *Journal of Advertising Research*, February 1971.
34. _____. "The Present and Potential Linkages Between the Microtheoretical Notions of Behavioral Science and the Problems of Advertising." In H. L. Davis and A. J. Silk (eds.), *Behavioral and Management Science in Marketing*. New York, 1978.
35. Sasieni, M. W. "Optimal Advertising Expenditure." *Management Science*, December 1971.
36. Simon, J. L. "Are There Economies of Scale in Advertising?" *Journal of Advertising Research*, June 1965.
37. _____. "New Evidence for No Effect of Scale in Advertising." *Journal of Advertising Research*, March 1969.
38. Simon, J. L., and Arndt, J. "The Advertising Response Function and Economies of Scale: The New Evidence." Working paper, 1978.
39. Strong, E. C. "The Spacing and Timing of Advertising." *Journal of Advertising Research*, December 1977.
40. Wärneryd, K. E. *Ekonomisk psykologi*. Stockholm, 1967.

THEORIES OF EXPLORATORY BEHAVIOR:

REVIEW AND CONSUMER RESEARCH IMPLICATIONS

P. S. Raju

OVERVIEW

This paper reviews several major psychological theories of exploratory behavior and attempts to apply them in the consumer context. Exploratory behavior, in simple terms, refers to so-called "nonpurposeful" behavior(s) with no easily discernible motives. Examples of such behaviors are those relating to novelty seeking and variety seeking.

The paper first introduces the concept of exploratory behavior and outlines its significance for consumer research. The study of exploratory behavior could lead to a more complete understanding of consumer behavior, and also provide a more complete explanation of specific behaviors in the consumer context such as

Research in Marketing, Volume 4, pages 223-249
Copyright © 1981 by JAI Press Inc.
ISBN: 0-89232-169-5

information search, brand switching, and response to advertising. Several psychological theories of exploratory behavior are then reviewed. The focus is not as much on providing descriptions of the individual theories as on the comparison of the theories in terms of the concepts and relationships proposed. Based on this review, conceptual issues that are likely to be faced in consumer research on exploratory behavior are identified and briefly discussed. It is proposed that researchers in consumer behavior modify existing frameworks to make them more applicable to the consumer context or develop a new framework using the existing concepts and theories. Two specific applications of exploratory behavior in the consumer context are then briefly discussed. These applications relate to the areas of information search and preference for stimuli over repeated exposures. The last part of the paper is devoted to the development of a theoretical framework which is likely to be more useful for conducting consumer research on exploratory behavior. The major feature of this framework is the division of environmental stimulation into two components; a positive component called the "novelty component" and a negative component called the "conflict component." Preference functions are postulated with respect to each component, and it is suggested that the overall preference for a stimulus is determined by the joint action of the two preference functions. It is also shown that the new framework can account for the relationships proposed in the literature with respect to preference for stimuli and exploration. Inferences resulting from the new framework and its benefits over existing frameworks are also briefly discussed.

INTRODUCTION

The need to understand consumers' behavior with respect to novel, complex, surprising, unfamiliar, and other such ambiguous stimuli has recently been emphasized by several researchers (Howard and Sheth [22]; Hansen [18]; Venkatesan [36]). The fact that individuals' approach or avoidance behavior with respect to such stimuli often seems to have no easily discernible "rational" motives makes it a conceptually intriguing area. As a first step, the term "exploratory behavior" can be used to describe such behaviors that result from motives that do not seem to conform to general expectations.

Hansen [18] postulates two kinds of activities related to the choice process; exploration and deliberation. Exploration affords access to environmental information that was not previously available, whereas deliberation refers to internal processes such as "thinking," "problem solving," and "memorizing." Exploration, thus, is an important aspect of the choice process. According to Berlyne [2, p. 79], exploratory activities are manifested to reduce the uncertainty about objects presently existing within the stimulus field or to bring receptors into contact with new stimulus objects. Theories of exploratory behavior seek to explain the psychological processes underlying such activities.

In the area of psychology, several studies have found strong evidence for exploratory tendencies in both lower animals and in human beings. Some of the earlier studies have shown that animals will engage in exploratory activities in the absence of any explicit reward, and that the opportunity to explore can itself act as a reward in learning specific responses. For instance, Harlow, Harlow, and Meyer [19] found that monkeys would work for hours on a complicated lock mechanism even though no reward was offered. Butler [6] showed that monkeys would bar-press in order to open a window that would allow them a brief glance at an electric train set. From experiments conducted on rats, Dember and Earl [8] suggested that there is a level of environmental complexity to which an organism is accustomed. Stimuli somewhat more complex than those usually encountered are interesting [8, 9]. There is also growing evidence from studies on human subjects that individuals prefer to maintain an optimal level of stimulation in their environment (Sales [33]; Walker [27]). Exploratory activities perform an important function in maintaining this optimal level. Further, in a classic experiment, Bexton, Heron, and Scott [1] showed that when environmental stimulation was reduced virtually to a zero level, subjects developed hallucinations and made attempts at self-stimulated increases in environmental stimulation. These studies and others show beyond doubt that exploratory activities are an important part of animal and human behavior.

In the consumer context, the existence of exploratory tendencies is at present mainly supported by indirect evidence. Preference for novelty, change, and variety has been found in several studies related to innovativeness and brand switching. For example, Cox [7] suggested that women sometimes become bored with the brand of shampoo they have been using and because of satiation buy a different brand. Haines [17] reported that 15 percent of his respondents gave ''newness'' as a reason for trying various products. Howard and Sheth [22] used the principles of exploratory behavior to derive the relationship between stimulus ambiguity and attention. The notion of ''psychology of complication'' suggested by Howard and Sheth also bears close relationship to exploratory behavior. This is the situation where the consumer gets bored of repetitive decision making and, therefore, complicates the decision process with considering new and unfamiliar brands or engaging in other forms of exploration.

Although the evidence accumulated thus far in the consumer domain is relatively sparse, the potential contribution of future research in this area stems from two reasons. First, the consideration of exploratory behavior would provide a more complete explanation of consumer behavior in general. It is typical in consumer research to concentrate on the so-called ''purposeful'' motives for behavior. However, such motives leave a large part of the variance in behavior unexplained. For instance, attitudes based on evaluative criteria alone may not explain brand-switching behavior because often such switching is manifested for variety or curiosity. If exploratory behavior can be incorporated systematically into existing frameworks for explaining and predicting behavior, it would prove to be extremely beneficial. Second, exploratory behavior might play a significant, and perhaps predominant, role in certain areas of consumer behavior. For instance, exploration plays a large part in the processes of attention and information search, and in the preference for stimuli over repeated exposures. These areas of behavior have tremendous relevance for marketing managers, particularly for advertising and introduction of new products.

To encourage further research on exploratory behavior in the consumer context, this paper presents a discussion of theoretical ideas with particular emphasis on their applicability to consumer behavior. The major objectives of the paper are: (1) to selectively review the major psychological theories of exploratory behavior and examine their common and divergent aspects, (2) to identify some major conceptual issues we are likely to encounter in consumer research on exploratory behavior, (3) to discuss selected applications of exploratory behavior in the consumer domain, and (4) to present some preliminary ideas toward a framework for studying exploratory behavior in the consumer context.

THEORIES OF EXPLORATORY BEHAVIOR

During the past thirty years several major theoretical frameworks and viewpoints have been advanced in the area of exploratory behavior. These conceptualizations have emerged predominantly in the field of psychology. Our objective here is not to discuss each of these theories in detail, but to discuss selected aspects of the theories in consideration of their relevance for consumer research and marketing. Consequently, the theories will not be presented individually and the discussion is structured on the basis of what the theories have to say about important concepts and relationships relevant to exploratory behavior. Readers who are interested in the theories themselves should refer to the original sources. Capsule versions of some of the major theories are also offered by Venkatesan [36] and Raju [32].

The Concept of Optimal Stimulation

The concept of optimal stimulation plays an important part in psychological explanations of exploratory behavior. In 1955, Hebb [21] and Leuba [26] independently formulated the "principle of optimal stimulation." Basically, they argued that every organism prefers a certain amount of stimulation which can be termed "optimal stimulation." When the actual level of stimulation is below optimum, an individual would attempt to increase stimulation, and when the actual stimulation is above optimum, the individual would try to reduce the stimulation. Essentially then, an inverted U-shaped relationship is postulated between stimulation and preference. All the major theories of exploratory behavior are in agreement with this principle in the sense that they consider an intermediate level of stimulation as most comfortable and satisfying to the individual than very low or high levels. The primary benefit of postulating this type of relationship is that one can now explain why individuals sometimes manifest responses aimed at increasing stimulation and sometimes manifest responses aimed at reducing stimulation.

Although theorists agree on the basic nature of the relationship between stimulation and preference, the precise shape of the relationship varies to an extent, thereby leading to somewhat different interpretations. This issue will be addressed later. Another major difference between the theorists is on the labeling of the abscissa. Precisely what is being optimized? Berlyne [2, 3], the most prominent psychologist in the area, believes that certain properties of stimuli have "arousal potential." These properties include novelty, uncertainty, surprisingness, complexity, change, incongruity, and other such properties that contribute to the ambiguity of the stimulus. Berlyne refers to these properties jointly as "collative properties" and their main feature is that they can influence arousal, a physiologic state which determines how ready the organism is to react and can be equated with the general degree of psychological activity ranging from sleep or coma at the lower extreme to states of frantic excitement at the other extreme. The basis mechanism motivating exploratory behavior, according to Berlyne is arousal-reduction. The concept of arousal is similar to the concept of drive in motivation theory. Just as decreases in drive are rewarding, decreases in arousal are also rewarding. However, at any particular time, an individual can attain the state of minimum possible arousal (the most desirable state) only if the arousal potential (novelty, uncertainty, etc.) of the environment is optimum. Exploration is aimed at altering the stimulus field so as to attain this optimum arousal potential.

Fiske and Maddi [13] use a dimension called "activation," an energizing mechanism in the central nervous system. The level of activation is a direct function of the variation, intensity, and ambiguity of the stimuli the individual is exposed to. Fiske and Maddi [13] propose that the individual finds an optimum level of activation to be most comfortable (contrast this with Berlyne's theory where a minimum of arousal is sought). Hence he attempts to maintain environmental ambiguity at an optimum through exploration. Although Fiske and Maddi's [13] conceptualization is different, the conclusion as far as environmental stimulation is concerned is the same as Berlyne's: an intermediate optimum level of environmental stimulation is sought.

Hunt [23] uses the term "incongruity" to refer to environmental stimulation. Incongruity occurs when environmental inputs fail to match expectations. An optimum of environmental incongruity is most preferred. Although this notion by itself is not unique, Hunt differs from the previous theorists in proposing an intrinsic motivation inherent within the organism's perceptual interaction with the environment which is the cause of exploratory behavior. This motivation is cognitive in nature as opposed to the physiologic motivating mechanism of the previous theories. Hunt proposes the term "motivation inherent in information processing and action" in reference to this motivation. Hunt's proposal of an intrinsic cognitive motivation derives primarily from his observation that "organisms do not become inactive in the absence of painful stimulation and homeostatic need." Hence one must assume some intrinsic motivation for exploration.

Streufert and Driver [34] also operationalize environmental stimulation in terms of "incongruity."[1] Incongruity occurs when information received by an organism is in disagreement with one or more stored concepts. Based on past experience, organisms come to expect certain levels of incongruity in the environments they encounter. This expectation can be considered synonymous to the optimum and represents the adaptation level (AL) of the organism. Thus, more or less incongruity than the expected amount is uncomfortable. Streufert and Driver (see also Driver and Streufert [12]) propose a GIAL (General Incongruity Adaptation Level) hypothesis as the basis for their theoretical framework. "General incongruity" refers to the total amount of novelty, ambiguity, surprise, imbalance, dissonance, disagreement, conflict, etc., which an organism encounters, on the average, across numerous situations. Through experience, organisms evolve general expectations for the "normal" amount of incongruity to encounter in their environment. This expectation of general incongruity is labeled GIAL. Organisms which have experienced a considerable amount of incongruity in the past will generally develop high GIAL and organisms which have experienced mostly routine and familiar situations in the past will generally develop low GIAL. Streufert and Driver further suggest that deviation from the GIAL motivates cognitive action to get back to the GIAL and hence exploratory behavior is manifested. Since arousal plays no direct role in this theory, it seems reasonable to assume that Streufert and Driver accept Hunt's [23] notion of an intrinsic cognitive mechanism that is responsible for exploratory behavior.

Although there is disagreement in the operationalization of environmental stimulation and the motivation behind exploration, one aspect on which researchers agree is that the optimum stimulation level varies from individual to individual. Further, it has been hypothesized that: (1) optimum stimulation level is related to several personality traits, such as intolerance of ambiguity, cognitive complexity, and flexibility, (2) optimum stimulation level is related to demographic variables, such as age and education, and (3) optimum stimulation level is correlated with the degree of exploratory behavior manifested. There is evidence in the psychological literature to support these hypotheses (Dent and Simmel [10]; Bieri [5]; Kish and Donneworth [25]; Kish and Busse [24]; Sales [22]).

Because there is strong support for the notion that optimum stimulation level is characteristic of an individual, several self-report instruments have been designed to measure it. Notable among these are: (1) the Sensation Seeking Scale of Zuckerman, Kolin, Price, and Zoob [40], (2) the Change Seeker Index of Garlington and Shimota [14], (3) the Stimulus Variation Seeking Scale of Penny and Reinehr [30], (4) the Similes Preference Inventory of Pearson and Maddi [29],

(5) the Arousal Seeking Tendency measure of Mehrabian and Russell [27], and (6) the GIAL measure of Driver and Streufert [12]. A discussion of these instruments is beyond the scope of this paper, although some information is available in Raju [32].

Optimum Stimulation and Affect

One important issue that has concerned researchers in the area of exploratory behavior is the relationship between environmental stimulation and affect. The question is: What degree of liking is associated with different levels of environmental stimulation? The object of many theorists has been to postulate a relationship that conforms with empirical findings in the area of exploratory behavior. Many types of relationships have been suggested and often there are conflicting viewpoints. Some of these suggestions are examined below.

According to Berlyne [2, 3], moderate levels of arousal potential are more attractive than extreme levels, and the optimum arousal potential value is most attractive. When arousal potential is below optimum the result is boredom, and when arousal potential is above optimum, the stimulus causes discomfort because it produces conflict. Conflict arises because the stimulus is in some ways similar to, and in some ways different from, stimuli experienced earlier. As a result, the individual is unsure as to exactly how to respond to the stimulus. Streufert and Driver [34] interpret Berlyne's theory to mean that arousal potential is never associated with positive affect. At below optimum levels the stimulus is associated with negative affect due to boredom and at above optimum levels it is associated with negative affect due to conflict. At the optimum, therefore, the stimulus should have zero affect. Maddi [26a] uses a similar argument to criticize Berlyne's theory, stating that it cannot account for the finding that people often enjoy novelty or variety, which in turn would imply the association of positive affect with arousal potential.

Streufert and Driver [34] suggest a relationship between environmental stimulation and affect. In this relationship (which they refer to as Model 3), moderate deviations from the GIAL are accompanied by positive affect whereas large deviations on either side are accompanied by negative affect.[2] This can eliminate the problem in Berlyne's relationship because moving closer to the optimum (or GIAL) is now associated with positive affect. This also seems to be the type of relationship implied by Fiske and Maddi [13] because they state that large deviations from the optimum level of activation (which in turn is directly associated with the variation, intensity, and ambiguity of environmental stimuli) are accompanied by negative affect.

McClelland [27], in trying to provide a general hedonistic explanation of behavior, also postulated a relationship between environmental stimulation and affect. According to his explanation, individuals are motivated to seek pleasant affect and avoid negative affect. He further stated that moderate discrepancies from the adaptation level will lead to positive affect and large discrepancies from the adaptation level will lead to negative affect. The adaptation level itself, which is based on past experience, will be associated with zero affect. Such a relationship, called a butterfly curve, has been supported by Haber [16] in an experiment dealing with preferences for temperature levels. The butterfly curve, however, has one major problem when applied to exploratory behavior. As Streufert and Driver [34] note, several studies have shown that, in the case of very novel stimuli, organisms first display fear (low affect). With continued exposure, the affect level increases. Beyond a certain degree of exposure the affect level again starts dropping, presumably due to boredom. This pattern of change in preference clearly supports the inverted U-shaped curve suggested by the previous theorists and not the butterfly curve.

What we find in the literature, therefore, is at least three major types of relationships between environmental stimulation and affect. These relationships are illustrated in Figure 1. Although it is difficult to rule out any of these relationships as being incorrect at this stage of theory development, an argument will be presented at a later stage as to why the Streufert and Driver [34] relationship appears to be the most logical and, therefore, appropriate to use as a basis for consumer research.

Figure 1.   Relationship Between Optimum Stimulation Level and Affect.

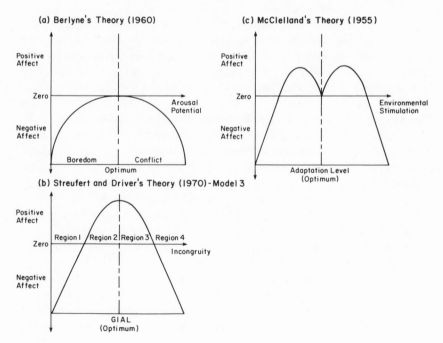

Optimum Stimulation Level and Exploratory Behavior

A variety of explanations have also been offered to show how environmental stimulation impacts on exploratory behavior. In Berlyne's theory exploratory behavior is manifested both when the arousal potential is below optimum and when it is above optimum. When the arousal potential is below optimum exploration is manifested in order to seek stimuli with higher arousal potential. A wide range of stimuli might serve the purpose of increasing arousal potential in this case. Berlyne [2, 3] uses the term "diversive exploration" to describe such exploration. When the arousal potential is above optimum, exploration is manifested in order to make the stimulus more familiar. This will serve to reduce the conflict caused by the stimulus and thereby reduce its arousal potential. Such exploration which is aimed at a particular stimulus in order to reduce conflict is termed "specific exploration" by Berlyne. At very high arousal potentials, however, exploration might not take place because the individual might go into a shock or daze. Such a condition, called supra-maximal inhibition, is a very rare occurrence and can be ignored for all practical purposes.

It might be useful at this point to also define certain other types of exploration Berlyne identifies. First, there is the distinction between *intrinsic* and *extrinsic* exploration. Intrinsic exploration results purely from a desire to maintain arousal potential at the optimum. Such exploration is an end in itself. When exploratory behavior is manifested as a means to an end, i.e., in order to attain specific goals it is termed extrinsic exploration. For instance, a consumer might manifest curiosity about a new product in order to solve a particular purchase problem. Another useful distinction is between exploratory responses and responses through which knowledge is acquired, although Berlyne admits that the two might often coincide. The latter is termed *epistemic behavior*. Epistemic behavior is often caused by conceptual conflict, i.e., conflict within the cognitive structure of the individual. Berlyne identifies certain other types of exploratory behaviors also, but they are not very pertinent to the present discussion.

Fiske and Maddi's [13] explanation of exploratory behavior bears some resemblance to Berlyne's approach but is different in other respects. According to their approach, exploratory behavior is manifested whenever the environment stimulation is below optimum in order to seek stimuli that are closer to the optimum. Such exploration is very similar to Berlyne's concept of diversive exploration. However, in above optimum conditions, Fiske and Maddi seem to imply that simulation can be reduced more easily by withdrawing from the novel or incongrous stimulus. Thus, they do not postulate any exploratory behavior arising due to the conflict caused by the stimulus. In fact, Maddi [26a] questions Berlyne's approach on this point—why should a person seek novelty or variety when it causes conflict, especially when he can more easily withdraw from the stimulus? Berlyne's [3, p. 321] response to this argument is that the capacity for symbolic representation in human beings will not allow the memory or thought of something puzzling, strange, or conflict-inducing to persist. Hence the individual will not be comfortable unless the conflict is faced and resolved. This argument, however, is not too convincing. Hunt's [23] explanation of exploratory behavior comes somewhat close to the Fiske and Maddi [13] approach. Hunt suggests that the optimum of incongruity determines the division of pleasant approach from unpleasant withdrawal. Hence Hunt [23] agrees with Fiske and Maddi [13] that withdrawal is more likely under above optimum conditions.

Streufert and Driver [34] do not rule out the possibility of exploratory behavior when incongruity is above optimum. They claim that objects and events that are moderately below optimum should be explored primarily to provide novel incongruous stimulation. Objects far below the optimum will not be explored, possibly due to boredom. Similarly, objects moderately above the optimum will be explored if they are likely to yield congruous information which will bring the incongruity closer to optimum. Objects far above the optimum will not be explored, possibly due to the fear they induce, and escape or withdrawal behavior is more likely. Referring back to Figure 1(b), one could safely assume that exploratory behavior is likely to be manifested for moderate deviations on either side of the optimum, *where the stimulus would still be associated with positive affect.* Exploration is not likely when the deviation is far below or far above optimum. In both these cases the stimulus is associated with negative affect; in the former case because the stimulus is too boring, and in the latter case because the stimulus is too threatening.

Summary of Theoretical Approaches

From the above discussion of the various theoretical frameworks it is clear that these frameworks have some similarities and some differences. The main point of agreement among the frameworks is that all of them, implicitly or explicitly, are based on the principle of optimum stimulation. They also agree that optimum stimulation level varies from individual to individual and is related to exploratory behavior and also certain personality traits.

On many points, however, the theories disagree. In order to compare and contrast the theories it is helpful to classify them on the basis of four major dimensions. These dimensions are: (1) the basic motivating mechanism, (2) the operationalization of environmental stimulation, (3) the relationship between environmental stimulation and affect, and (4) the relationship between environmental stimulation and exploratory behavior. Table 1 presents the classification scheme. It is perhaps useful to emphasize that one can gain the maximum insight into theoretical developments in the area of exploratory behavior by examining the similarities and differences between the various frameworks. Further, it is possible that certain specific aspects of each framework can be used to develop a new framework suitable for consumer research. An attempt at such an integration will be made later in this paper.

Table 1. Comparison of Theories Related to Exploratory Behavior

Theory	Basic Motivating Mechanism	Dimension of Environmental Stimulation	Env. Stimulation -- Affect Relationship	Env. Stimulation -- Exploratory Beh. Relationship
Berlyne (1960, 1963)	Minimization of Arousal	Arousal Potential	Affect always negative, below optimum--boredom, above optimum--conflict	Below optimum--diversive exploration due to boredom, above optimum--specific exploration due to conflict
Fiske and Maddi (1961)	Activation is Optimized	Variety, Intensity, Ambiguity, etc.	Large deviations from optimum accompanied by negative affect	Below optimum--exploration, above optimum--withdrawal
Hunt (1963)	Motivation Inherent in Information Processing	Incongruity	Not rigorously specified	Below optimum--exploration, Above optimum--withdrawal
Streufert and Driver (1970)	Deviation from GIAL leads to cognitive action	Incongruity	GIAL and moderate deviations from GIAL accompanied by positive affect, large deviations by negative affect	Below optimum--exploration to increase incongruity, above optimum--exploration to decrease incongruity
McClelland (1955)	Hedonistic Tendency	Not Specified	Butterfly curve--moderate deviation from AL accompanied by maximum affect	Not Specified

CONCEPTUAL ISSUES FOR CONSUMER RESEARCH ON
EXPLORATORY BEHAVIOR

Although the existing theoretical approaches have relevance for consumer research they also pose some conceptual problems. The author has identified three
major problems which have to be resolved, at least to a degree, in order to
advance consumer research in the area of exploratory behavior. These problems
are briefly discussed below.

Optimal Level of What?

Table 1 shows that researchers have made various suggestions with respect to
operationalizing environmental stimulation. However, actual measures of environmental stimulation, especially those suitable for application in the consumer
context, are not available. Berlyne considers arousal potential of a stimulus to be
a function of its novelty, incongruity, uncertainty, etc., but does not provide
specific suggestions to measure it. Similarly, Hunt [23] and Streufert and Driver
[34] propose the dimension of incongruity but do not address the issue of measurement. One important task for consumer researchers, therefore, is to determine what is the best method of operationalizing environmental stimulation and
to design specific measures for this purpose.

Extrinsic vs. Intrinsic Motives in Exploration

Another problem consumer researchers are likely to face is the determination
of which behaviors are exploratory and which are not. In order to put this
problem in perspective, let us begin with the notion that exploratory behavior
essentially represents an act of stimulus selection or choice among stimuli. At
any point in time an individual has the choice of staying with the stimulus he is
faced with or seeking out some other stimulus. For example, an analogy in the
consumer context is that an individual has the choice of sticking with his current
brand or purchasing a new brand. The issue in question is whether the purchase
of a new brand is really an act of exploration. Should we not look at the reasons
why the purchase was made and see if it was influenced by the novelty, uncertainty, etc., of the item? A moment's thought will reveal that the real issue here is
the distinction made earlier between extrinsic and intrinsic motives. Essentially,
should the definition of exploration be detached from the motive(s) for the
exploration or should we consider a behavior as exploratory only if it was caused
by instrinsic motives?

If we go the first route of detaching the definition of exploration from the
motives that caused it, we would have to find independent criteria for specifying
which behaviors constitute exploration. For instance, we could say that an act
constitutes exploration as long as it brings an individual in contact with some-

thing not encountered earlier, such as a new brand. We could then postulate that there are both intrinsic and extrinsic motives behind buying the new brand. Thus, the consumer bought the new brand partly because of its novelty (intrinsic motive) and partly because it helped him solve a particular purchase problem (extrinsic motive).

If we go the second route of defining exploration on the basis of motives, we would say that the act of buying a new brand *a priori* does not constitute exploration. It can be considered exploratory only if it was caused by intrinsic motives, such as a desire for novelty. Extending this argument, we could then say that any behavior could have an exploratory component. The degree of this exploratory component (i.e., whether the behavior is completely exploratory, partially exploratory, or not exploratory) depends on the extent to which intrinsic motives played a part in the behavior.

Personally, the author prefers the second approach, primarily because it eliminates the problem of having to decide *a priori* which behaviors are exploratory and which are not. It would be correct to say, on the basis of this viewpoint, that the goal of researchers in this area is to study the exploratory component of behavior, no matter what behavior it is.

Which Existing Framework to Adopt?

A third problem, and perhaps the most important, facing consumer researchers is the selection of a framework for studying exploratory behavior. Are any of the existing frameworks ideally suited to study exploratory behavior in the consumer context? If not, it might be necessary to develop a new framework retaining the good aspects of existing frameworks and eliminating the bad aspects. Although it is difficult to say which approach is best without rigorous empirical testing, it might be worthwhile at this stage to develop some logical arguments which can aid the selection process or be instrumental in the development of a new eclectic approach.

In comparing the approaches, we find that Berlyne's [2, 3, 4] work is very rich in conceptual detail. The concept of arousal potential, the role of conflict in exploratory behavior, and the specification of different types of exploratory behaviors can be extremely useful in furthering consumer research on this topic. However, in specifying the relationships of environmental stimulation with affect and exploratory behavior, Berlyne's approach runs into some problems. First, there seems to be no positive affective state associated with environmental stimulation in Berlyne's approach. Stimuli are either boring or conflict-provoking. Second, Berlyne's contention that under conditions of above optimum arousal potential it is conflict that causes exploration is perhaps true. However, experience tells us that people sometimes approach conflict-provoking stimuli and sometimes withdraw from them. Berlyne's approach is not able to distinguish clearly when conflict will cause exploration and when it will cause withdrawal.

These problems with Berlyne's approach can be remedied if we accept the relationship between environmental stimulation and affect proposed by Streufert and Driver [34]. First, this approach allows for the existence of both positive and negative affect. Moderate deviations from the optimum stimulation are associated with positive affect and large deviations are associated with negative affect. Hence it is easier to understand why moving closer to the optimum is pleasurable. Second, it can clearly specify the manifestation of both exploration and withdrawal. Withdrawal is more likely when a stimulus is associated with negative affect either due to very low stimulation (boredom) or very high stimulation (fear). Exploration is more likely for moderate deviations on either side of the optimum under conditions of positive affect. The objective of the exploration is to move closer to the optimum.

What we have done in the preceding paragraphs is to lay the foundation for the development of a new approach combining Berlyne's ideas [2, 3] with those of Streufert and Driver [34]. Further extensions of this new approach will be discussed later. At present, we will discuss some specific applications of theories of exploratory behavior in the consumer context.

SELECTED APPLICATIONS IN CONSUMER BEHAVIOR

Theories of exploratory behavior can be used to explain many facets of consumer behavior such as buying new products, brand switching, information search, and response to advertising. These specific applications are illustrated in this section. First, exploratory behavior is used as the basis for understanding "information search." The term "information search" is used in a braod sense because, as Berlyne [2] states, all exploratory activities provide access to information that was not previously available. Second, the principles of exploratory behavior are used to explain preference for stimuli over repeated exposures. This forms the basis for brand switching and preference for repetitious advertising. Third, the optimal stimulation concept is linked with individual differences in exploratory behavior. This would be useful for market segmentation especially since optimum stimulation level also seems to be related to personality and demographics.

Information Search

The relationship between environmental stimulation and affect suggested by Streufert and Driver [34] is used as the basis for explaining information search behavior. The choice of this approach is favored by certain advantages over other approaches, as explained earlier, and because Streufert and Driver have made specific attempts to link their approach to information search behavior. The reader is referred to the work of Streufert and Driver for an elaborate discussion of their theory in relation to information search. What is presented here is a very simplified discussion whose primary purpose is to show the relationship between exploration and information search.

Let us refer back to the relationship between environmental stimulation and affect (Figure 1) proposed by Streufert and Driver [34]. The abscissa has been divided into four regions. In other words, the stimulus an individual is exposed to, at a point in time, might fall into any one of the four regions in terms of its incongruity or stimulation value. The type of search behavior manifested by the individual is likely to be different in each of the four regions.

In region 1, the stimulation value is very low. The stimulus causes negative affect due to boredom. Since the stimulus is very far from the optimum, efforts by the individual to seek out novel aspects within the stimulus through exploration are likely to be unsuccessful. Hence the most likely behavior is escape. In other words, the individual will be actively engaged in the search for an entirely new or different stimulus which is closer to the optimum.

In region 2, the present stimulus is somewhat below optimum but is still associated with positive affect. Due to the positive affect, the individual will not actively seek out another stimulus. However, he would be passively receptive to other stimuli which can move him closer to the optimum. He might also attempt to increase the stimulation value by unearthing novel aspects and incongruities in the present stimulus, or by perceiving the stimulus in a new or different way.

In region 3, the stimulus is slightly above optimum. As in region 2, the affect value is still positive. Therefore, the individual will not actively seek out another stimulus but may be passively receptive to other stimuli which are closer to the optimum. He might also attempt to decrease the stimulation value of the present stimulus through exploration aimed at familiarizing himself more with the stimulus or reducing its novelty, incongruity, etc.

In region 4, the stimulus is again much above the optimum and accompanied by negative affect. Since exploration is not likely to bring the stimulation value to the optimum in a short span of time, the individual would manifest escape behavior and actively seek out another stimulus that is closer to the optimum.

Table 2 summarizes the type of information sought and the type of search activity that is likely in each region. Application of these principles in the consumer context leads to some interesting conclusions. When a stimulus, say a brand, is extremely familiar due to repeated buying, it will most likely fall in region 1. The consumer, thus, would be very likely to buy another brand because of its novelty. Region 2 represents a consumer who has purchased a brand a few times and hence is only slightly bored with it. He would explore the present brand for information that makes it more interesting, novel, or incongruous. Thus, information put out by a competitor about a negative aspect of the brand might catch the eye of the consumer due to its incongruity value, which would make the purchase more challenging or exciting. Also, information on previously unimportant dimensions may be sought in order to learn something new about the brand. Region 3 represents a typical cognitive dissonance situation. Here the

Table 2.   Environmental Stimulation and Information Search

Env. Stimulation From Current Stimulus	Type of Info. Sought	Type of Search Activity
Very Low (Region 1)	Unfamiliar, incongruous	Active search for new stimulus
Low (Region 2)	Unfamiliar incongruous	Exploration of current stimulus. Passive receptivity to other stimuli with greater stimulation value
High (Region 3)	Familiar, congruous	Exploration of current stimulus. Passive receptivity to other stimuli with lower stimulation value
Very High (Region 4)	Familiar, congruous	Active search for more familiar stimulus

consumer might have bought a new brand out of necessity only to find that it is a little too novel, unfamiliar, or incongruous. Hence the consumer might find congruous information reassuring, such as from others who have bought the brand. Region 4 typifies a consumer who chooses not to buy a brand because it is too novel or different. A couple of additional hypotheses are suggested by the above discussion:

1. In regions 1 and 2 the consumer is likely to be more receptive to information about competing brands due to its incongruity value.
2. In regions 3 and 4 emphasizing the similarity of a new brand to existing alternatives should make the brand appear more familiar and hence make the information more persuasive. In regions 1 and 2, on the other hand, the appeal of novelty or dissimilarity from existing alternatives should work better.

Preference Over Repeated Exposures

Thus far it has been implied, but not explicitly stated, that the stimulation value (hereafter called arousal potential) of a stimulus is not a fixed quantity. The arousal potential of a stimulus decreases as it becomes more familiar. Thus, if a stimulus has optimum arousal potential to begin with, it would become less attractive over time due to the decrease in arousal potential. In cases where the arousal potential is initially above optimum, increased familiarity would increase the attractiveness of the stimulus until the stimulus attains optimum arousal potential. Beyond that, increase in familiarity would decrease attractiveness. The inverted U-shaped relationship thus provides an answer to the controversy in the psychological literature as to whether familiarity increases or decreases the attractiveness of a stimulus. Some studies (Zajonc [38]; Harrison [20]; Zajonc and Rajecki [39]) have found attractiveness of a stimulus to increase over repeated exposures while Berlyne [4] and some others have found just the opposite relationship. Perhaps they are considering stimuli that are above and below the optimum arousal potential. Berlyne himself uses such an explanation to resolve the contradictory findings. According to the two-factor theory he proposes there are two effects of exposure to a stimulus. The first effect, positive habituation, increases the liking for a stimulus and occurs as the stimulus moves from a higher arousal potential to the optimum. The second effect, tedium, decreases the liking for a stimulus and occurs when the arousal potential decreases below the optimum level.

Just as continued exposure to a stimulus leads to a decrease in arousal potential, a period of nonexposure to a familiar stimulus can cause it to regain at least some of the lost arousal potential. It is reasonable to assume that this regain in arousal potential can occur only to a limited degree because novel of complex stimuli, once explored, can never be as novel or complex again. It is not clear what factors determine the rate of decrease in arousal potential with exposure or the rate of increase in arousal potential with nonexposure. There is no reason to expect that the rate of decrease or increase will be constant over time (i.e., a linear function).

The above framework can be applied fruitfully to repetition of advertising. Advertising that is quite novel or that contains complex information will benefit by repetition. However, this effect will last only until the advertising attains optimum arousal potential. Beyond that, it would not be worthwhile repeating the advertisement. In fact, advertising should never be repeated to the point that it becomes very boring, leading to negative affect. Once a novel advertisement has attained optimum arousal potential, it would be wise to alternate periods of exposure with periods of nonexposure so that the advertising never becomes boring. Hence media schedules would have to be planned carefully to take this into consideration.

Another area where these principles can be applied is brand switching, especially for repetitively purchased product classes with very little brand differentiation. A consumer might buy a certain brand (say brand A) repeatedly until he tires of it. At this point he might switch to another brand (say brand B) because its novelty makes it closer to his optimum arousal potential. This switching from brand A to B will now cause the arousal potential of B to start declining with continued purchase and the arousal potential of A to start increasing due to nonexposure. At some point, therefore, brand A could regain enough of its previous arousal potential so that it is now closer to the optimum. The consumer would thus switch back from brand B to brand A. In cases where a number of brands are available, this phenomenon might cause the consumer to keep switching from brand to brand for variety.

Individual Differences in Exploratory Behavior

As stated earlier, there is evidence in the psychological literature to show that "optimum stimulation level" varies from individual to individual and is related to certain personality traits and demographic variables. Also "optimum stimulation level" seems to be directly related to the degree of exploratory behavior manifested. These relationships have been examined in the consumer context only to a limited degree but seem to have considerable potential for application.

Two recent studies have investigated optimum stimulation level in relation to consumer behavior. Grossbart, Mittelsteadt, and Devere [15] found stimulation needs to be related to consumers' acceptance of recycled urban retail facilities because these facilities offered shopping experiences different from the typical shopping situation. Mittelstaedt, Grossbart, Curtis, and Devere [28] examined the relationship between optimum stimulation level and the adoption decision process for new products and services. They hypothesized that high-sensation seekers (corresponds to those with high optimum stimulation levels) are likely to exhibit a greater awareness of and a greater tendency to evaluate, symbolically accept, try, and adopt new products and retail facilities. Most of their hypotheses were supported. In addition, their study showed that high-sensation seekers have a significantly shorter decision time from awareness to trying new products. They attributed this result to the fact that high- and low-sensation seekers behave differently with respect to trial; the former use trial to make the adoption decision whereas the latter first symbolically evaluate the alternative and try it only if it is acceptable. High-sensation seekers, therefore, proceed quickly to the trial stage and take a great risk that the product will be acceptable.

In another study, Raju [31] examined the relationship of optimum stimulation level with certain selected personality traits, demographics, and exploratory behavior. Both homemaker and student samples were used. In the case of personality traits, both "intolerance of ambiguity" and "rigidity" were found to have significant negative correlations with optimum stimulation level. "Dogmatism" did not have a significant correlation with optimum stimulation level. With respect to demographics, those with higher optimum stimulation levels were found to be younger, better educated, and more likely to be employed. Relationships between optimum stimulation level and intentions to engage in various types of behaviors produced some striking results. Risk taking and innovativeness had the highest correlations with optimum stimulation level; brand switching and the tendency to engage in repetitive behavior had intermediate correlations; and interpersonal communication, information seeking, and interest in shopping had the least correlations. These three sets of behaviors seem to correspond roughly to the dimensions of *risk taking, variety seeking,* and *curiosity.* On this basis it would seem that stimulation needs are satisfied most by risk taking, followed by variety seeking, and the least by curiosity.

The above results have considerable significance for the promotion of new products and for segmenting consumers based on their response to new products. For example, it may not always be to the marketer's advantage to place the promotional emphasis on reducing perceived risk. This could turn away those who prefer to take risks. Also, further research might reveal that those with higher optimum stimulation levels are different with respect to their decision process relating to new products. This issue is worth pursuing in future research.

A NEW FRAMEWORK FOR CONSUMER RESEARCH

Earlier it was suggested that we could perhaps develop a new approach by integrating the theoretical ideas of existing frameworks, an approach that would, we hope, be easier to operationalize in consumer research. Such an attempt is made in this section. The suggested new approach stems predominantly from Berlyne [2, 3] and Streufert and Driver [34] in the conceptualization, yet it has aspects which are very different from either of these theories.

Arousal Potential and Its Components

To start, we shall accept Berlyne's notion of arousal potential in referring to the stimulation value of the environment or any particular stimulus. Properties such as novelty, surprisingness, change, incongruity, uncertainty, and ambiguity contribute to the arousal potential of a stimulus. We shall now deviate substantially from Berlyne's theory in suggesting that the arousal potential of a stimulus is composed of two major components—a positive component which we shall call the "novelty component," and a negative component which we shall call the "conflict component."

The "novelty component" represents the joint effect of all the "positive" properties related to arousal potential. By "positive" we mean that an increase in these properties is always welcomed by the individual. Examples are novelty and surprisingness. On the other hand, the "conflict component" represents the joint effect of all the "negative" aspects of arousal potential. Negative aspects include uncertainty, ambiguity, incongruity, etc., in which increases are always unwelcome.

The preference or affect for a stimulus is now a type of approach-avoidance phenomenon. A person would like to approach a stimulus because of its "novelty component" but would like to avoid it because of its "conflict component." The overall preference for the stimulus is thus determined by a summation of these two independent dimensions. Generally, a person would attempt to seek stimuli with high degrees of the "novelty component" and low degrees of the "conflict component."

Preference Functions of the Components

Having proposed these two independent components—independent in the sense that the degree of one component contained in a stimulus is not dependent on the degree of the other component—we need to resolve some important issues. First, we should be able to explain the inverted-U relationship between arousal potential and affect proposed in the literature and supported by many empirical studies. Second, if optimum arousal potential is characteristic of an individual, what is the connection between it and the two independent components? Fortunately, the new approach can provide some answers to these questions. First, we shall postulate a preference function associated with each component.

As stated earlier, higher degrees of the "novelty component" contribute to increases in affect. However, the value of this affect can be negative or positive, depending on the magnitude of this component in the environment. For instance, stimuli with very little of the novelty component may have negative affect because they are boring or too routine. On the other hand, stimuli with somewhat higher degrees of the novelty component might be considered interesting, and therefore associated with positive affect. We are essentially assuming a certain degree of the novelty component which divides positive affect from negative affect. A second assumption we make about this component is that increases in affect arising from increases in this component follows the "law of diminishing marginal utility." In other words, if we consider successive increases of equal magnitude in this component, the increase in affect associated with these successive increases will diminish. As we keep increasing the "novelty component" we will, therefore, ultimately reach what we call a "novelty saturation point," a point above which an increase in the novelty component contributes very little to affect.

In the case of the "conflict component," we assume that the affect associated with the component is always negative. An increase in this component can only contribute to a decrease in affect (or an increase in negative affect). With respect to the preference function, it is reasonable to assume that there is a "threshold effect" operating in the case of this component. Up to a certain point the conflict caused by a stimulus (through its uncertainty, ambiguity, etc.) is tolerable and hence is associated with very little negative affect. Beyond this point the conflict becomes unbearable and further increases in the conflict component are associated with large increases in negative affect.

We have now postulated two different preference functions associated with the "novelty component" and the "conflict component." These preference functions are illustrated in Figure 2. We can now state that what has been observed to be the individual characteristic "optimum stimulation level" is really the joint manifestation of the preference functions associated with the two independent components over many situations. In other words, the individual will always seek out more of the "novelty component" and less of the "conflict component." Since stimuli with larger degrees of one component are usually also associated with larger degrees of the other component (although not always), the approach toward one component and the avoidance of the other will produce a joint effect closely resembling preference for an optimum combination of the two components, i.e., an optimum stimulation level. To illustrate this, consider the combined preference function for the two components shown in Figure 2. It is immediately apparent that this is the same relationship suggested by Streufert and Driver [34] where extreme levels of stimulation are associated with negative affect and intermediate levels are associated with positive affect. The point where affect is maximized corresponds to the optimum stimulation level of the individual.

Figure 2. Preference Functions for the Novelty Component and the Conflict Component.

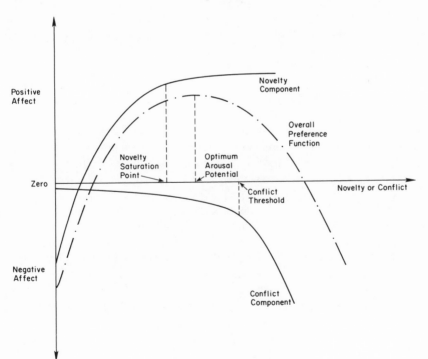

The approach suggested, therefore, can explain the inverted-U relationship so popular in the psychological literature related to exploratory behavior and also why individuals seem to have an optimum level of stimulation. A few additional aspects need to be considered, namely, the preference for a stimulus over repeated exposures and the manifestation of exploratory behavior.

Preference over Repeated Exposures and Exploration

In the case of a particular stimulus, it may derive its arousal potential primarily through the novelty component or the conflict component even though all stimuli have both components. Our approach, therefore, allows room for saying that a stimulus is very novel but not very conflict provoking, or vice versa. This seems very logical on the basis of everyday experience. It has also an advantage not possessed by any of the existing theoretical frameworks, all of which treat environmental stimulation as a single dimension although it is determined by stimulus characteristics like novelty and ambiguity. The postulation of independent preference functions associated with the novelty component and the conflict component which jointly determine the overall preference function leads to some interesting inferences with respect to preference over repeated exposures and exploration.

With repeated exposures of a stimulus, the change in preference would depend on the initial degrees of the novelty component and the conflict component. Let us consider some different cases. First, if the stimulus is initially characterized by high novelty as well as high conflict, both of these will decrease over exposures. The preference over repeated exposures, in this case, will follow the overall preference curve of Figure 2. Preference will first increase and then decrease, leading ultimately to negative affect due to boredom. Second, if a stimulus initially has high novelty but very little associated conflict, preference over repeated exposures will primarily depend on the "novelty component." Hence, preference will drop over repeated exposures until the stimulus becomes very boring. Third, in the case where a stimulus is initially very conflict-provoking but not novel (for example, something familiar but complex), preference over repeated exposure would depend primarily on the conflict component. Here, preference would first increase with the decrease in conflict over repeated exposures. However, after most of the conflict has been resolved, increases in preference resulting from further decreases in conflict will be minimal. At this point, since the novelty was initially low, the stimulus would also become quite boring. Hence, for such a stimulus, preference would first increase due to conflict resolution and then preference would decrease due to boredom. Since conflict and boredom are both associated with negative affect, these changes in preference will take place over the negative range of effect.

Based on the above arguments, it is apparent that preference over repeated exposures will follow an inverted-U curve whenever the stimulus is initially associated with high conflict. This is in conformity with the findings of many psychological studies dealing with repeated exposures of stimuli.

Another aspect to consider is exploration. According to our approach, exploration will be manifested either to increase the novelty component or to decrease the conflict component. Due to the opposite effects of novelty and conflict we can say that under conditions of low novelty and low conflict, an individual will be receptive to information where the increase in preference due to greater novelty exceeds the decrease in preference due to any increased conflict. Similarly, under conditions of high novelty and high conflict, the individual would be receptive to information whose positive effect of decreasing conflict exceeds any negative effect of decreasing novelty. As discussed earlier under the section on "information search," we could state that under conditions of very low novelty or very high conflict, exploration would primarily take the form of escape from the present stimulus due to the high negative affect associated with such conditions. Under conditions of intermediate novelty and conflict, on the other hand, exploration is likely to take the form of seeking specific kinds of information to supplement the existing stimulus, such as information to make the stimulus more novel or information to reduce its conflict.

The Effect of Extrinsic Motives

So far, we have primarily emphasized the desire to increase novelty or decrease conflict. These can be classified as intrinsic motives. Again, everyday experience tells us that our overall preference for stimuli are not determined by intrinsic motives alone. There is also the instrumental value of the stimulus in solving particular problems, which can be considered an extrinsic motive. As a final step in our framework, therefore, we postulate, in addition to preference associated with the "novelty component" and the "conflict component," preference associated with an "extrinsic component." Thus, we have the following equation

$$P_o = P_N + P_C + P_E$$

where

P_o = Overall Preference for an object or stimulus,
P_N = Preference due to the "novelty component,"
P_C = Preference due to the "conflict component," and
P_E = Preference due to the "extrinsic component."

It might be worthwhile to provide some clarification of the extrinsic component at this stage. First, the extrinsic component helps explain many instances where individuals still approach or choose stimuli which are very boring or conflict provoking. Second, in most instances the preference due to the "extrinsic component" can be represented quite accurately by the typical expectancy-value attitude models which encompass evaluative beliefs with respect to the stimulus. Third, the preference due to the extrinsic component is likely to be far more stable over time than the other two components. Thus, it is not likely to change much over time or with repeated exposures of a stimulus, except under conditions where the individual encounters information that changes his attitudes resulting from evaluative beliefs.

The New Approach: Additional Considerations

We shall consider here some benefits of the new approach over existing approaches. One of the benefits is that the new approach clearly distinguishes between the positive and negative aspects of environmental stimulation. We can therefore talk of stimuli having different levels of the ''novelty component'' and the ''conflict component'' without lumping these together under one heading. By doing so, we explicitly recognize that stimulation from novelty is not the same as stimulation from conflict, the two having very different effects on preference and exploration. A second major benefit relates to operationalization of the framework. We find that in talking of the preference for a particular stimulus we no longer have to consider how much it deviates from the optimum stimulation level of an individual, which is necessary in other frameworks. Instead, we can compare stimuli with respect to their degrees of the ''novelty component'' and the ''conflict component'' and thereby predict which one should be preferred more. This is likely to be extremely useful in the consumer context because the measurement of novelty or conflict associated with a stimulus can, perhaps, be accomplished more easily than deviation from the optimum arousal potential. A third benefit relates to the explicit inclusion of extrinsic motives in the framework. Again, this would be important in the consumer context because prediction of preference or choice based on intrinsic motives alone may not be accurate. Apart from these explicit benefits, the framework can explain the relationship of environmental stimulation to preference and exploration postulated by other theorists.

It should be emphasized here that in spite of the benefits enumerated, the new approach is merely a preliminary statement of some ideas designed to improve the applicability of exploratory behavior concepts in consumer research. Considerable work still needs to be done with respect to operationization and testing of the framework and this is left for future research in the area to accomplish.

IMPLICATIONS

So far the paper has reviewed several psychological theories of exploratory behavior, discussed their application in consumer research, and developed a new framework for studying exploratory behavior. As a last step, we will briefly review some broad implications of exploratory behavior for consumer research and marketing management.

In the case of consumer research, study of exploratory behavior could lead to better operationalizations of stimulus characteristics such as novelty, incongruity, ambiguity, etc., and a better understanding of the effects of these characteristics on behavior. It is also possible that such dimensions could be useful to characterize environments or situations. A second possible application is in the personality area. It would be beneficial to know if individual differences in optimum arousal potential are systematically related to other psychological traits, demographics, and to exploratory behavior manifested in the consumer context. Raju [31] has done some preliminary work in this area. A third possible application in consumer research is the testing and operationalization of the proposed new framework. In this case it would be necessary to operationalize the "novelty component" and the "conflict component" and develop the preference functions for these components. Then we could see if preference can be predicted by the extrinsic, novelty, and conflict components.

For marketing management the implications are primarily in the areas of new product introduction, advertising, and brand switching. Stimulus characteristics such as novelty, conflict, etc., are related to innovative behavior and brand switching. Low-priced, repetitively purchased products will especially benefit from a better understanding of this relationship. In the case of advertising there are implications for both message content as well as repetition of advertising. Messages can be designed to contain specific characteristics to maximize the attention of the consumer. For example, messages can be complex or simple, novel or routine, and emphasize similarity of the product to existing alternatives or emphasize differences. Also, the number of times a commercial or an advertisement could be repeated would depend on the degree of specific characteristics such as novelty and complexity it has to begin with. Some of these implications were discussed earlier in relation to preference for stimuli over repeated exposures. If the new framework suggested in this paper can be operationalized it might also make the principles of exploratory behavior more applicable to marketing management.

ACKNOWLEDGMENTS

The author is grateful for the helpful comments of Flemming Hansen, Jerry C. Olson, and Jagdish N. Sheth on earlier drafts of this paper.

NOTES

1. Although reference is made in this paper consistently to Streufert and Driver [34], the reader is also referred to an earlier article by Driver and Streufert [12] and the later work of Streufert and Streufert [35] for an elaborate treatment of their theory.

2. Streufert and Driver [34] suggest that the true relationship between environmental stimulation and affect can be determined only through rigorous empirical testing. However, in the absence of

such data, the proposed Model 3 seems to eliminate many of the problems associated with other relationships suggested in the literature.

REFERENCES

1. Bexton, W., Heron, W., and Scott, T. "Effects of Decreased Variation in the Sensory Environment." *Journal of Psychology* 8, (1954) 70–76.
2. Berlyne, D. E. *Conflict, Arousal, and Curiosity.* New York: McGraw-Hill, 1960.
3. _____. "Motivational Problems Raised by Exploratory and Epistemic Behavior." In *Psychology: A Study of a Science,* S. Koch (ed.). New York: McGraw-Hill, 1963.
4. _____. "Novelty, Complexity, and Hedonic Value." *Perception and Psychophysics* 8 (1970): 279–286.
5. Bieri, J. "Complexity-Simplicity as a Personality Variable in Cognitive and Preferential Behavior." In *Functions of Varied Experience,* D. W. Fiske and S. R. Maddi (eds.). Homewood, Ill.: The Dorsey Press, 1961.
6. Butler, R. A. "Incentive Conditions Which Influence Visual Exploration." *Journal of Experimental Psychology* 48 (1954): 19–23.
7. Cox, D. F. *Risk Taking and Information Handling in Consumer Behavior.* Boston: Harvard University Press, 1967.
8. Dember, W. N., and Earl, R. W. "Analysis of Exploratory, Manipulatory, and Curiosity Behavior." *Psychology Review* 64 (1957): 91–96.
9. Dember, W. N., Earl, R. W., and Paradise, N. "Response by Rats to Differential Stimulus Complexity. *Journal of Comparative and Physiological Psychology,* 50 (1957): 514–518.
10. Dent, O. B., and Simmel, E. C. "Preference for Complex Stimuli as an Index of Diversive Exploration." *Perceptual and Motor Skills* 26 (1968): 896–898.
11. Driver, M. J., and Streufert, S. "The 'General Incongruity Adaptation Level' (GIAL) Hypothesis: An Analysis and Intergration of Cognitive Approaches to Motivation." Paper No. 114, Institute for Research in the Behavioral, Economic, and Management Sciences, Herman C. Krannert Graduate School of Industrial Administration, Purdue University, Lafayette, Ind., 1965.
12. Driver, M. J., and Streufert, S. "An Objective Measure of the General Incongruity Adaptation Level." Purdue University, Lafayette, Ind. (mimeo, copyrighted), 1966.
13. Fiske, D. W., and Maddi, S. R. (eds.). *Functions of Varied Experience,* Homewood, Ill: The Dorsey Press, 1961.
14. Garlingon, W. K., and Shimota, H. E. "The Change Seeker Index: A Measure of the Need for Variable Stimulus Input." *Psychological Reports* 14 (1964): 919–924.
15. Grossbart, S. L., Mittelstaedt, R. A., and Devere, S. P. "Consumer Stimulation Needs and Innovative Shopping Behavior: The Case of Recycled Urban Places." In *Advances in Consumer Research,* B. B. Anderson (ed.), Association for Consumer Research, 1976.
16. Haber, R. N., "Discrepancy from Adaptation Level As A Source of Affect." *Journal of Experimental Psychology* 56 (1958): 370–375.
17. Haines, G. H. Jr., "A Study of Why People Purchase New Products." In *Science, Technology, and Marketing,* R. M. Haas (ed.). Fall Conference Proceedings of the American Marketing Association, pp. 685–697, 1966.
18. Hansen, F. *Consumer Choice Behavior: A Cognitive Theory.* New York: The Free Press, 1972.
19. Harlow, H. F., Harlow, M. K., and Meyer, D. R. "Learning Motivated by A Manipulation Drive." *Journal of Experimental Psychology* 50 (1950): 228–234.
20. Harrison, A. A. "Response Competition, Frequency, Exploratory Behavior, and Liking." *Journal of Personality and Social Psychology* 9 (1968): 363–368.
21. Hebb, D. O. "Drives and the C.N.S. (Central Nervous System)." *Psychological Review* 62 (1955): 243–254.

22. Howard, J. A., and Sheth, J. N. *The Theory of Buyer Behavior*. New York: John Wiley, 1969.

23. Hunt, J. McV. "Motivation Inherent in Information Processing and Action." In *Motivation and Social Interaction: Cognitive Determinants,* O. J. Harvey (ed.), New York: Ronald Press pp. 35–94, 1963.

24. Kish, G. B., and Busse, W. "Correlates of Stimulus-Seeking: Age, Education, Intelligence, and Aptitudes." *Journal of Consulting and Clinical Psychology* 32 (1968): 633–637.

25. Kish, G. B., and Donneworth, G. V. "Interests and Stimulus-Seeking." *Journal of Consulting Psychology* 16 (1969): 551–556.

26. Leuba, C. "Toward Some Integration of Learning Theories: The Concept of Optimal Stimulation." *Psychological Reports* 1 (1955): 27–33.

26a. Maddi, S. R. "The Pursuit of Consistency and Variety." In *Theories of Cognitive Consistency: A Sourcebook,* R. P. Abelson et al. (eds.), Skokie, Ill.: Rand McNally, pp. 267–274, 1968.

27. McClelland, D. C. *Studies in Motivation*. New York: Appleton-Century-Crofts, 1955.

27a. Mehrabian, A., and Russell, J. A. *An Approach to Environmental Psychology*. Cambridge, Mass.: MIT Press, 1974.

28. Mittlestaedt, R. A., Grossbart, S. L., Curtis, W. W., and Devere, S. P. "Optimum Stimulation Level and the Adoption Decision Process." *Journal of Consumer Research,* Vol. 3, No. 2 (1976): 84–94.

29. Pearson, P. H., and Maddi, S. R. "The Similes Preference Inventory: Development of a Structured Measure of the Tendency Toward Variety." *Journal of Consulting Psychology* 30 (4) (1966): 301–308.

30. Penney, R. K., and Reinehr, R. C. "Development of a Stimulus-Variation Seeking Scale for Adults." *Psychological Reports* 18 (1966): 631–638.

31. Raju, P. S. "Exploratory Behavior in the Consumer Context." Unpublished doctoral dissertation. University of Illinois at Urbana-Campaign, 1977.

32. ———. "Theoretical Perspectives On Exploratory Behavior: A Review and Examination of Their Relevance for Consumer Research." Paper #67, *Working Series in Marketing Research,* Pennsylvania State University, 1977.

33. Sales, S. M. "Need for Stimulation As A Factor in Social Behavior." *Journal of Consulting Psychology* 19 (1), (1971): 124–134.

34. Streufert, S., and Driver, M. J. "The General Incongruity Adaptation Level (GIAL)." Technical Report #32. Homewood, Ill.: Dorsey Press, 1971.

35. Streufert, S., and Streufert, S. C. *Behavior in the Complex Environment*. Washington, D.C.: V. H. Winston, 1978.

36. Venkatesan, M. "Cognitive Consistency and Novelty Seeking." In *Consumer Behavior: Theoretical Sources,* S. Ward and T. S. Robertson (eds.), Englewood Cliffs, N.J.: Prentice-Hall, 1973.

37. Walker, E. L. "Psychological Complexity as a Basis for a Theory of Motivation and Choice." *Nebraska Symposium on Motivation* 12 (1964): 47–97.

38. Zajonc, R. B. "Attitudinal Effects of Mere Exposure." *Journal of Personality and Social Psychology,* Monograph Supplement 9 (2, Pt. 2), (1968): 1–27.

39. Zajonc, R. B., and Rajecki, D. W. "Exposure and Affect: A Field Experiment." *Psychonomic Science* 17 (1969): 216–217.

40. Zuckerman, M., Kolin, E. A., Price, L., and Zoob, I. "Development of a Sensation Seeking Scale." *Journal of Consulting Psychology* 28 (6), (1964): 477–482.

SOME ISSUES IN THE CONSTRUCTION OF MODELS FOR MARKETING DECISIONS

Vithala R. Rao and Darius Jal Sabavala

I. INTRODUCTION

Analytical modeling of marketing systems began in the early sixties, and since then there has been a growing interest in building models of market processes. This thrust is evidenced by the number of articles that are published on this general subject and by the existence of journals largely devoted to the dissemination of such research. Prediction of future behavior of subsystems in the marketing environment owing to changes in elements of marketing programs for products and brands has been a general concern of these analytical studies. The desire to obtain good predictions is not merely due to scientific considerations. The survival of business corporations itself implicitly depends upon such accurate predictions.

Research in Marketing, Volume 4, pages 251–272
Copyright © 1981 by JAI Press Inc.
ISBN: 0–89232–169–5

Marketing model building has generally been of a partial equilibrium nature. That is to say, only selected components of the marketing process have been usually looked at in any one model. Grandiose attempts at building models to include all subsystems demand large amounts of data. They tend to be highly detailed, taking the form of a large-scale simulation.

Specification and estimation of a market response function—which postulates the nature of relationships between marketing inputs, i.e., marketing mix elements and marketing outputs, e.g., market share or sales, have been the crux of several model building efforts. Various specifications do exist in literature and different types of data have been utilized in estimating the response functions.

Knowledge of market response functions is essential to management in making economically judicious allocation of marketing resources among competing means. Users can enrich the modeling efforts by providing guidance in the choice of situations or phenomena to be modeled as well as developing criteria for choice among alternative models that may be used for the same situation. Interaction between model builders and model users should augment the capabilities of either group.

Two significant streams of research on analytical marketing models for the firm may be identified: macro and micro. The macro-analytic models attempt to develop and test models for the firm's behavior utilizing global or aggregate measures of the market. The micro-analytic models, on the other hand, attempt to build and test descriptive models with regard to an individual consumer's overt behavior or components of the behavioral process (e.g., perceptions, attitudes, and preferences). Understanding of the dynamics of the behavioral process is an implicit goal of either approach. While the micro-analytic models are being diffused in academic research, as yet there seems to be no strong evidence of incorporating them to enrich the macro models for the firm. Previous attempts, notably those of Amstutz [1] at large-scale simulation of market response, although steps in this direction, have not achieved the necessary integration.

Against this background, the major objective of this paper is to develop an integrative, theoretical framework for looking at the marketing mix effects on market response and discuss some main issues in the construction of marketing mix models. A selective review will be made of some previous models in light of the proposed framework.

The subject matter of marketing mix models can be very broad. Therefore, some comments on the scope of this paper are in order. First, the paper deals with marketing mix decisions for established as well as new brands. In either case, the decisions of place, promotion and price are included in the discussion. However, the decisions with respect to product will be taken as given for established brands. The issue of product design modeling will be treated for the case of new brands. Second, the question of implementation of marketing mix plans (e.g., sales force allocations, media planning, etc.) are not included in this discussion. Similarly, the issue of evaluation of market preformance of new products is not covered here. A third aspect of the scope relates to the question of deciding the product/market boundary—the decision on what is being offered (i.e., need) and to whom it is being offered (i.e., segments). This decision has broad strategic implications for the firm's offering as a whole. The discussion in this paper begins with the premise that the product-market definition has been made.

The remainder of this paper is organized into three main sections. Section 2 describes the integrative theoretical framework or model. Section 3 provides a brief review of and classification of major models in marketing in terms of their dealing with components of the framework. Finally, Section 4 identifies some unresolved issues and directions for future research.

II. AN INTEGRATIVE MODEL FOR MARKETING MIX

This section will describe an integrative framework to examine the basic problems of marketing management, namely, that of prediction of changes in sales or market share due to changes in the marketing mix for an existing brand and that of prediction of market share for a new brand. In this framework, some of the recent developments in areas related to marketing (such as economics and psychology) can be synthesized with the conceptions of a marketing system and consumer behavior for looking at marketing mix effects. The objective of this framework is the same as that of the BRANDAID model [28], but we believe that this model will attempt a more formal structure than the input-output format. We believe it provides a deeper understanding of the marketing process. Further, this discussion might assist in pinpointing some basic research areas of interest to the marketing management. Some of these ideas have been previously discussed by Rao [40]. Some discussion as it relates the problem of new products was presented by Urban in his PERCEPTOR model [49].

The ensuing discussion will be in two main parts. First, a number of premises for marketing management will be stated. These premises may be construed to be *a* synthesis of the marketing substantive knowledge to date. Next, an outline of this intergrative model will be discussed. The research issues will be briefly touched upon.

A. Premises of The Model

The various premises of this integrative model can be stated:

1. At the individual consumer level, a brand of a product is considered in relation to others fulfilling the same need. The set of such alternatives looked at has been called the evoked set in the literature. Sometimes, this is loosely referred to as a product category.
2. Any brand of a product category can be fully described as a profile on a number of attributes. In fact, it is the relative position of one brand to

another that is relevant to the consumer's decision of purchase. This is also important to the marketer in most cases. Further, these attributes are both physical and psychological.

3. Consumers derive utility or satisfaction through the attributes of the brands. Lancaster [26] elaborates this point, but considers only objective attributes of a product. We claim that this is perhaps a restricted view.

4. Marketers of brands can influence the relative positioning of the brands on the attributes (also called the attribute space or perceptual space) by changing their marketing mix programs.

5. Markets can be partitioned into a small number of market segments, each of which considers the brands in an almost homogeneous manner. That is, the perceptual spaces of brands are the same for every member of the market segment, and further, these spaces differ from one segment to another. That is to say, perceptual differences lead to segments.

6. Consumers of any one market segment differ in the manner of evaluating the brands. The rules of evaluation could be quite simple (such as conjunctive rule) or quite complicated (such as a strategy of both lexicographic rule followed by a linear compensatory rule). The thresholds, or weights used in the evaluation process may depend upon several descriptions (economic, social, psychological) of the consumer.

7. The probability of purchase (choice) of a brand is a direct function of the derived utility from it as evaluated by each consumer. A mapping of the derived utility to choice is feasible.

B. Outline of the Mathematical Model

The above premises are translatable into a model for marketing mix effects. Before doing that, it is necessary to differentiate the technology (data collection, analysis, etc.) from the conceptual part of the model. It is technically feasible to analyze various marketing research data, using specialized methods if necessary, to do the following:

a. Identification of the evoked set;
b. Identification of the relevant attributes;
c. Identification of market segments;
d. Derivation of perceptual spaces; and
e. Paramorphically determine the rules of evaluation.

Notice that there have been significant developments in the technology for doing the above. In fact, a majority of current research in marketing is still directed to improving the methods for these.

For convenience of simplicity, we will write the model in terms of an average consumer for any segment. The model can be extended to deal with distributions around this average. We introduce the following notation for the model.

b = number of brands in the evoked set;

r = number of attributes describing each brand;

s = number of market segments;

ℓ = number of periods of lag;

t = current time period;

N_i = size of the ith market segment, $i = 1,2,\ldots,s$.

$\Pi_{1i}^{(t)}$ = probability of a member of ith segment purchasing the product class at time t;

$\Pi_{2ij}^{(t)}$ = conditional probability that a member of the ith segment buys brand j at time t;

$\Pi_{2i}^{(t)}$ = vector of conditional probabilities of buying the b brands for a member of the ith segment at time t;

$K_{ij}^{(t)}$ = purchase rate (quantity bought) of brand j by a consumer of the ith segment at time t;

$\Psi_i^{(t)}$ = matrix of perceptual space for the ith segment at time t; a typical element of this matrix is $\Psi_{ijk}^{(t)}$ which is the value of the jth brand on kth attribute at time t in the perceptual space of the ith market segment;

$BV_i^{(t)}$ = set of background variables describing the members of ith segment at time t;

$X^{(t)}$ = matrix of physical characteristics, market mix elements for the b brands at time t; each row of this matrix refers to one brand. One of the columns is price of the brand, others refer to product quality, advertising, etc.;

S_{jt} = sales of brand j at time t.

We may write the sales of the jth brand at time t as:

$$S_{jt} = \sum_{i=1}^{s} N_i^{(t)} \Pi_{1i}^{(t)} \Pi_{2ij}^{(t)} K_{ij}^{(t)} \tag{1}$$

The variables $N_i^{(t)}$ in this equation can be determined from secondary data. Marketing research data can in fact estimate the remainder of these for any time. But there is a need to formulate relationships of the variables in terms of what can be controlled by the firm. This can be done using the premises stated earlier.

Several constructs appear in this framework. These are: (a) background variables, BV; (b) marketing mix decisions, X; (c) perceptual space, ψ; (c) probability of purchasing the product class, Π_1; (d) conditional probability of purchasing a brand, Π_2; and (e) purchase rate, K. The integrative framework identifies some

Figure 1.   Flowchart of the Integrative Framework

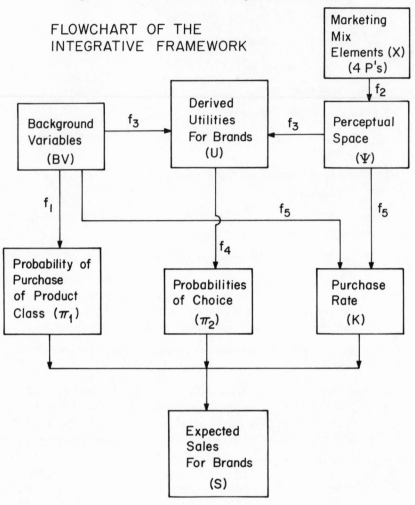

FLOWCHART OF THE
INTEGRATIVE FRAMEWORK

Marketing
Mix
Elements (X)
(4 P's)

f_2

Background
Variables
(BV) f_3

Derived
Utilities
For Brands
(U) f_3

Perceptual
Space
(Ψ)

f_1 f_5 f_5

f_4

Probability of
Purchase
of Product
Class (π_1)

Probabilities
of Choice
(π_2)

Purchase
Rate
(K)

Expected
Sales
For Brands
(S)

significant relationships among these constructs. These are shown as a flowchart in Figure 1, omitting the various subscripts (including time) involved.

The following equations state the model rather compactly. The reader may note that not all variables noted would enter the functions. This is written for convenience. Particular versions must be developed for specific situations.

$$\Pi_{1i}^{(t)} = f_1(BV_i^{(t)}) \qquad (2)$$

$$\Psi_i^{(t)} = f_{2i}(X^{(t)}, \phi_i^{(t-\ell)}) \qquad (3)$$

$$U_i^{(t)} = f_{3i}(\Psi_i^{(t)}, BV_i^{(t)}) \tag{4}$$

$$\Pi_{2i}^{(t)} = f_{4i}(U_i^{(t)}, \Pi_{2i}^{(t-\ell)}) \tag{5}$$

$$K_i^{(t)} = f_5(of_i^{(t)}, \Psi_i^{(t)}) \tag{6}$$

Equations (2) through (6) comprise one particular representation of a marketing system. There are two driving forces in this structure. First is the X-matrix, which consists of the marketing mix decisions for the brands. The other is the set of background variables for each segment. The reader may note that equation (2) is a scalar equation while equations (3) through (6) are vector or matrix equations.

Brief comments are in order for equations (2) through (6). Equation (2) is an expression that the background variables alone determine the individual's probability to purchase the product class. This statement ignores any generic demand effects due to the combined advertising in the industry, which is generally the case for several product classes. Some adjustments can be made in this equation for cases where the generic effects are large. Much of the work in demand analysis is directed at determining these functions.

Equation (3) says that the perceptual space of the brands is obtained as a transformation of the X-matrix. It provides for differences in such transformations due to segment differences. Further, it allows for the possibility of carryover effects in the individual's perception of brands. More specifically, it states that perceptions of brands at any time are the resultant of current marketing mix decisions as well as previously held perceptions by consumers. The period of lag is denoted as l; it needs to be determined empirically. Thus, this equation postulates some form of updating procedure of perceptions. When a new brand enters the market, this set of functions might require a respecification and reestimation.

Equation (4) simply states that the derived utilities for brands are dependent upon the perceptual space and the individual characteristics. The specific manner in which the space is utilized, i.e., the function f, could vary for each segment. Much of the current research is arrived at these so-called composition rules that determine the derived utilities. In these functions we could introduce other variables such as ideal points to describe alternative utility formation processes.

Equation (5) provides for a mapping of the derived utilities to choice or purchase of the brands. These relationships could be as simple as the rule, "choose the brand with highest utility" which leads to deterministic choices. Alternatively, relationships for some probabilistic choices could be formulated by specifying the nature of the function, f_4.

Equation (6) is an expression that relates the purchase rate to the background variables and elements of perceptual space. All aspects of perceptual space may not be relevant here, however.

C. Illustration of Relationships

The relationships of the model may be clarified by tracing through the effects of two typical (frequently) occurring phenomena in the marketing of a brand. For this purpose, let us consider Brand A versus competition and two particular changes in the marketing mix (X) for Brand A, namely, increase in advertising expenditure and decrease in its price through a promotion. The effect of increase in ad expenditure will initially be felt in the perceptual space (Ψ) of all the brands—either through changes in the positions of the brands (Brand A in particular) or through changes in the saliences of the dimensions of the space. One would hypothesize that these changes would occur in a direction favorable to Brand A. This change will reflect itself in the utilities (U) derived for each of the brands and will ultimately translate into changes in the probabilities of choice (Π_2). The effect of these changes in the perceptual space (occurring due to advertising) may be minimal on the purchase rate of the brand, which is more directly affected by perception of economy of the brand. The resultant effect of all of these changes would be an increase in the expected sales for Brand A and a possible lasting change in the perceptual space.

With regard to the price promotion of Brand A, the expected effects are very straightforward. Brand A will be perceived to have a higher economic value in relation to other brands. This effect is typically transitory in nature since the promotion runs for a limited time. Hence the derived utilities for brands may be minimally altered. Thus, we hypothesize minimal changes in the purchase probabilities of brands, but expect higher purchase rates of Brand A. These effects would manifest in a higher stocking up of the brand (an usual phenomenon observed in the sales rates of brands under price deals).

Similar relationships may be postulated for other variables of marketing mix for the brand as well as dynamics of competitive forces in the marketplace. Once a set of such hypotheses are formulated from the model, it should be possible to devise procedures to test them empirically.

D. Some Dynamics

The framework and the model are described in terms of an existing product category with established brands. However, the effects due to new brand/product introduction (ΔX) can be explicated by considering the changes on the purchase probability for the product (Π_1) as well as the changes in the perceptual space. These changes can be incorporated using the behavioral theories and diffusion of innovation.

An additional aspect of the model relates to the dynamics of the managerial and consumer decisions based upon the outcomes of the process. From the management viewpoint, the outcome is the actual sales of the brand. An evaluation of actual versus expected or target sales would enable the marketing management of the firm to alter the mix decision (X) for the brand. Similarly, the derived satisfactions or dissatisfactions due to consumption of the brand would enable consumers to reevaluate their perceptions of brands (Ψ). Such a feedback would have an impact on the subsequent brand choice probabilities. These dynamics can be considered as extensions to the basic model.

E. Aggregation

The conceptual model is stated in terms of (a) an individual consumer; (b) a given point in time; (c) a given situation or context of purchase; and (d) a given set of outcomes or competing alternatives in the product category. The framework is useful when certain aggregations are considered since it would almost be impossible to acquire the necessary data at the level of detail at which the model is described. The several possibilities of aggregation may be indicated below for each of the four aspects that specify the conceptual model.

Aspect of Model	*Possible Aggregations*
(a) Individual consumer	—All consumers as one group —Many segments (geographic, social, economic or other bases)
(b) Point of Time	—Choice occasions —Calendar period of time (week, month, etc.)
(c) Situation/context	—All uses of the product category and all contexts —By use situation (e.g., at home or outside) —By context of purchase (e.g., own use or for gift)
(d) Set of Outcomes	—Items defined by brand X size as outcomes —Individual brands as outcomes —Subset of brands as outcomes (e.g., firm's brand versus all others)

By appropriate aggregations, we could translate the structure of Figure 1 to any level of marketing system. Each aggregation is a particular combination of the alternatives under the four aspects that specify the model. For example, the model may be cast in terms of sales formation for geographic territories in each month for all uses of the firm's brand versus competition. From the firm's point of view, aggregated models using data for its brand versus competition would be highly useful in making marketing mix decisions; many of the econometric models in marketing are of this type.

III. A REVIEW OF RECENTLY DEVELOPED MODELS

Several published models in marketing may be thought of particular aggregations of the structure described above. We intended to provide a selective review of recently developed models building on the framework described. Most of the models we review may be classified either as aggregate models that do not explicitly study the underlying *process* or as models that have addressed parts of the process shown in Figure 1.

A. Relationships Between X and Ψ

Table 1 summarizes several research efforts that have been concerned with directly estimating the relationship between the marketing mix variables (X) and the sales outcome (S). Table 1 shows how the X and S variables were operationalized and other details concerning the model and the empirical applications, if any. These models have typically been built with the objective of providing information for managerial decisions on resource allocation or mix manipulation and have been formulated at highly aggregate levels. The individual consumer's process is treated as a black box. We examine here only the controllable variables (X) and the outcome variables (S). These models are often inconsistent with the underlying micro-theory but must be viewed as approximations to the appropriate aggregate model. This point is discussed further in Section IV, below.

B. Relationships Between X and Ψ

The methodology of multidimensional scaling has contributed significantly to the problem of determining the perceptual space of a set of alternatives as viewed by consumers. Typically, the dissimilarity judgments on all pairs of alternatives are analyzed using metric or nonmetric algorithms. Both individual and group analyses are performed on the data. This research focussed on the issue of determining the perceptual space (Ψ) and the marketing mix variables are only used in interpreting the space. In this process, individual's ratings on X-variables (some of which may be construed to be perceptual variables) are related to the dimensions of the perceptual space.

Table 2 reviews selected attempts in this area of modeling relationships between X and Ψ. We must note that this work has been methodologically motivated in the beginning. Some recent attempts (e.g., Pessemier [36]) have tended to focus on the managerial problem of designing products or communication strategies on the basis of empirical relationships between X and Ψ. Since many of the variables used in the X-set are ratings on attributes, a moot issue relates to one's ability to translate the attribute ratings into implied marketing mix decisions. The difficulty of such translation has led to the growth of research and

Table 1. Review of Models of X → S Relationships

Reference	Operationalisation		Data			Additional Comments
	X	S	Method/Technique/Functional Form	Aggregation	Product	
Balachandran & Gensch [4]	AS, RP, ΔP, D, PS, DI	SL	Linear & log-linear; Optimal conditions derived using geometric programming	Montly; Market segment	Beer	
Beckwith [5]	AS	MS	Linear dynamic; Alternative econometric estimation techniques	Monthly; National	Frequently purchased consumable	Simultaneous estimation of brand response functions.
Clarke [9]	A (mostly)	SL (mostly)	Review of dynamic (Koyck/distributed lag/ partial adjustment) models	Several levels	Several	Shows effect of time on lag estimates. Review paper.
Eskin & Baron [11]	P, A	SL	Experimental; ANOVA (fixed effects)	City (store panel); Monthly	Household cleaner snack food, specialty food, baked good	
Gensch & Welam [13]	P, (A/D)	SL, II	Convex programming	Market segment	Consumer products	Provides comparison versus econometric models based on the same data.
Helmer & Johannsen [19]	A	SL	Box-Jenkins Transfer function	Annual	Lydia Pinkham	Determines optimal duration of the promotion.
Kinberg & Rao [23]	D	II	Stochastic model	IE	IE	
Kinberg, Rao & Shakun [24]	D	SL	Stochastic model	IE	IE	Examines competitive strategies and cooperative versus non-cooperative behavior.
Lambin [25]	DIS, AS	MS	Several alternative functional forms	Semi-annual (?); Market area	Gasoline	
Little [28]	D, A, P	SL, MS	Multiplicative indices, subjective parameter estimation	—	—	Interactive model.
McCann [29]	P, AS, D	MS	Linear, additive model; Random Coefficient Regression	Segment; Bi-monthly	NA	Emphasis on segment differences.
Montgomery, Silk & Zaragoza [32]	A (by media type)	MS	Log-linear, dynamic	Monthly; National	Ethical Drugs	Focuses on the communications mix. Develops short & long run elasticities.
Parsons [33]	DI, A	SL	Linear; Generalized least squares estimation	Bi-monthly; New brands only; National	Frequently purchased consumer product	Focuses on new product introduction. Includes model of distribution retail availability.

(continued)

Table 1. Review of Models of X → S Relationships (Continued)

Reference	Operationalisation		Method/Technique/Functional Form	Data		Additional Comments
	X	S		Aggregation	Product	
Parsons & Bass [34]	A	SL	Log-linear, simultaneous	Bi-monthly National (?)	Frequently purchased consumer product	Simultaneous estimation.
Prasad & Ring [37]	P, A	MS	Linear, dynamic Stepwise Regression Matched panels	Market Weekly	Frequently purchased canned food item	Examines price, advertising, advertising effects and interactions.
Rao [39]	A, AS	SL, MS	Several	Annual	Cigarettes	Comparison of estimation methods and alternative model specifications.
Rao & Lilien [38]	D, P	SL	Linear with some interactions Least squares estimation applied separately to components in the model	Monthly 19 Markets	Gasoline	Promotion effects superimposed on a time series model.
Schultz [43]	A AS	SL (industry) MS (company)	Linear, log-linear Lagged	Quarterly One-sector, one-way	Airlines	Simultaneous estimation of market share models. Comparison of alternative forms.
Sexton [44]	AS, RP	MS	Exponential Least squares estimation	Weekly based on panel data Market area	Three closely substitutable frequently purchased consumer products	Models built at brand and category levels.
Tapiero [48]	A	SL	Stochastic model Analytical "least squares" estimates	IE	IE	Diffusion approximation to the Vidale-Wolfe model.
Weinberg [51]	A	SL	Linear, dynamic	Uses previously published data	Uses previously published data	Examines normative implications of ignoring carry-over effects beyond the planning horizon.
Wittink [53]	RP, AS	MS	Log-linear, dynamic Several econometric estimation methods	Metro areas Monthly	Frequently purchased branded consumable	

Key to Table 1: Π, Profits; SL(MS), Sales (Market share); P(RP), Price (Relative price); A(AS), Advertising (Relative advertising or advertising share); D(DS), Dealing or promotion (relative dealing or dealing share); DI(DIS), Distribution (relative distribution or distribution share); PS, Personal selling; NA, Not available; IE, Illustrative example only, possibly hypothetical.

Table 2. Selected Models Relating X to Ψ

Reference	Operationalization of		Data			
	X	Ψ	Method/Technique/ Functional Form of Model	Level of Aggregation	Product	Additional Comments
Green and Rao [16]	Ratings on product attributes	Dimensions of perceptual space obtained from similarity judgments	Several competing methods and models of perceptual analysis for Ψ and linear and nonlinear correlation methods for relating X and Ψ	Sample as a whole and analysis by subsamples	Breakfast foods	The reference contains comparisons of algorithms for deriving perceptual space.
Wilkie and[1] Pessemier [52]	Ratings on item attributes	Attitude toward item	Several issues and methods dealt with; linear functions	Individual as well as group	Several	Review paper.
Green [14]	Ratings on product attributes	Dimensions of similarity space	Several issues and methods dealt with; linear and monotone relationships	Individual and group	Several	Review article.
Moinpour, McCullough & Maclachlan [31]	Persuasive communication on product attributes	Dimensions of perceptual space obtained from similarity	INDSCAL model for deriving Ψ and a matching procedure to test effects of changes in X and multivariate analysis of variance; metric models	Sample as a whole in each treatment group	Toothpaste	This is a longitudinal study.
Johnson [22]	Ratings on product attributes	Dimensions of best discriminating space	Multiple discriminant analysis using items as "groups"; linear relationships	Sample as a whole	Houses	The "model" is a technique of multidimensional scaling. It yields relationship between X and Ψ directly.
Pessemier [36]	Ratings on product attributes	Dimensions of best discriminating space	Multiple discriminant analysis to derive the perceptual space; linear relationships	Group level analysis	Automobiles	The procedure extends to linking X to U (see table 3).

[1]Depending upon the point of view, this multi-attribute-attitude modeling may be viewed also as relating X to U.

models that related X directly to U (i.e., implicitly bypassing the intermediate steps of relating X to Ψ and then Ψ to U).

C. Relationships between X and U

The models relating X to U have typically utilized the methodology of conjoint analysis. The major focus has been on the "actionable" variables in the X-set which typically included product design characteristics. Table 3 reviews selected attempts in this area. There exists a close connection between these models and the methods of multidimensional scaling reviewed in Table 2.

Research to date has covered a wide range of alternative functional forms that relate X to U, alternative estimation techniques as well as competing data collection methods. Typically, however, hypothetical product profiles—each described on a number of attributes in accordance with a fractional factorial design—are presented to a subject and evaluations on each profile are elicited. These evaluations are then decomposed into contributions of each attribute. As revealed by Table 3, several alternatives do exist for this decomposition.

The models that relate X to U have found significant managerial acceptance owing to the ract that they yield predictions of future sales of new products (which are deemed to be new combinations of existing attributes). The work on this front requires a translation of utility (U) into probabilities of choice (Π_2). We must note that this part of the overall framework (described in Figure 1) has not been fully investigated; only simple rules of transformation (e.g., choose the brand with highest utility) have been used in the market simulations built in specific applications.

D. Other Relationships

A number of research efforts that do not fall into the three classes mentioned above have appeared. The theoretical framework (Figure 1) provides an appropriate perspective for these efforts too. Some examples are provided here. The LINMAP methodology of Shocker and Srinivasan [45] links X (essentially product features) to Ψ to Π_2 with the objective of identifying new product ideas. An ideal point model is specified and estimated at the individual level and these are aggregated across individuals for locating the best product opportunities. Urban's PERCEPTOR model [49] also links product attributes (X) through Ψ to Π_2, at the aggregate level. Best [6] relates Π_2 to Ψ in an examination of the predictive ability of joint-space models. The choice probability is a function of the distance from the consumer's ideal point to the brand in the perceptual space for that consumer. Horsky [20] builds a model which relates X (advertising) to Π_2. That is, it is an aggregate market share model which is nonlinear and provides an opportunity for some rigorous testing.

Another set of models and methods have dealt essentially with the problems of

Table 3. Selected Models Relating X to U

Reference	Operationalization of		Data			Additional Comments
	X	U	Method/Technique/Functional Form of Model	Level of Aggregation	Product	
Green and Wind [17]	Product design variables	Evaluations of product profiles on criteria such as "goodness" of buy	Several models and functional forms examined (metric, nonmetric, categorical models)	Individual as well as group	Several	Contains comparison of models.
Davidson [10]	Product design variables	Same as above	Multiplicative model developed from pairwise attribute–profile evaluations	Sample as a whole	STOL service defined on 13 attributes	Shows good predictions.
Johnson [21]	Product design variables	Same as above	Multiplicative model developed for product attributes	Individual or sample	Several	Describe the technique.
Rao [41]	Product design variables	Same as above	Describes several algorithms and technical issues	Individual or sample	—	Technical paper.
Pessemier [36]	Product design and communication strategy variables	Product preference ratings	Joint space analysis using PREFMAP is included in specific models of DESIGNR and STRATOP	Individual and by segment	Automobiles	Shows the economic consequence of strategy changes.
Green and Srinivasan [15]	Product design variables	Same as above	Several issues and models dealt with; partworth function models; ideal point models and LINMAP included	Individual as well as group	Several	Review article.
Rao and Winter [42]	Product design variables	Intention to buy	Multivariate-probit-model	Individual analysis	Cameras	Estimates purchase probabilities by segment.

265

designing, evaluating and predicting sales for new products or services. Some of the recent efforts in this area have moved toward the theoretical framework we propose by enriching previous models, integrating ideas and methods and thereby incorporating several components of the Figure 1 framework. Examples of these are Blattberg and Golanty [7], Huser and Urban [18] and Silk and Urban [46]. The Hauser and Urban methodology focuses on the managerial design process and evaluates product ideas based on individual consumer models. The individual evaluations are aggregated by segments (defined with respect to homogeneous preferences) into choice probabilities for the competing alternatives. The Silk and Urban paper presents a methodology for predicting sales potential for a new product prior to market testing. Finally, the Blattberg and Golanty paper deal with the problem of making early (during test market) predictions of a product's sales. Their model integrates some product design aspects and marketing planning aspects.

IV. SOME ISSUES AND DIRECTIONS FOR RESEARCH

In spite of the several research efforts reviewed in the previous section and many others, there remain a number of issues that pervade the entire model-building process in marketing. These issues provide fertile areas for research and point to the need for integrative research and model development. There are four distinct but related questions that we will address in this section. First, given that our theoretical understanding of consumer and market behavior is at the individual consumer level and that the bulk of the research is conducted at aggregate levels, are the macro and micro approaches consistent? If they are not, what can be done to develop macro models which are appropriate aggregations of the theory-based micro models? Second, are there pragmatic benefits to be derived from the macro models that outweigh the theoretical inconsistency? Third, even if one adopts an ad hoc aggregate model building approach, what are some of the relevant issues and opportunities for research? Finally, what is the scope for extensions to the theoretical framework (which has been the core of the paper)? We will elaborate these issues below.

A. Aggregation: Micro → Macro Consistency

Our theoretical framework and most of the theory development have been based on individual consumers. Yet, most of the research that is published has used models which have been directly formulated (ad hoc) at the aggregate level. (The merits of this approach are discussed in Section IV B.) An appropriate question is whether the macro model is an appropriate aggregation of the implicitly assumed or explicitly stated micro models. The simple case would be one where the researcher was willing to assume that individuals were homogeneous (this is a sufficient but not necessary condition). However, this is an assumption most researchers in marketing would be unwilling to make. It is very likely that most ad hoc macro models, which have plausible functional forms, could not have resulted from the aggregation of a plausible micro model. It should be noted that the stochastic models of brand choice and purchase timing (Π_2 and Π_1) have explicitly treated the heterogeneity of consumers and the aggregate models derived have been quite tractable. However, here too, researchers have fallen prey to inappropriate aggregation. For example, if individuals behave according to a zero order multinomial brand choice process and if the choice probabilities may vary across individuals, we will not find a zero-order process in an examination of the *aggregate* of consumers; the process will be of a higher order.

What can be done to improve the micro-macro consistency? First, and most important, is the application of market segmentation principles. This will identify homogeneous groups of consumers making the aggregation process simpler. Second, it is necessary to specify the individual level process and then aggregate upwards to the desired level. This is easier said than done, since very quickly the aggregation becomes intractable. However, the attempts may be worthwhile in suggesting how the ad hoc model may be enriched so as to provide a better approximation to the desired aggregate specification. Finally, a number of general ad hoc approaches exist that permit variability of the parameters of a model across consumers. One example of this is random coefficient regression; see, for example, Swamy [47].

B. Appropriateness of Ad Hoc Macro Models

There are at least two distinct objectives in model building in marketing—understanding consumer/market behavior and using the model's results for managerial decision making. While the first objective often focuses at the micro level, the latter objective requires dealing with aggregates. Therefore, even when the macro model is not consistent with micro theory, it may be that the model is a sufficiently good approximation *for the managerial objectives*. Problems of estimation and implementation often dictate the need for simple models. Therefore, the pragmatic merits of the ad-hoc macro-model may outweigh its departure from theory.

C. Issues in Formulation of Ad Hoc Macro Models

While the work on ad hoc macro model building is laudable, some issues on the process of constructing such models can be raised. These deal with questions of functional forms, interdependence of marketing mix variables, simultaneity, and use of control theory to enable the models to represent the real world in a better manner. We will comment on each of these briefly.

Functional Forms.   The functional forms that are used in marketing have often been simplistic. For example, most relationships are specified to be linear. No doubt, this is due to the versatility of the linear approximation and one's ability to estimate the model parameters. Model builders can capture the richness of the market process within the confines of the linear structure by two possible techniques. First of these involves use of second-order terms (e.g., $X_1 X_2$) in the model, retaining the ability to estimate the parameters with linear theory. The second possible technique involves specifying models in terms of changes in the variables (e.g., Δ market share) rather than the variables themselves yet retaining the linear form. This second technique would enable one to deal with a nonlinear model using a linear structure.

As noted earlier, the choice of a linear form has been largely dictated by availability of estimation techniques. The emergence of efficient numerical computerized methods for estimating general nonlinear functions should advance the use of more complicated relational forms.

Interdependence of Mix Effects.   While there exists some experimental evidence (in addition to managerial wisdom) to indicate that marketing mix variables interact with each other, most modeling effort has neglected this aspect. Inclusion of the interaction effects would naturally make the functional form nonlinear. The methods indicated above could assist in handling this issue. Some explicit ways of including interactions include use of $X_1 X_2$ terms, use of log-linear relationships, and specification of models in terms of changes in variables.

Simultaneity.   The outcomes of marketing system are a set of complex phenomena; for example, outcomes of consumer behavior can be thought of as brand choice, amount of satisfaction with the brand, information search, and repeat choice. From the firm's point of view, the outcomes could be market share, sales volume, returns, and net earnings. Model builders in marketing have often focused on one dependent variable despite the need to consider the set of relationships among the outcomes simultaneously. Models of systems to handle the simultaneity can be set up. The issues of identifiability and estimation do arise for simultaneous systems, but theory is available to handle these technical problems.

Potential Use of Control Theory.   So far, effort in modeling has largely been restricted to determining *ex ante* the effects of possible changes in marketing mix elements. However, a managerially more useful model would be to determine the values of marketing mix so that the outputs (profit or market share) follow a desired course of action. These models are called control models and are becoming popular in economics (Aoki [2]; Chow [8]). While such models have been proposed earlier by Little [27] and Fitzroy [12] in the context of advertising experiments for adaptive decisions, the developments have not been significant.

A recent paper by Pekelman and Tsi [35] treats the subject further. These attempts have been restricted to one decision variable only. Work is needed to determine optimal control policies for several of the marketing mix elements. Such an effort would have a desirable impact on the practice of marketing management.

Effort in modeling control phenomenon should begin with specification of the dynamics (changes) in the outputs of a marketing system. This may result in nonlinear system of the type $\dot{X} = a(t) X + B(t) U$ where X is the vector of outputs, U is a vector of controllable variables, and A(t) and B(t) are matrices with time dependent coefficients of appropriate dimensions. Properties of such systems including controllability and observability, and techniques for determining optimal control policies are well studied by electrical engineers (Athens and Falb [3]). Marketing academicians may benefit from looking at this approach.

The control theory approach also would enable consideration of tradeoffs that exist among multiple objectives (or outcomes) of the marketing function. An initial formulation of this problem is discussed by McCann and Rao [30].

D. Extensions to the Theoretical Framework

The theoretical framework we proposed in this article is particularly appealing because of its generality and parsimony. However, there are several opportunities for enriching this framework and we mention these below:

(i) Incorporating feedback elements: for example what is the impact of a new brand on the perceptual space (Ψ) and utility (U)? Or, what is the impact, at the aggregate level, of sales outcomes (S) on the managerial marketing decisions (X)?

(ii) Incorporating time effects: the model was presented for a single decision—how does the process take place over time? This would include incorporating leads, lags and other dynamic effects.

(iii) Identifying sub-systems: from a systems perspective, can we identify subsystems which may be studied separately?

(iv) Providing a general aggregation methodology: finally, and this has been a central point in this paper, can the framework be extended so as to provide a "natural" aggregation scheme?

REFERENCES

1. Amstutz, Arnold E. *Computer Simulation of Market Response*. Cambridge, Mass: M.I.T. Press, 1967.
2. Aoki, Masanao. *Optimal Control and System Theory in Dynamic Economic Analysis*. New York: American Elsevier Publishing Company, Inc., 1976.

3. Athens, Michael, and Falb, Peter L. *Optimal Control: An Introduction to the Theory and Its Applications*. New York: McGraw-Hill Book Company, 1976.

4. Balachandran, V., and Gensch, D. H. "Solving the 'Marketing Mix' Problem Using Geometric Programming." *Management Science* 21, No. 2 (October 1974): 160–171.

5. Beckwith, N. E. "Multivariate Analysis of Sales Responses of Competing Brands to Advertising." *Journal of Marketing Research* 9 (May 1972): 168–176.

6. Best, R. J. "The Predictive Aspects of a Joint Space Theory of Stochastic Choice." *Journal of Marketing Research* 13, (May 1976): 198–204.

7. Blattberg, R., and Golanty, J. "Tracker: An Early Test Market Forecasting and Diagnostic Model for New Product Planning." *Journal of Marketing Research* 15 (May 1978): pp. 192–202.

8. Chow, Gregory C. "How Much Could Be Gained by Optimal Stochastic Control Policies." *Annals of Economic and Social Measurement*, 1, No. 4 (1972): 391–406.

9. Clarke, D. G. "Econometric Measurement of the Duration of Advertising Effect on Sales." *Journal of Marketing Research* 13, (November 1976): 345–357.

10. Davidson, J. D. "Forecasting Traffic on STOL." *Operational Research Quarterly* 24 (1973): 561–569.

11. Eskin, G. J., and Baron, P. H. "Effects of Price and Advertising in Test-Market Experiments." *Journal of Marketing Research* 14 (November 1977): 499–508.

12. Fitzroy, Peter F. "An Adaptive Model for Promotional Decision Making." Special Report, Marketing Science Institute, April 1967.

13. Gensch, Denis H., and Welam, Peter Ulf. "Optimal Price and Promotion for Interdependent Market Segments." *Operations Research* 22, July-August 1974: 746–755.

14. Green, P. E. "Marketing Applications of MDS: Assessment and Outlook." *Journal of Marketing* 39 (January 1975): 22–31.

15. Green, P. E., and Srinivasan, V. "Conjoint Analysis in Consumer Research: Issues and Outlook." *Journal of Consumer Research* 5, September 1978.

16. Green, Paul E., and Rao, Vithala R. *Applied Multidimensional Scaling*. New York: Holt, Rinehart and Winston, 1972.

17. Green, Paul E., and Wind, Yoram. *Multiattribute Decisions in Marketing*. Hinsdale, Ill: Dryden Press, 1973.

18. Hauser, John R., and Urban, Glen L. "A Normative Methodology for Modeling Consumer Response to Innovation." *Operations Research* 25, No. 4, July–August, 1977: 579–619.

19. Helmer, R. M., and Johansson, J. K. "An Exposition of the Box-Jenkins Transfer Function Analysis with An Application to the Advertising-Sales Relationship." *Journal of Marketing Research* 14, May 1977: 227–239.

20. Horsky, D. "Market Share Response to Advertising—An Example of Theory Testing." *Journal of Marketing Research* 14, February 1977: 10–21.

21. Johnson, R. M. "Trade-off Analysis of Consumer Values." *Journal of Marketing Research* 11 (1974): 121–127.

22. Johnson, R. M. "Multiple Discriminant Analysis: Marketing Research Applications." In J. N. Sheth (ed.), *Multivariate Methods for Market and Survey Research*. Chicago: American Marketing Association, 1977, pp. 65–80.

23. Kinberg, Y., and Rao, A. G. "Stochastic Models of a Price Promotion." *Management Science* 21, No. 8, April 1975: 897–907.

24. Kinberg, Y., Rao, A. G., and Shakun, M. F. "A Mathematical Model for Price Promotion." *Management Science* 20, No. 6, February 1974: 948–959.

25. Lambin, Jean-Jacques. "A Computer On-Line Marketing Mix Model." *Journal of Marketing Research* 9, May 1972: 119–126.

26. Lancaster, Kelvin. *Consumer Demand: A New Approach*. New York and London: Columbia University Press, 1971.

27. Little, John D. C., "A Model for Adaptive Control of Promotional Spending." *Operations Research* 14, No. 6 (1966): 1075–1096.
28. Little, John D. C. "BRANDAID: A Marketing Mix Model, Part 1: Structure." *Operations Research* 23: 628–655.
29. McCann, J. M. "Market Segment Response to the Marketing Decision Variables." *Journal of Marketing Research* 11, No. 4, November 1974: 399–412.
30. McCann, J. M., and Rao, V. R. "Marketing Planning and Control via Discrete Stochastic Optimal Control." Working Paper, Cornell University, May 1977.
31. Moinpour, Reza, McCullough, James M., and MacLachlan, Douglas L. "Time Changes in Perception: A Longitudinal Application of Multidimensional Scaling." *Journal of Marketing Research* 13 (August 1976): 245–253.
32. Montgomery, David B., Silk, A. J., and Zaragoza, C. E. "Multiproduct Sales Effort Allocation Model," *Management Science* 17 (December 1971): 3–24.
33. Parsons, L. M. "A Rachet Model of Advertising Carryover Effects." *Journal of Marketing Research* 13, February 1976: 938–947.
34. Parsons, L. J., and Bass, F. M. "Optimal Advertising—Expenditure Implications of a Simultaneous Equation Regression Analysis." *Operations Research* 19; No. 3, May–June 1971: 822–831.
35. Pekelman, Dov, and Tsi, Edison. "Experimentation and Control in Advertising, An Adaptive Control Approach." Working Paper No. 76-04-01, University of Pennsylvania, March, 1976.
36. Pessemier, Edgar A. *Product Management: Strategy and Organization.* New York: John Wiley and Sons, 1977.
37. Prasad, V. K., and Ring, L. W. "Measuring Sales Effects of Some Marketing Mix Variables and Their Interactions." *Journal of Marketing Research* 13, November 1976: 391–396.
38. Rao, A. G., and Lilien, G. "A System of Promotional Models." *Management Science,* Vol. 19, No. 2, October 1972, pp. 152–160.
39. Rao, V. R. "Alternative Econometric Models of Sales-Advertising Relationships." *Journal of Marketing Research* 9, May 1972: 177–181.
40. Rao, Vithala R. "A View of the Competitive Marketing Mix Model." In Thomas V. Greer (ed.), *1973 Combined Proceedings,* American Marketing Association, Chicago, 1973.
41. Rao, V. R., "Conjoint Measurement in Marketing Analysis." In J. N. Sheth (ed.), *Multivariate Methods for Market and Survey Research,* Chicago: American Marketing Association, 1977, pp. 257–286.
42. Rao, V. R., and Winter, F. W. "An Application of the Multivariate Probit Model to Market Segmentation and Product Design." *Journal of Marketing Research* 15, August 1978: 361–368.
43. Schultz, R. L. "Market Measurement and Planning with a Simultaneous Equation Model." *Journal of Marketing Research* 8, May 1971: 153–164.
44. Sexton, D. E. Jr. "Estimating Marketing Policy Effects on Sales of a Frequently Purchased Product." *Journal of Marketing Research* 7, August 1970: 338–347.
45. Shocker, A. D., and Srinivasan, V. "A Consumer-based Methodology for the Identification of New Product Ideas." *Management Science* 20, No. 6, February 1974, pp. 921–937.
46. Silk, A. J., and Glen L. Urban. "Pre Test Market Evaluation of New Packaged Goods: A Model and Measurement Methodology." *Journal of Marketing Research* 15, May 1978: 171–191.
47. Swamy, P. "Statistical Inferences in Random Coefficient Regression Model," *Econometrica* 38, 1970, pp. 311–323.
48. Tapiero, C. S. "On-line and Adaptive Optimum Advertising Control by a Diffusion Approximation." *Operations Research* 23, No. 5, September-October 1975: 890–907.
49. Urban, Glen L. "PERCEPTOR: A Model for Product Positioning," *Management Science,* Vol. 21, No. 8, (April, 1975), pp. 858–871.

50. Urban, Glen L. "SPRINTER MOD III: A Model for the Analysis of New Frequently Purchased Consumer Products." *Operations Research* 18 (September–October, 1970): 805–853.
51. Weinberg, C. B. "Dynamic Correction in Marketing Planning Models." *Management Science* 22, No. 6, February 1976: 677–687.
52. Wilkie, William, and Pessemier, Edgar A. "Issues in Marketing's Use of Multi-attribute Attitude Models." *Journal of Marketing Research,* Vol. 10 (November 1973), pp. 428–441.
53. Wittink, D. R. "Exploring Territorial Differences in the Relationship Between Marketing Variables." *Journal of Marketing Research,* 14, No. 2, May 1977: 145–55.

PSYCHOLOGY OF INNOVATION RESISTANCE:

THE LESS DEVELOPED CONCEPT
(LDC) IN DIFFUSION RESEARCH

Jagdish N. Sheth

INTRODUCTION

As one reviews and evaluates the vast literature on diffusion of innovations [3, 4, 6, 7, 14], he gets a distinct impression that most researchers in the area have a pro-change bias. This is indicated by the following research emphasis:

1. Learning and understanding the psychology of innovators and early adopters rather than that of the followers.
2. Profiling the early adopters with respect to demographic, life style and communication characteristics to identify and differentiate them.
3. Developing communication and other strategies with which to accelerate the process of adoption and diffusion.

Research in Marketing, Volume 4, pages 273-282
Copyright © 1981 by JAI Press Inc.
All rights of reproduction in any form reserved.
ISBN: 0-89232-169-5

4. Utilization of early adopters as change agents in a two-step flow of communication and influence.
5. Labeling the change resistors as laggards with a clear derogatory perspective toward them.

According to Rogers [5],

the second important bias found in most diffusion research is an inherent pro-change bias, which assumes that the innovations are "good" and should be adopted by everyone. Undoubtedly hybrid corn *was* profitable for each of the Iowa farmers in the Ryan and Gross [10] study, but most other innovations that have been studied do not have this high degree of relative advantage. Many individuals, for their own good, should *not* adopt them (p. 229).

In fact, the vast majority of people who have no *a priori* desire to change may be more typical and even more rational than a small minority of individuals who seek change for its own sake rather than, or in addition to, the intrinsic value of the innovation. Therefore, it is about time we paid respect to individuals who resist change, understand their psychology of resistance and utilize this knowledge in the development and promotion of innovations rather than thrust upon them preconceived innovations which may or may not have any value to the masses. There are several compelling reasons for this conclusion.

First, the research evidence suggests that the true innovators (the first 2-3 percent adopters) are more likely to be social deviants, abnormal in their epistemic drive, and adopt innovations indiscriminately rather than based on any rational choice calculus. Why should we understand them and motivate others to emulate their behavior?

Second, we have developed and promoted many technological innovations without properly understanding or even examining their side effects or longer-term effects on human life. This seems to be particularly true in the twentieth-century era which has pushed the society from a mechanical-electrical age to a chemical-electronic age of mankind with the immediate prospect of migrating into the nuclear age.

Third, many critics in Europe and Asia argue that the pro-change attitudes of scientists and marketers generates planned obsolescence which, in turn, encourages waste and overutilization of natural scarce resources.

Fourth, most marketing innovations fail in the market place. This entails a tremendous amount of waste of scientific and marketing resources. Perhaps the knowledge about why people resist change may motivate scientists and marketers to become more realistic in channeling their expertise and efforts and thus become more productive.

Fifth, the pro-change bias leads to increased inequity according to Röling [8]. In fact, some even charge that the rapid development and promotion of innovations are the root cause for the increasing gap between the "haves" and the "have nots" of the world, which in turn results in greater tensions and conflicts among nations and people.

Finally, it is argued that the quality of life has deteriorated rather than improved in the technologically driven mass consumption societies. Products that break down frequently, increased number of consumer complaints and consumer dissatisfaction as well as the emergence of consumerism are cited as examples of lessening the quality of life.

Perhaps it is none of these reasons but simply a consequence of the aging process which is motivating me to theorize about the psychology of innovation resistance.

HABIT AND RISK CONSTRUCTS

It seems easier to theorize about individuals who resist innovations rather than those who embrace them. The two psychological constructs which seem most useful in understanding the psychology of innovation resistance are: (a) Habit toward an existing practice or behavior, and (b) Perceived risks associated with innovation adoption.

1. Habit toward Existing Practice

The strength of habit associated with an existing practice or behavior is hypothesized to be the single most powerful determinant in generating resistance to change. Without this motivational incentive, an individual is not likely to voluntarily pay attention to innovation communication or to voluntarily commit himself to try it out. In fact, his perceptual and cognitive mechanisms are all likely to be tuned in to preserve the habit because the typical human tendency is to strive for consistency and status quo rather than to continuously search for, and embrace new behaviors. In other words, formation and sustenance of habits is much more prevalent than innovativeness among people.

One exception to the above proposition is when the motivation underlying the formation and continuity of an existing behavior or practice is weakened by satiation or replaced by other motivations due to aspiration or adaptation processes. However, these changes in motivational structure are more evolutionary and do not match in velocity the rapidity with which innovations are developed and marketed. While variety seeking (Russell and Mehribian [9], curiosity behavior (Berlyne [1], and psychology of complication (Howard and Sheth [2] do occur in reality, they still represent only a small percentage of total human behavior except perhaps in those individuals with an abnormal dominance of the epistemic trait.

Habit toward an existing practice includes all the behavioral steps involved in the process of selecting, acquiring and using an existing alternative. In consumer behavior, it includes all the behavioral acts associated with shopping (time and place choices), procuring (money and effort choices), and consuming (storage, packaging and serving choices) the product. In other words, habit includes the total behavioral stream as a system rather than the terminal act.

The following propositions emerge with respect to habit and innovation resistance relationship:

a. The stronger the habit toward an existing practice or behavior, the greater the resistance to change and the innovations associated with that change. While this is a monotonic relationship, it is not likely to be linear. The hypothesis is that it is a curvilinear relationship with a logistic function possessing both a lower asymptote and an upper asymptote.
b. Those innovations which generate change for the total behavioral stream will be resisted more strongly than other innovations which generate change for a single behavioral act in the stream of selection, acquisition, and usage.
c. While habit is a major determinant for generating resistance to change, it is not the sole determinant. Thus, even in the absence of strong habits, resistance to change may be present due to other factors. One such other factor is perceived risks associated with the innovation.

2. Perceived Risks Associated with Innovations

A second major determinant of innovation resistance is the perception of different risks associated with the adoption of an innovation. There are three major types of risks: (i) aversive physical, social or economic consequences; (ii) performance uncertainty; and (iii) perceived side effects associated with the innovation.

The following propositions are suggested for the risk-resistance relationship:

a. The higher the perceived risk, the greater the innovation resistance. While the risk-resistance relationship is monotonic, it is not likely to be linear. The hypothesis is that the curvilinear relationship is a logistic function with both lower and upper asymptotic properties.
b. Innovations which are discontinuous (Robertson [3]) are likely to be resisted more than continuous innovations since they entail all the three types of risks.
c. Perceived risk is a major determinant of innovation resistance but it is not a sole determinant. Thus, even in the absence of any risk, people will resist change due to habits toward an existing practice.

A TYPOLOGY OF INNOVATION RESISTANCE

Based on the habit-risk constructs, it is possible to create a typology of innovations in terms of the degree and nature of resistance they might encounter if developed and marketed. Table 1 summarizes the four types of innovations. Each is described below.

Table 1. A Typology of Innovation Resistance.

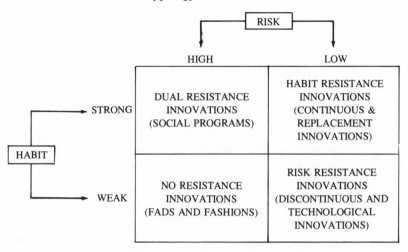

1. Dual Resistance Innovations

These are innovations which face the strongest resistance from people due to both strong prior habits and high risk perceptions about the innovation. Many innovations in the area of planned social change or social programs fall in this category. Examples include education, welfare, population control, nutrition and conservation (Sheth and Wright [13]).

Dual resistance innovations have the highest prospects of failure. It is, there-fore, not surprising to observe the high failure rate in social programs and the consequent frustrations experienced by the social policy makers and their change agents.

Dual resistance innovations must work backward by first focusing on the psychology of innovation resistance and then developing specific innovative programs which will minimize risk perceptions, on the one hand, and work through the existing habits rather than attempt to replace them. The classical examples in this area come from the failures of high protein, low-cost foods. In less developed countries, Sheth and Sudman [12] recommend that social policymakers will be better off offering nutrition in beverages rather than in solid foods since habits are much more strongly embedded for solid foods, and per-formance uncertainty and social risks are far greater with new types of processed foods in many cultures.

2. Habit Resistance Innovations

Innovations which are low risk but require changes in existing habits and practices are classified as habit-resistance innovations. Many of the continuous innovations which attempt to replace existing products fall in this category. As Rogers [5] points out, most of these replacement innovations offer very little relative advantage to motivate the farmers to change. I think that a vast majority of product innovations in marketing are of this kind: They offer very little above and beyond the existing products and consumers perceive them as "me too" products or artificial differences, and consequently reject them. This is presumably the classic reason for the failure of freeze-dried coffee: Housewives perceived it as no better than existing instant or regular coffees on the marketplace despite the enormous technical differences in the manufacturing process.

Only those replacement innovations succeed which improve rather than change the existing habits and practices by offering cost or performance or social advantages. Examples include electronic calculators, light beer for heavy drinkers or low-tar-and-nicotine cigarettes.

3. Risk Resistance Innovations

Certain types of innovations face resistance primarily because of high risk perceptions although they do not replace existing habits but instead generate altogether new habits. These are the most radical and discontinuous innovations. According to Howard and Sheth [2], there is no prior product class for these innovations and the innovation itself defines a new product class. Many technological breakthroughs such as nuclear energy, birth-control pills and picturephone are examples of risk-resistance innovations. They generate new habits but, at the same time, also raise risk perceptions in terms of both main effects and side effects.

It should be pointed out that those technological breakthroughs which are perceived to be low risk face minimal or no resistance at all. Examples include the adoption of the telephone, the television and the computer.

4. No-Resistance Innovations

Those innovations which neither contain any risks nor attempt to change existing habits are labeled as no-resistance innovations. The most common examples of no-resistance innovations are the fads and fashions. Similarly, innovations which offer high relative advantage and low risk (Sheth [11]) should face no resistance.

Unlike other types of innovations, the no-resistance innovations are likely to have exponential growth functions as opposed to the more common logistic growth functions associated with their diffusion. Fads and fashions clearly suggest this to be true.

The above typology of innovations resistance will, it is hoped, be helpful to policymakers and change agents in realizing what types of innovations may be most difficult to diffuse, and therefore, knowing situations in which it may be desirable to work backwards from understanding the psychology of resistance.

MODELING INNOVATION RESISTANCE

It seems possible mathematically to model innovation resistance. Figure 1 suggests how habit and risk factors are related to innovation resistance.

The following equation represents the model:

$$R = k/(1 + bp^H) + a/(1 + cq^{PR})$$

where

R = Innovation resistance

H = Habit toward existing practice

PR = Perceived Risks associated with innovation.

and k, a, b, c, p and q = constants.

There are two problems associated with the above equation. First, habit and perceived risk are multi-attribute phenomena. As we discussed earlier, habit represents conditioning toward the total behavioral stream associated with selec-

Figure 1. Modeling Psychology of Innovation Resistance.

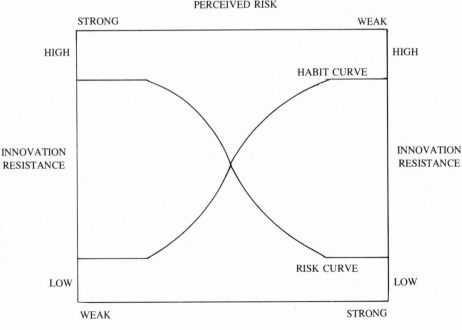

tion, acquisition and utilization processes. Similarly, perceived risk consists of aversive consequences, performance uncertainty, and side effects. One way to reduce the multi-attribute profiles of habit and perceived risk is to transform them into indices. Rather than averaging or summing, it is proposed that a principal components analysis be performed on each profile and extract a general component or factor as representing the index of habit and perceived risk, respectively.

Second, it is difficult to simultaneously estimate parameters with two logistic functions in the above equation. There are three separate procedures one can utilize for parameter estimation.

1. Aggregate Curve Fitting

In this option, we should combine the habit and perceived risk factor scores for each observation and thereby reduce the problem to a bivariate curvilinear curve fitting. In other words, innovation resistance is optimally related to the aggregate sum score of habit and perceived risk, and the parameters estimated are for the aggregate function.

The equation will appear as follows:

$$R = d/(1 + fk^{HR})$$

where

HR = sum of habit and perceived risk factor scores.

d, f, and k = constants

and

R = innovation resistance.

2. Two-Stage Parameter Estimation

This procedure entails estimating parameters with respect to one determinant of innovation resistance, calculating the residuals, and then estimating parameters for the second determinant by curve fitting of the residual scores. Since habit is hypothesized as the stronger determinant, it is possible to suggest the following two-stage procedure:

$$R = k/(1 + bp^{h})$$

and

$$R_{Res} = a/(1 + cq^{PR})$$

where

R_{Res} = Residual Values of innovation resistance and all other terms as before.

3. Linear Approximation Analysis

The third and the simplest option is to approximate the logistic relationships of each factor by a linear approximation. It is obvious that the linear approximation will underestimate innovation resistance when habit and risk are weak and overestimate it when they are strong. In other words, the parameters will generate biased estimations in the extreme values of observations by presuming a linear relationship. If the asymptotic constants in the logistic function are not very large, the linear approximation will produce a good fit.

The following equation represents the linear approximation for the model:

$$R = B_1 (H) + B_2 (PR)$$

where

B_1 and B_2 = regression parameters

H = habit factors score

PR = perceived risk factor score

and

R = innovation resistance.

Among the three approaches, the two-stage process and linear approximation may be more relevant and useful, if the policy makers are interested in estimating the relative contributions of habit and perceived risk in generating resistance to a particular innovation. On the other hand, if the interest is in forecasting the overall resistance toward a particular innovation, the aggregate curve fitting may be quite adequate.

CONCLUSIONS

This paper attempts to theorize about why people resist innovations. Since the vast majority of people either have no a priori desire to change or actually resist change, it is argued that we might learn more by concentrating on the psychology of innovation resistance rather than on the psychology of adoption. Indeed, the literature of diffusion and adoption seems to be so pro-change in its bias, that psychology of innovation resistance has, so far, remained a less developed concept.

Two factors which determine innovation resistance are habit toward an existing practice and perceived risk associated with the innovation. Both are hypothesized to have a logistic function relationship with innovation resistance. Several statistical methods are suggested for estimating the parameters of the two logistic curves including aggregate parameter estimation, two-stage curve fitting and linear approximation procedures.

Finally, the paper provides a typology of innovation resistance. Dual resistance innovations are those which are high risk and attempt to change existing practice. Risk-resistance innovations are those high-risk technological breakthroughs which create new habits. Habit resistance innovations are those which attempt to replace existing practices; and finally, no-resistance innovations are those which are either highly advantageous—low-risk technological innovations or fads and fashions which encounter no resistance either due to habit or due to perceived risks.

REFERENCES

1. Berlyne, D. E. "Curiosity and Exploration," *Science* 153, (3731): 25–33, 1966.
2. Howard, J. A., and Sheth, J. N. *The Theory of Buyer Behavior*. New York: John Wiley, 1969.
3. Robertson, T. S. *Innovative Behavior and Communication*. New York: Holt, Rinehart and Winston, 1971.
4. Rogers, E. M. *Diffusion of Innovations*. New York: Free Press, 1962.
5. _____. "New Product Adoptiong and Diffusion," In R. Ferber (ed.), *Selected Aspects of Consumer Behavior*, NSF, Washington, D.C. Government Printing Office, pp. 223–238, 1977.
6. Rogers, E. M., and Shoemaker, F. F. *Communication about Innovations*. New York: Free Press, 1971.
7. Rogers, E. M., and Thomas, P. C. *Bibliography on the Diffusion of Innovation*, Department of Population Planning, University of Michigan.
8. Röling, N., Ascroft, J., and Chege, F. "Innovation and Equity in Rural Development." Paper presented at the World Congress on Sociology, Toronto, 1974.
9. Russell, J. A., and Mehrabian, A. "Environmental Variables in Consumer Research." *Journal of Consumer Research* 3: 62–63, 1976.
10. Ryan, B., and Gross, N. C. "The Diffusion of Hybrid Seed Corn in Two Iowa Communities." *Rural Sociology* 8: 15–24, 1943.
11. Sheth, J. N. "Word of Mouth Communication in Low-Risk Innovations." *Journal of Advertising Research* 11: 15–18, 1971.
12. Sheth, J. N., and Sudman, S. "Malnutrition and Marketing." In Sheth and Wright (eds.), *Marketing Analysis for Societal Problems*, Bureau of Economic and Business Research, University of Illinois.
13. Sheth, J. N., and Wright, P. L. (eds.) *Marketing Analysis for Societal Problems*, Bureau of Economic and Business Research, University of Illinois, 1974.
14. Zaltman, Gerald. "Strategies for Diffusing Innovations." In Sheth and Wright (eds.), *Marketing Analysis for Societal Problems*, Bureau of Economic and Business Research, University of Illinois, 1974.

Research in Marketing

A Research Annual

Series Editor: **Jagdish N. Sheth**
Department of Business Administration,
University of Illinois.

Volume 1.   **Published 1978**   Institutions: $ 32.50
ISBN 0-89232-041-9   330 pages   Individuals: $ 16.25

CONTENTS: Foreword, *Jagdish N. Sheth.* **Research in Productivity Measurement for Marketing Decisions,** *Louis P. Bucklin, University of California, Berkeley.* **Simulation of Risk Attitudes in Joint Decision Making by Marketing Firms in Competitive Markets,** *Ralph L. Day, Indiana University and Jehoshua Eliashberg, University of Missouri.* **Interpretative Versus Descriptive Research,** *Ernest Dichter, Ernest Dichter Associates International, Ltd.* **The Household as a Production Unit,** *Michael Etgar, State University of New York, Buffalo.* **Some New Types of Fractional Designs for Marketing Experiments,** *Paul E. Green, University of Pennsylvania, J. Douglas Carroll, Bell Laboratories, and Frank J. Carmone, Drexel University.* **Optimizing Research Budgets: A Theoretical Approach,** *Flemming Hansen, Copenhagen School of Business Administration and Economics.* **Choosing the Best Advertising Appropiation When Appropiations Interact Over Time,** *Haim Levy, The Hebrew University and Julian Simon, University of Illinois.* **Advertising and Socialization,** *John G. Myers, University of California, Berkeley.* **Multi-Product Growth Models,** *Robert A. Peterson, University of Texas - Austin and Vijay Mahajan, Ohio State University.* **Advocacy Advertising: Corporate External Communications and Public Policy,** *S. Prakash Sethi, University of Texas - Dallas.* **An Empirical-Simulation Approach to Competition,** *Randall L. Schultz, Purdue University and Joe A. Dodson, Jr., N.W. Ayer A.B.H. International.* **Field Theory Applied to Consumer Behavior,** *Arch G. Woodside, University of South Carolina and William O. Bearden, University of Alabama.*

Volume 2.   **Published 1979**   Institutions: $ 32.50
ISBN 0-89232-059-1   357 pages   Individuals: $ 16.25

CONTENTS: Preface. **Canadian and American National Character as a Basis for Market Segmentation,** *Stephen J. Arnold, Queen's University, and James G. Barnes, Memorial University of Newfoundland.* **The Products-Needs Matrix as a Methodology for Promoting Anti Consuming,** *Michael A. Belch, San Diego State University and Robert Perloff, University of Pittsburgh.* **The Cereal Antitrust Case: An Analysis of Selected Issues,** *Paul N. Bloom, University of Maryland.* **Gift - Giving Behavior,** *Russell W. Belk, University of Utah.* **A Process Model of Interorganizational Relations in Marketing Channels,** *Ernest R. Cadotte, University of Tennessee and Louis W. Stern, Northwestern University.* **The Product Audit System as a Tool of Marketing Planning,** *C. Merle Crawford, University of Michigan.* **Rudiments of Numeracy,** *A.S.C. Ehrenberg, London Business School.* **Evaluating the Competitive Environment in Retailing Using Multiplicative Competitive Interactive Model,** *Arun K. Jain, State University of New York - Buffalo and Vijay Mahajan, Ohio State University.* **The Parametric Marginal Desirability Model,** *John F. McElwee, Jr., University of Laverne, Leonard J. Parsons, Georgia Institute of Technology.* **Carry-Over Effects in Advertising Communication,** *Alan Sawyer, Ohio State University and Scott Ward, Harvard University.* **Redlining in Mortgage Markets: Research Perspectives in Marketing and Public Policy,** *Thaddeus H. Spratlen, University of Washington.* **Psychological Geography,** *William D. Wells, Needham, Harper & Steers Advertising, Inc. and Fred D. Reynolds, University of Georgia.*

Please see reverse side for Volumes 3 & 5.

Research in Marketing

A Research Annual

Series Editor: **Jagdish N. Sheth**
Department of Business Administration
University of Illinois.

Volume 3.   **Published 1980**   **Institutions: $ 32.50**
ISBN 0-89232-060-5   **325 pages**   **Individuals: $ 16.50**

In Preparation — Available Summer 1981

Volume 5.   **Cloth**   **Institutions: $ 35.00**
ISBN 0-89232-211-X   **Ca. 325 pages**   **Individuals: $ 17.50**

INSTITUTIONAL STANDING ORDERS *will be granted a 10% discount and be filled automatically upon publication. Please indicate initial volume of standing order*
INDIVIDUAL ORDERS *must be prepaid by personal check or credit card. Please include $1.50 per volume for postage and handling.*
Please encourage your library to subscribe to this series.

JAI PRESS INC., P.O. Box 1678, 165 West Putnam Avenue, Greenwich, Connecticut 06830.

Telephone: 203-661-7602   **Cable Address: JAIPUBL**